ECCE ROMANI IB

A LATIN
READING PROGRAM

FOURTH EDITION

Boston, Massachusetts
Glenview, Illinois
Shoreview, Minnesota
Parsippany, New Jersey
Upper Saddle River, New Jersey

This North American edition of *Ecce Romani* is based on *Ecce Romani: A Latin Reading Course*, originally prepared by The Scottish Classics Group © copyright The Scottish Classics Group 1971, 1982, and published in the United Kingdom by Oliver and Boyd, a division of Longman Group.

Photo Credits appear on page 185, which constitutes an extension of this copyright page.

Cover illustration: Lin Wang
Text art: Lin Wang
Maps: John Burgoyne

13-digit ISBN: 978-0-13-361093-2
10-digit ISBN: 0-13-361093-4

4 5 6 7 8 9 10 V054 14 13 12 11

Series Editor: Gilbert Lawall
Professor Emeritus of Classics
University of Massachusetts, Amherst, Massachusetts

AUTHORS AND CONSULTANTS

Timothy S. Abney
Marquette High School
Chesterfield, Missouri

Jim Bigger
McLean High School
McLean, Virginia

Melissa Schons Bishop
Windermere, Florida

Peter C. Brush
Deerfield Academy
Deerfield, Massachusetts

Penny R. Cipolone
Gateway Regional High School
Woodbury Heights, New Jersey

Gail A. Cooper
Academy of the New Church
Bryn Athyn, Pennsylvania

Sally Davis
Arlington Public Schools
Arlington, Virginia

Pauline P. Demetri
Cambridge Rindge &
Latin School
Cambridge, Massachusetts

Dennis De Young
Montgomery Bell Academy
Nashville, Tennessee

Katy Ganino
Wayland Middle School
Wayland, Massachusetts

Jane Hall
National Latin Exam
Alexandria, Virginia

Sally Hatcher
Winsor School
Boston, Massachusetts

Thalia Pantelidis Hocker
Old Dominion University
Norfolk, Virginia

Anthony L.C. Hollingsworth
Roger Williams University
Bristol, Rhode Island

Dexter Hoyos
Sydney University
Sydney, Australia

Joan C. Jahnige
Kentucky Educational Television
Lexington, Kentucky

Caroline Switzer Kelly
Covenant Day School
Charlotte, North Carolina

Glenn M. Knudsvig
University of Michigan
Ann Arbor, Michigan

Richard A. LaFleur
University of Georgia
Athens, Georgia

Shirley G. Lowe
Wayland Public Schools
Wayland, MA

Maureen O'Donnell
W.T. Woodson High School
Fairfax, Virginia

Ronald B. Palma
Holland Hall School
Tulsa, Oklahoma

David J. Perry
Rye High School
Rye, New York

Kathleen M. Robinson
Harbor Day School
Corona del Mar, CA

Debra Pennell Ross
University of Michigan
Ann Arbor, Michigan

Andrew Schacht
St. Luke's School
New Canaan, Connecticut

Judith Lynn Sebesta
University of South Dakota
Vermillion, South Dakota

**The Scottish Classics
Group**
Edinburgh, Scotland

David M. Tafe
Rye Country Day School
Rye, New York

Rex Wallace
University of Massachusetts
Amherst, Massachusetts

Allen Ward
University of Connecticut
Storrs, Connecticut

Elizabeth Lyding Will
Amherst College
Amherst, Massachusetts

Philip K. Woodruff
Lake Forest High School
Lake Forest, Illinois

CONTENTS

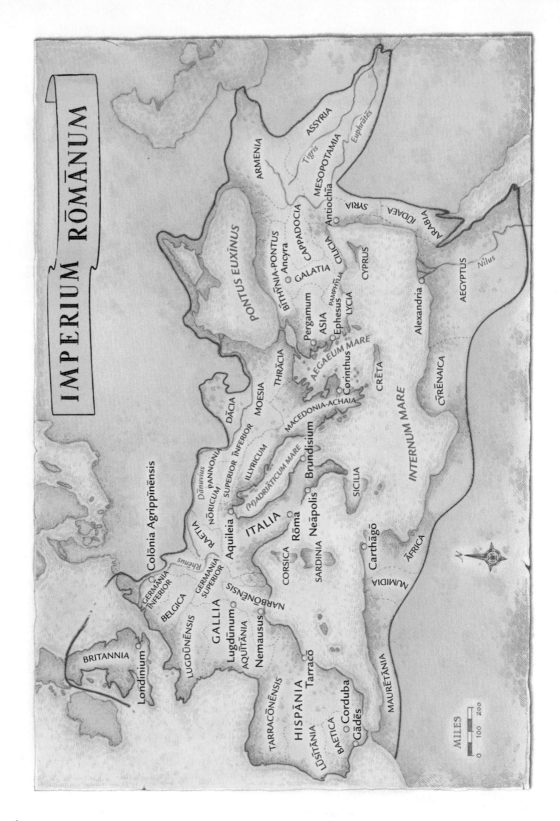

IMPERIUM RŌMĀNUM

BRITANNIA
Londinium

GERMANIA INFERIOR
Colōnia Agrippīnēnsis
BELGICA
GERMANIA SUPERIOR
Rhēnus
RAETIA
NŌRICUM PANNONIA
SUPERIOR INFERIOR
Dānuvius

GALLIA
LUGDŪNĒNSIS
Lugdūnum
AQUĪTĀNIA
NARBONĒNSIS
Nemausus
Aquileia

ITALIA
Rōma
Neāpolis
Brundisium

CORSICA
SARDINIA
SICILIA
Carthāgō
ĀFRICA
NUMIDIA
MAURĒTĀNIA

HISPĀNIA
TARRACŌNĒNSIS
Tarracō
LŪSĪTĀNIA
BAETICA
Corduba
Gādēs

DĀCIA
MOESIA
ILLYRICUM
THRĀCIA
MACEDONIA-ACHAIA
Corinthus
Aegaeum MARE
(H)ADRIĀTICUM MARE
CRĒTA

PONTUS EUXĪNUS

ARMENIA
ASSYRIA
MESOPOTAMIA
Tigris
Euphrātēs

BITHŸNIA-PONTUS
GALATIA
Ancyra
CAPPADOCIA
Pergamum
ASIA
Ephesus
PAMPHŸLIA
LYCIA
CILICIA
CYPRUS
Antiochīa
SYRIA
IŪDAEA
ARABIA

CRĒTA

CŸRĒNAICA
Alexandria
AEGYPTUS
Nīlus

INTERNUM MARE

MILES
0   100   200

N

ROMANVM

vi INTRODUCTION

INTRODUCTION

Welcome to the second part of the first level of *Ecce Romani*. In this book you will follow the adventures of the family of Cornelius as they complete their journey to Rome and as Eucleides shows the children around the city and takes them to the chariot races in the famed Circus Maximus. The book begins with the family spending a night at an inn, where Cornelius and the boys hear a terrifying tale of murder. You will learn of both the splendors and the dangers of life in Rome as Eucleides takes the children on a tour of the great buildings of the city and as Marcus has a nightmarish dream of being attacked by ruthless thieves.

While following this story, you will learn much about the cultural life of the Romans as you experience life in an ancient inn, travel over ancient roads, and view the excitement of life in the great city. You will learn about the aqueducts that the Romans constructed to make urban life possible by providing an adequate supply of water, and you will witness one of the most popular forms of entertainment in Rome, the fiercely competitive chariot races. By reading the passages from Latin authors in *The Romans Speak for Themselves* that accompany Chapters 19, 21, 23, 25, and 27 of *Ecce Romani*, you will gain insight into how the ancient Romans themselves viewed the products and practices of their culture, and you may draw comparisons with the culture of your own world today.

You will also be introduced to life on the frontiers of the Roman empire in northern Europe and in north Africa, and you will begin to explore the process of cultural assimilation through which Roman practices and values came to be accepted in lands far removed from the city of Rome.

You will expand your knowledge as you follow the development of Roman history from the establishment of a republican form of government after the expulsion of the last of the king in 509 B.C. through a period of legendary heroes and the consolidation of Roman power in Italy to Rome's victory over its archenemy Carthage and the extension of Roman power into the eastern Mediterranean world, with Rome becoming the leader of a far-flung empire.

As you continue to study Latin words and their English derivatives, you will be making many connections and comparisons between these two languages. You will learn the meaning of Latin expressions that have been taken over directly into English, and you will learn the meaning of prefixes that were attached to Latin words and that continue to be used in our English today.

Go Online: Every chapter of your book contains a Web Code that will allow you to Go Online to the *Ecce Romani* Companion Web Site. This Web Site contains activities for additional practice with vocabulary, grammar, and culture and a Self-Test that corresponds to the Review sections in your book. In order to Go Online, go to www.PHSchool.com, type in the Web Code you'd like to access, and click on the "Go" button. In order to access additional information and links that will be useful to you throughout the year, use the following Web Code:

Go Online
PHSchool.com
Web Code: jfd-0018

ARRIVAL AT THE INN

Raeda in fossā haerēbat. Cornēliī per viam ībant ad caupōnam, quae nōn procul aberat. Cornēlia, quae nōn iam lacrimābat, cum Eucleide ambulābat. Puerōs, quod praecurrēbant, identidem revocābat Cornēlius. Aurēlia, quamquam in caupōnā pernoctāre adhūc nōlēbat, lentē cum Cornēliō ībat.

Mox ad caupōnam appropinquābant. Nēminem vidēbant; vōcēs tamen hominum audiēbant. 5

Subitō duo canēs ē iānuā caupōnae sē praecipitant et ferōciter lātrantēs Cornēliōs petunt. Statim fugit Sextus. Stat immōbilis Mārcus. Aurēlia perterrita exclāmat. Cornēlius ipse nihil facit. Cornēlia tamen nōn fugit sed ad canēs manum extendit.

"Ecce, Mārce!" inquit. "Hī canēs lātrant modo. Nūllum est perīculum. Ecce, Sexte! 10 Caudās movent."

Eō ipsō tempore ad iānuam caupōnae appāruit homō obēsus, quī canēs revocāvit.

"Salvēte, hospitēs!" inquit. "In caupōnā meā pernoctāre vultis? Hīc multī cīvēs praeclārī pernoctāvērunt. Ōlim hīc pernoctāvit etiam lēgātus prīncipis."

"Salvē, mī Apollodōre!" interpellāvit Eucleidēs. "Quid agis?" 15

"Mehercule!" respondit caupō. "Nisi errō, meum amīcum Eucleidem agnōscō."

"Nōn errās," inquit Eucleidēs. "Laetus tē videō. Quod raeda dominī meī in fossā haeret immōbilis, necesse est hīc in caupōnā pernoctāre."

"Doleō," inquit caupō, "quod raeda est in fossā, sed gaudeō quod ad meam caupōnam nunc venītis. Intrāte, intrāte, omnēs!" 20

3 praecurrō, praecurrere, *to run ahead*
5 **homō, hominis,** m., *man*
7 sē praecipitant, (*they*) *hurl themselves, rush*
8 **fugiō, fugere,** *to flee*
9 **manum,** *hand*
10 hī canēs, *these dogs*
   modo, adv., *only*
11 cauda, -ae, f., *tail*
12 **appāruit,** (*he*) *appeared*
   obēsus, -a, -um, *fat*

revocāvit, (*he*) *called back*
14 **pernoctāvērunt,** (*they*) *have spent the night*
   ōlim, adv., *once (upon a time)*
   lēgātus, -ī, m., *envoy*
15 **Quid agis?** *How are you?*
16 Mehercule! interj., *By Hercules! Goodness me!*
   nisi errō, *unless I am mistaken*
   agnōscō, agnōscere, *to recognize*
19 doleō, dolēre, *to be sad*

EXERCISE 18a Respondē Latīnē:

1. Quō ībant Cornēliī?
2. Volēbatne Aurēlia in caupōnā pernoctāre?
3. Quid canēs faciunt?
4. Quālis homō ad iānuam caupōnae appāruit?
5. Quālēs cīvēs in caupōnā pernoctāvērunt?
6. Cūr necesse est in caupōnā pernoctāre?

Go Online
PHSchool.com
Web Code: jfd-0018

FORMS

Adjectives: 1st/2nd Declension and 3rd Declension

You learned in Chapter 16 that some adjectives have endings like those of 1st and 2nd declension nouns. There are also other adjectives, which have 3rd declension endings, as shown in the right-hand column in the following chart:

Number Case	1st and 2nd Declensions			3rd Declension		
	Masc.	Fem.	Neut.	Masc.	Fem.	Neut.
Singular						
Nominative	mágn**us**	mágn**a**	mágn**um**	ómn**is**	ómn**is**	ómn**e**
Genitive	mágn**ī**	mágn**ae**	mágn**ī**	ómn**is**	ómn**is**	ómn**is**
Dative	mágn**ō**	mágn**ae**	mágn**ō**	ómn**ī**	ómn**ī**	ómn**ī**
Accusative	mágn**um**	mágn**am**	mágn**um**	ómn**em**	ómn**em**	ómn**e**
Ablative	mágn**ō**	mágn**ā**	mágn**ō**	ómn**ī**	ómn**ī**	ómn**ī**
Vocative	mágn**e**	mágn**a**	mágn**um**	ómn**is**	ómn**is**	ómn**e**
Plural						
Nominative	mágn**ī**	mágn**ae**	mágn**a**	ómn**ēs**	ómn**ēs**	ómn**ia**
Genitive	magn**ṓrum**	magn**ā́rum**	magn**ṓrum**	ómn**ium**	ómn**ium**	ómn**ium**
Dative	mágn**īs**	mágn**īs**	mágn**īs**	ómn**ibus**	ómn**ibus**	ómn**ibus**
Accusative	mágn**ōs**	mágn**ās**	mágn**a**	ómn**ēs**	ómn**ēs**	ómn**ia**
Ablative	mágn**īs**	mágn**īs**	mágn**īs**	ómn**ibus**	ómn**ibus**	ómn**ibus**
Vocative	mágn**ī**	mágn**ae**	mágn**a**	ómn**ēs**	ómn**ēs**	ómn**ia**

Be sure to learn these forms thoroughly.

NOTES

1. Some 1st and 2nd declension adjectives end in *-er* in the masculine nominative singular, e.g., **miser**, and keep the **-e-** before the **-r** in all other forms. The feminine and neuter of this adjective are **misera** and **miserum**. Compare the 2nd declension noun **puer**, gen., **puerī**, which also keeps the **-e-** in all its forms.

   Some 1st and 2nd declension adjectives that end in *-er* in the masculine nominative singular drop the **-e-** in all other forms, e.g., **noster, nostra, nostrum**; gen., **nostrī, nostrae, nostrī**. Compare the 2nd declension noun **ager**, gen., **agrī**.

2. Most 3rd declension adjectives have identical forms in the masculine and feminine, as does **omnis** above.

3. The ablative singular of 3rd declension adjectives ends in *-ī* (not *-e*), and the genitive plural ends in *-ium*. The neuter nominative and accusative plurals end in *-ia*. Compare these endings with those of 3rd declension nouns that you learned in Chapters 11, 13, and 15.

4. You have met the following 3rd declension adjectives:

   brevis, -is, -e, *short*   **omnis, -is, -e,** *all, the whole, every, each*
   immōbilis, -is, -e, *motionless*   **Quālis, -is, -e...?** *What sort of...?*
   incolumis, -is, -e, *unhurt, safe and sound*

In future vocabulary lists, most 3rd declension adjectives will be given in this way, with the masculine nominative singular form spelled out in full and only the endings given for the feminine and neuter nominative singular forms.

BUILDING THE MEANING

Go Online
PHSchool.com
Web Code: jfd-0018

Nouns and Adjectives: Agreement II

You learned in Chapter 16 that adjectives agree with the nouns they modify in gender, case, and number. Consider the following sentence:

Multās vīllās, multōs agrōs, multās arborēs vident.

Since **vīllās** is a feminine noun in the accusative plural, **multās** has a feminine accusative plural ending. Similarly, **multōs** is masculine accusative plural agreeing with **agrōs**, and **multās** is feminine accusative plural agreeing with **arborēs**. An adjective will agree with the noun it describes in gender, case, and number.

You already know that 1st and 2nd declension adjectives may be used to modify nouns of any declension (see the example above). Third declension adjectives may also be used to describe nouns of any declension:

Omnēs vīllās, omnēs agrōs, omnēs arborēs vident.

Note that the adjective **omnēs** has the same endings all three times in this sentence while two different forms, **multās** and **multōs**, are used in the sentence above. Why is this?

What Noun Does an Adjective Modify?
How Do You Decide?

Gender, Case, and Number

Identifying the gender, case, and number of an adjective will help you decide what noun it modifies.

EXERCISE 18b

Read each sentence aloud. What noun does each adjective modify?
Explain your decisions. Then translate:

1. Canis magnus ossa habet.   os, ossis, n., *bone*
2. Meus canis magna ossa habet.
3. Ossa multī canēs habent.
4. Canis magnum os habet.
5. Ossa magnus canis habet.
6. Dominus bonum canem habet.
7. Dominus obēsus canem habet.
8. Canem magnum dominus habet.

Position

In English, adjectives usually come immediately before the nouns they modify, e.g., "the good boy," "the good girls." The opposite is true in Latin; the more significant word comes first, and usually this is the noun and not the adjective:

> Ad iānuam caupōnae appāruit **homō** obēsus. (18:12)

Numbers, adjectives meaning *this* and *that*, and adjectives expressing quantity, however, normally precede the nouns they modify:

> duo canēs   hī canēs   multī cīvēs   omnēs cīvēs

The adjective **bonus, -a, -um** also often precedes the noun it modifies: **Māter bonās puellās laudat**, *The mother praises the good girls*. In Latin, an adjective may be placed before a noun for emphasis; observe how the adjective **meus, -a, -um** is placed sometimes before (for emphasis) and sometimes after the noun it modifies in the story at the beginning of this chapter (lines 13, 15, 16, 17, and 19). Examples of these rules for the placement of adjectives may be found in the sentences in Exercise 18b. Note that **magnus, -a, -um** may be placed before or after the noun it modifies.

An adjective may be separated from the noun it modifies. This often occurs in prepositional phrases, e.g., **magnīs in aedificiīs**, *in big buildings*, and **magnā cum cūrā**, *with great care*.

Sense

In the following sentence, both position and sense suggest that the adjective goes with the preceding rather than the following noun:

> **Puellam** ignāvam epistulam scrībere iubēmus.
> *We order the lazy girl to write a letter.*

EXERCISE 18c

Read each sentence aloud. Identify all 3rd declension adjectives. Tell what noun each modifies and what gender, case, and number each is. Then translate:

1. Omnēs viātōrēs ad caupōnās vesperī adveniēbant.
2. Apollodōrus est dominus omnium servōrum quī sunt in caupōnā.
3. In omnī urbe sunt magna aedificia.
4. Aurēlia nōn est fēmina fortis, nam in caupōnīs perīculōsīs pernoctāre nōn vult.
5. Omnēs līberī erant laetī quod Syrus, raedārius bonus, raedam celerrimē agēbat.
6. Cornēlia laudat Mārcum, puerum fortem, quī omnēs lupōs magnā in silvā repellit.
7. Puer fortis canēs nōn timet.
8. Canēs manum puellae fortis olfaciunt.
9. Sextus omnēs arborēs ascendere vult.
10. Brevia itinera laetī saepe facimus.

omnis, -is, -e, *all, every*   **fortis, -is, -e,** *brave, strong*
viātor, viātōris, m., *traveler*   laudō, -āre, *to praise*
vesperī, *in the evening*

Go Online
PHSchool.com
Web Code: jfd-0018

LEGENDARY HEROES OF EARLY ROME

Once Tarquinius Superbus had been expelled for tyranny in 509 B.C., the monarchy was replaced by a republican form of government, in which two consuls, elected annually, held equal power and ruled with the advice of the Senate. For the next 250 years, Rome's history was one of constant struggle and conflict, as she vied with other city-states for supremacy in Italy. The story of Rome's conquests is studded with patriots, whose actions reflect the character of early Rome and emphasize the virtue of **pietās**, firm loyalty and devotion to one's country, gods, and family. The stories of these patriots were told by the Roman historian Livy (1st century B.C.–1st century A.D.), on whom the following accounts are based.

Horatius at the Bridge

The king of Clusium in Etruria, Lars Porsenna, was goaded by Tarquinius Superbus into leading an army to attack Rome and restore the monarchy. As the Etruscans advanced to cross the Pons Sublicius, the access route into the city across the Tiber, they were thwarted by one man, Horatius Cocles. He instructed his fellow citizens to demolish the bridge behind him, promising to hold back the attack of the enemy as well as one man could. The sight of a single armed man standing at the entrance to the bridge astounded the Etruscan army. Two comrades helped Horatius stave off the first attack and then retired into the city over what still remained of the bridge. Horatius taunted the Etruscans and

The goddess Victory crowns Horatius Cocles as he defends the bridge. Father Tiber, with water jar, watches (*below*). Horatius Cocles Defending the Bridge, *oil on canvas, 1643, Charles LeBrun*

with his shield blocked the many spears they threw at him as they advanced. As the last of the bridge fell, the loud crash behind him and the cheers of the Romans inside the city stopped the advancing enemy in their tracks. "Father Tiber," prayed Horatius, "receive these weapons and this soldier in your kind waters!" and he jumped into the river and swam through a shower of spears to safety with his fellow citizens in the city.

Mucius Scaevola

Porsenna then decided to besiege the Romans into submission. Gaius Mucius, a young Roman noble, got permission from the senators to infiltrate the Etruscan camp and kill the king. Mucius happened to arrive at the camp on the soldiers' payday. As he mingled with the crowd, he noticed that two similarly dressed important people were talking with the troops from a raised platform. Since Mucius realized he could not ask someone in the crowd, "Which one is King Porsenna?" he made a guess, pulled his sword, and slew the king's scribe. Seized by the royal bodyguards and dragged before the king, he said, "I am a Roman citizen. They call me Mucius. As an enemy I wanted to kill my enemy, nor do I have less courage for death than for killing." When the furious king threatened to have Mucius burned alive, "Watch this," he said, "so you may know how cheap the body is to men who have their eye on great glory." With that, Mucius plunged his right hand into the fire on an altar and held it there. The king, astounded because Mucius showed no feeling of pain, jumped up and ordered his guards to pull him from the fire. "Go back," said Porsenna, "since you do more harm to yourself than to me." After informing the king that he was but one of a number of young Romans who had sworn to assassinate the king, Mucius returned to Rome, where he received rewards of honor and the cognomen Scaevola, "Lefty."

Cloelia

Frightened by the news that others like Mucius Scaevola would attempt to kill him, Porsenna offered to withdraw his troops in exchange for Roman hostages. Cloelia was one of the girls included among the hostages. Inspired by Mucius's act of heroism, when she realized that the Etruscan camp was near the Tiber, Cloelia led a group of girls to elude their guards, swim across the river through a shower of spears, and reach safety on the Roman side. Incensed, Porsenna demanded Cloelia's return, only to honor her by sending her home with other hostages of her choosing and calling her deed greater than those of Cocles and Mucius. After friendship had thus been restored and the treaty renewed, the Romans honored Cloelia by setting up in the Forum a statue of a girl seated on a horse.

Cincinnatus

Lucius Quinctius Cincinnatus was a model Roman citizen-farmer, a statesman idolized in legend for virtues other than being a fine patriot and military leader. In 458 B.C., the Aequi, a neighboring people with whom the Romans had been fighting for half a century,

History and myths of antiquity are full of legendary women, some of whom are pictured here.
Great Women of Antiquity, *pencil and watercolor, 1902, Frederick D. Wallenn*

had surrounded a Roman army and its commander, a consul, near Mt. Algidus in the Alban Hills southeast of Rome. Deeming the other consul not up to the challenge of rescuing the besieged army, the Senate decreed that Cincinnatus should be named dictator, a special office that in times of crisis permitted them to put the best qualified citizen in charge of the state for up to six months. The Senate's representatives found Cincinnatus at his four-acre farm across the Tiber, intent on his work of digging ditches and plowing. After an exchange of greetings, they asked him to put on his toga and hear the Senate's instructions. The startled Cincinnatus ordered his wife to run to their hut and fetch his toga. Once he had wiped off the dust and sweat and put on his toga, the senators hailed him as dictator, asked him to come to the city, and explained the dangerous circumstances of the army. The next day Cincinnatus ordered every citizen of military age to muster on the Campus Martius, armed, provided with five days' supply of food, and each carrying twelve poles to be used for building a palisade. With this army Cincinnatus marched from Rome and arrived at Mt. Algidus at midnight. In the darkness he deployed his troops in a circle, surrounding the enemy. On command, his army started shouting as they dug a trench and built a palisade that fenced the Aequi in between the two Roman armies. The enemy quickly surrendered. Within days Cincinnatus resigned his dictatorship and returned to his farm. Here, indeed, was a Roman driven by **pietās** rather than by hunger for wealth or power.

The Romans passed along legendary anecdotes such as these about their heroes from generation to generation as an inspiration to their children.

1. Explain how each of these heroes embodied **pietās**.
2. All Roman children learned these stories as part of their education. How do *you* react to heroes such as Horatius Cocles and Cloelia?
3. George Washington was referred to as a modern Cincinnatus. In what ways do you find this comparison appropriate or inappropriate?

Word Study V

Latin Suffixes -*(i)tūdō* and -*(i)tās*

Some Latin adjectives may form nouns by adding the suffix -*(i)tūdō* or the suffix -*(i)tās* to their bases. The base of a Latin adjective may be found by dropping the ending from the genitive singular, e.g., the base of **magnus** (genitive, **magnī**) is **magn-**. Nouns formed in this way are in the 3rd declension, they are feminine, and they convey the meaning of the adjective in noun form:

	Adjective			Base	Noun
Nom.	*Gen.*				
magnus	**magnī**	*big, great*		**magn-**	**magnitūdō, magnitūdinis**, f., *size, greatness*
obēsus	**obēsī**	*fat*		**obēs-**	**obēsitās, obēsitātis**, f., *fatness*

In English words derived from these nouns, -*(i)tūdō* becomes -*(i)tude* and -*(i)tās* becomes -*(i)ty*. The meaning of the English derivative is usually the same as that of the Latin noun, e.g., *magnitude* (size), *obesity* (fatness).

EXERCISE 1

Give the Latin nouns that may be formed from the bases of the adjectives below. In numbers 1–4, use the suffix -*(i)tūdō*, and in numbers 5–10, use the suffix -*(i)tās*. Give the English word derived from each noun formed, and give the meaning of the English word:

1. **sōlus, -a, -um**
2. **multus, -a, -um**
3. **longus, -a, -um**
4. **sollicitus, -a, -um**
5. **ūnus, -a, -um**
6. **brevis, -is, -e**
7. **īnfirmus, -a, -um**
8. **timidus, -a, -um**
9. **vīcīnus, -a, -um**
10. **hūmānus, -a, -um**

Manus manum lavat. *One hand washes the other.* (Petronius, *Satyricon* 45)

Errāre est hūmānum. *To err is human.* (Seneca)

Nōn omnia possumus omnēs. *We cannot all do everything.* (Vergil, *Eclogues* VIII.63)

Latin Suffixes -*īlis*, -*ālis*, -*ārius*

The suffixes -*īlis*, -*ālis*, and -*ārius* may be added to the bases of many Latin nouns to form adjectives. The base of a Latin noun may be found by dropping the ending from the genitive singular, e.g., the base of **vōx** (genitive, **vōcis**) is **vōc-**. Adjectives formed in this way mean *pertaining to* the meaning of the noun from which they are formed:

	Noun			Base	Adjective
Nom.	*Gen.*				
vir	**virī**	*man*		**vir-**	**virīlis, -is, -e,** *pertaining to a man or men, manly*
vōx	**vōcis**	*voice*		**vōc-**	**vōcālis, -is, -e,** *pertaining to the voice, vocal*
statua	**statuae**	*statue*		**statu-**	**statuārius, -a, -um,** *pertaining to statues*

Some adjectives ending in -*ārius* are used as nouns, e.g., **statuārius, -ī,** m., *sculptor*. Can you think of similar words made from the nouns **raeda, -ae,** f., *coach*, and **tabella, -ae,** f., *tablet, document*?

English words derived from these adjectives make the following changes in the suffixes:

> -*īlis* becomes -*il* or -*ile*, e.g., **virīlis,** *virile*
> -*ālis* becomes -*al*, e.g., **vōcālis,** *vocal*
> -*ārius* becomes -*ary*, e.g., **statuārius,** *statuary*

The meaning of the English derivative is similar to or the same as that of the Latin adjective, e.g., **virīlis** in Latin and *virile* in English both mean "manly." Sometimes the English word ending in -*ary* may be used as a noun, e.g., *statuary*, "a group or collection of statues," "sculptor," or "the art of sculpting."

EXERCISE 2

For each English word below, give the following:
  a. the Latin adjective from which it is derived
  b. the Latin noun from which the adjective is formed
  c. the meaning of the English word

You may need to consult a Latin and an English dictionary for this exercise.

auxiliary	principal
civil	puerile
literary	servile
nominal	temporal

Combining Suffixes

Some English words end with a combination of suffixes derived from Latin. For example, the English word *principality* (domain of a prince) is derived from the Latin **prīnceps, prīncipis**, m., base **prīncip-** > English *prīncip-* plus the suffixes *-al* (from Latin *-ālis*) and *-ity* (from Latin *-itās*).

EXERCISE 3

For each word below, give the related English noun ending in the suffix *-ity*. Give the meaning of the English word thus formed and give the Latin word from which it is derived:

civil	immobile
dual	partial
facile	servile
hospital	virile

English Replaced by Latin Derivatives

In the following exercise, the italicized English words are not derived from Latin. Note that these words are usually simpler and more familiar than the Latin derivatives that replace them. Latin can help with the meanings of many of these more difficult English words.

EXERCISE 4

Replace the italicized words with words of equivalent meaning chosen from the pool on the next page. Use the Latin words in parentheses to determine the meanings of the English words in the pool:

1. Staying at an inn was much too *risky* for Aurelia.
2. While he was away, Cornelius left the children in the *guardianship* of Eucleides.
3. Although the driver *handled* the reins skillfully, he was unable to avoid disaster.
4. It was *easy to see* that Eucleides was a friend of the innkeeper.
5. The *runaway* slave was captured and returned to the farm.
6. The innkeeper offered his *friendly welcome* to the Cornelii.
7. The heat made the slaves' work more *burdensome*.
8. The Via Appia is full of *traveling* merchants, who sell their wares from town to town.
9. Cornelia cast a *sorrowful* glance as she waved goodbye to Flavia.
10. This *country* inn was host to all the local farmers.

custody (**custōs**)	hospitality (**hospes**)
itinerant (**iter**)	fugitive (**fugere**)
apparent (**appārēre**)	perilous (**perīculum**)
doleful (**dolēre**)	onerous (**onus**)
manipulated (**manus**)	rustic (**rūsticus**)

Latin Words in English

Some Latin words are used in English in their Latin form. Many of these words have become so familiar in English that they are pluralized using English rules:

senator	plural: *senators*
area	plural: *areas*

Others retain their Latin plurals:

alumnus	plural: *alumni*
alumna	plural: *alumnae*
medium	plural: *media*

Sometimes both an English and a Latin plural are used:

index	plurals: *indexes, indices*
memorandum	plurals: *memorandums, memoranda*

Occasionally the use of two plurals reflects more than one meaning of the word. For example, the word *indexes* usually refers to reference listings in a book, whereas *indices* are signs or indicators, e.g., "the indices of economic recovery."

EXERCISE 5

Look up these nouns in both an English and a Latin dictionary. For each noun, report to the class on similarities or differences between the current meaning in English and the original meaning in Latin. Be sure to note carefully the English plurals and their pronunciation (one word does not have an English plural):

antenna	consensus	formula
appendix	crux	stadium
campus	focus	stimulus

SETTLING IN

Cūnctī in caupōnam intrāvērunt.

"Nōnne cēnāre vultis?" inquit caupō. "Servī meī bonam cēnam vōbīs statim parāre possunt."

"Ego et Cornēlia hīc cēnāre nōn possumus," inquit Aurēlia. "Dūc nōs statim ad cubiculum nostrum." 5

Servōs caupō statim iussit cēnam Cornēliō et Mārcō et Sextō parāre. Ipse Aurēliam et Cornēliam ad cubiculum dūxit. Aurēlia, ubi alterum duōrum lectōrum vīdit, gemuit.

"Hic lectus est sordidus," inquit. "Neque ego neque Cornēlia mea in sordidō lectō dormīre potest. Necesse est alium lectum in cubiculum movēre."

Caupō respondit, "Cūr mē reprehendis? Multī viātōrēs ad meam caupōnam venīre 10 solent. Nēmō meam caupōnam reprehendit."

Iam advēnit Eucleidēs. Ubi Aurēlia rem explicāvit, Eucleidēs quoque caupōnem reprehendit.

Caupō mussāvit, "Prope Viam Appiam caupōnam meliōrem invenīre nōn potestis. In caupōnā meā nūllī lectī sunt sordidī." 15

Sed servōs iussit alium lectum petere. Brevī tempore servī alium lectum in cubiculum portāvērunt. Caupō iam cum rīsū clāmāvit, "Ecce, domina! Servī meī alium lectum tibi parāvērunt. Nōnne nunc cēnāre vultis?"

"Ego nōn iam ēsuriō," inquit Cornēlia. "Volō tantum cubitum īre."

"Ego quoque," inquit Aurēlia, "sum valdē dēfessa." 20

Nōn cēnāvērunt Aurēlia et Cornēlia, sed cubitum statim iērunt. Aurēlia mox dormiēbat sed Cornēlia vigilābat.

1 **intrāvērunt,** *(they) entered*	**sordidus, -a, -um,** *dirty*
2 **cēnō, cēnāre,** *to dine, eat dinner*	12 **rem explicāre,** *to explain the situation*
cēna, -ae, f., *dinner*	14 **melior,** *better*
vōbīs, *for you* (pl.)	17 **tibi,** *for you* (sing.)
6 **iussit,** *(he) ordered*	19 **ēsuriō, ēsurīre,** *to be hungry*
Cornēliō, *for Cornelius*	**cubitum īre,** *to go to bed*
7 **dūxit,** *(he) led*	20 **valdē,** adv., *very, very much, exceedingly*
lectus, -ī, m., *bed*	21 **iērunt,** *they went*
8 **hic lectus,** *this bed*	22 **vigilō, vigilāre,** *to stay awake*

Go Online
PHSchool.com
Web Code: jfd-0019

EXERCISE 19a Respondē Latīnē:

1. Quid servī caupōnis parāre possunt?
2. Vultne Aurēlia statim cēnāre?
3. Quid fēcit Aurēlia ubi lectum vīdit?
   Quid fēcit…? *What did…do?*
4. Quid servī in cubiculum portāvērunt?
5. Cūr Cornēlia cēnāre nōn vult?
6. Quid faciēbant Aurēlia et Cornēlia?

Verbs: Perfect Tense I

Compare the following pairs of sentences:

Caupō **mussat**.	*The innkeeper **mutters**.*
Caupō **mussāvit**.	*The innkeeper **muttered**.*
Dāvus servōs **iubet** canēs dūcere.	*Davus **orders** the slaves to lead the dogs.*
Caupō servōs **iussit** cēnam parāre.	*The innkeeper **ordered** the slaves to prepare dinner.*
Mārcus **gemit**.	*Marcus **groans**.*
Aurēlia **gemuit**.	*Aurelia **groaned**.*
Mārcus nūntium in vīllam **dūcit**.	*Marcus **leads** the messenger into the house.*
Cornēliam ad cubiculum **dūxit**.	*He **led** Cornelia to the bedroom.*

In each of the pairs of examples listed above, the verb in the first example is in the present tense, and the verb in the second example is in the *perfect tense*.

Meanings and translations of the perfect tense:

1. The perfect tense ("perfect" comes from Latin **perfectus**, *completed*) refers not to an action that *is happening* (present tense) or that *was happening* (imperfect tense; "imperfect" = "not completed"), but to an action that *happened* or to something that someone *did* in past time:

   Present:
   Caupō **mussat**.   *The innkeeper **mutters**.*

   Imperfect:
   Caupō **mussābat**.   *The innkeeper **was muttering/used to mutter**.*
                              (imperfect = continuous or repeated action in past time)

   Perfect:
   Caupō **mussāvit**.   *The innkeeper **muttered**.*
                              (perfect = a single action, completed in the past)

Note that in questions, emphatic statements, or denials we may use the helping verb "did" in translating a verb in the perfect tense:

Cēnāvitne Aurēlia?	***Did*** Aurelia ***eat*** dinner?
Cēnāvit Aurēlia.	Aurelia ***did eat*** dinner.
Aurēlia nōn **cēnāvit**.	Aurelia ***did*** not ***eat*** dinner.

2. The perfect tense may also refer to an action that someone *has completed* as of present time:

Servus meus alium lectum tibi **parāvit**.	*My slave **has prepared** another bed for you.*
Hīc multī cīvēs praeclārī **pernoctāvērunt**.	*Many famous citizens **have spent the night** here.*

In the perfect tense, the ending of the 3rd person singular is *-it*; the ending of the 3rd person plural is *-ērunt*.

In many verbs, the stem for the perfect tense ends in **-v-** or **-s-** or **-u-** or **-x** :

mussāv-	iuss-	gemu-	dūx-

The perfect endings are then added to the perfect stem:

mussāv*it*	iuss*it*	gemu*it*	dūx*it*
mussāv*ērunt*	iuss*ērunt*	gemu*ērunt*	dūx*ērunt*

The perfect stems of some verbs are recognized not by letters such as those given above but by a lengthened vowel:

Iam Eucleidēs **advenit**. (present)	*Now Eucleides **arrives**.*
Iam Eucleidēs **advēnit**. (perfect)	*Now Eucleides **arrived**.*

Note how **currō** forms its perfect stem; its perfect tense is **cucurrit**, and its perfect stem is <u>**cucurr-**</u>. This is called a *reduplicated stem*.

Sometimes there are no letters such as **-v-**, **-s-**, **-u-**, or **-x-** or any other marker for the perfect stem, and the perfect stem is the same as the present. Third conjugation verbs of this sort are spelled the same in the 3rd person singular in the present and the perfect tenses, and only the context can tell you the tense of the verb (find an example in lines 12–13 of the story).

EXERCISE 19b

Give the missing forms and meanings to complete the following table:

Perfect Tense		Perfect Stem Marker	Infinitive	Meaning
Singular	*Plural*			
intrāvit	intrāvērunt	-v-	intrāre	to enter
_____	custōdīvērunt	_____	_____	_____
timuit	_____	_____	_____	_____
_____	cēnāvērunt	_____	_____	_____
_____	trāxērunt	_____	_____	_____
mīsit	_____	_____	_____	_____
spectāvit	_____	_____	_____	_____
doluit	_____	_____	_____	_____
_____	mānsērunt	_____	_____	_____
_____	voluērunt	_____	_____	_____
haesit	_____	_____	_____	_____

EXERCISE 19c

Read aloud, paying special attention to tenses of verbs. Then translate:

Cornēliī per viam ad caupōnam lentē ambulābant.

Sextus, "Nōnne ille tabellārius equōs vehementer incitāvit, Mārce?"

Cui respondit Mārcus, "Ita vērō! Eōs ferōciter verberāvit. Equī cisium celeriter trāxērunt. Raedārius noster, 'Cavē, sceleste!' magnā vōce exclāmāvit. Tum raedam dēvertēbat, sed frūstrā. Tabellārius tamen neque cisium dēvertit   5 neque raedam vītāvit. Itaque equī raedam in fossam trāxērunt. Gemuit raedārius; gemuērunt pater et māter; lacrimāvit Cornēlia."

"Pater tuus certē īrātus erat," interpellāvit Sextus. "Statim virgam arripuit et miserum raedārium verberābat. Cornēlia, ubi hoc vīdit, iterum lacrimāvit. 'Pater! Pater!' inquit. 'Nōlī miserum hominem verberāre!'"   10

"Tum pater," inquit Mārcus, "Cornēliam tacēre iussit. Omnēs sollicitī caelum spectāvērunt quod iam advesperāscēbat. Pater igitur Eucleidem nōs ad caupōnam dūcere iussit."

2 **vehementer,** adv., *very much, violently, hard*
3 cui, *to whom, to him, to her*

8 **certē,** adv., *certainly*
  arripuit, *he seized*
9 **hoc,** *this*

EXERCISE 19d

Locate all verbs in the perfect tense in the story above. Copy them onto a sheet of paper in six columns, each headed with one of the markers of the perfect stem ("-v-," "-s-," "-u-," "-x-," "lengthened vowel," and "no stem marker").

ADDITIONAL READING:
The Romans Speak for Themselves: Book I: "Stopping at an Inn," pages 53–58.

Go Online
PHSchool.com
Web Code: jfd-0019

GRAFFITI FROM ANCIENT INNS

Numerous graffiti were scratched or painted on the walls of inns and taverns in Pompeii, and many of them have been recovered by archaeologists while excavating this city that was destroyed by the eruption of Mount Vesuvius in A.D. 79. Some of the graffiti were written by the proprietors, others by the guests. They concern food, drink, conditions at the inn, and experiences of the guests. Sometimes they are prose, sometimes verse, and sometimes they are in dialogue form. Here is a sample:

I

Viātor, audī. Sī libet, intus venī:
tabula est aēna quae tē cūncta perdocet.
Traveler, listen. Come inside if you like:
there's a bronze tablet that gives you all the information.

II

Assibus hīc bibitur; dīpundium sī dederis, meliōra bibēs;
    quattus sī dederis, vīna Falerna bibēs.
A drink is had here for one as; if you pay two, you'll drink better (wines);
    if you pay four, you'll drink Falernian.

III

Tālia tē fallant utinam mendācia, caupō:
    tū vēndis aquam et bibis ipse merum.
I hope these deceptions get you into trouble, innkeeper:
    you sell water and drink the pure wine yourself.

IV

Mīximus in lectō. Fateor, peccāvimus, hospes.
    Sī dīcēs, "Quārē?" Nūlla matella fuit.
I wet the bed. I have sinned, I confess it, O host.
    If you ask why: there was no chamber-pot.

Write a graffito that one of our characters might write after a night at the inn.

Scene from an inn at Pompeii. Sausages and meat hang from the rack.

Go Online
PHSchool.com
Web Code: jfd-0019

ROMAN TRAVEL

Gaius Cornelius and his family traveled by land from Baiae to Rome along a section of the Via Appia, which ran south from Rome to Brundisium—a distance of 358 miles or 576 kilometers. It was part of a network of major highways that radiated from the Golden Milestone (**mīliārium aureum**) in the Forum at Rome to all parts of the Empire. These roads, originally built by the legions to make easy movement of troops possible, were laid on carefully made foundations with drainage channels at both sides and were usually paved with slabs of basalt. Although land travel was safer and easier than at any time before the "Railway Age," it was nevertheless extremely slow by modern standards. The **raeda** seldom averaged more than five miles or eight kilometers per hour; a man walking might manage twenty-five miles or forty kilometers a day; an imperial courier on urgent business might, with frequent changes of horse, manage to cover over 150 miles or 240 kilometers in twenty-four hours. Since carriage wheels had iron rims and vehicles lacked springs, a journey by road was bound to be uncomfortable. Some **raedae** were open or covered only with a canopy and would subject travelers to clouds of dust and attacks of insects. Others were enclosed with leather, cloth, or wood but could be uncomfortable in hot weather.

1. Via Aemilia (187 B.C.)
2. Via Appia (312–244 B.C.)
3. Via Aurēlia
4. Via Flāminia (220 B.C.)
5. Via Latīna
6. Via Postumia (148 B.C.)
7. Via Valeria
8. Via Iūlia Augusta
9. Via Domitiāna
10. Via Traiāna
11. Via Cassia
12. Via Popillia
13. Via Salāria

VIAE ITALIAE ROMANAE

SCALE OF MILES
0   50   100

Whether a journey was over land or water, the trip was filled with hazards and discomforts. The following passage illustrates some of these discomforts:

> When I had to make my way back from Baiae to Naples, to avoid the experience of sailing a second time, I easily convinced myself that a storm was raging. The whole road was so deep in mud that I might as well have gone by sea. That day I had to endure what athletes put up with as a matter of course: after being anointed with mud, we were dusted with sand in the Naples tunnel. Nothing could be longer than that prison-like corridor, nothing dimmer than those torches that do not dispel the darkness but merely make us more aware of it. But even if there were light there, it would be blacked out by the dust, which, however troublesome and disagreeable it may be in the open, is, as you can imagine, a thousand times worse in an enclosed space where there is no ventilation and the dust rises in one's face. These were the two entirely different discomforts that we suffered. On the same day and on the same road we struggled through both mud and dust.

Seneca, Moral Epistles LVII

Roman mosaic showing travel by boat on the Nile
Mosaic, Landscape crossed by the Nile, Palestrina, second to third century B.C.

Horace's Journey

The Roman poet Horace describes a journey that he took on the Appian Way from Rome to Brundisium in 38 or 37 B.C. He describes some of the hazards with which travelers might be faced:

After I had left great Rome, I put up in Aricia in a humble inn. My companion was Heliodorus, a teacher of rhetoric. From there we went to Forum Appii, a town packed with boatmen and grasping innkeepers. We were idle enough to take this part of the journey in two stages; for the more energetic it is only one; the Appian Way is less tiring for leisurely travelers. Here, because of the water, which is very bad, I suffered an upset stomach; and it was in a bad temper that I waited for my companions to finish their evening meal. As we were about to go on board, the boatmen began to argue. A whole hour went past while the fares were being collected and the mule harnessed. The vicious mosquitoes and marsh-frogs made sleep impossible, while the boatman, who had drunk too much cheap wine, sang of his absent girlfriend, and a passenger joined in the singing.

At last the weary passengers fell asleep, and the idle boatman turned the mule out to graze, fastened its halter to a stone, and lay on his back snoring.

At dawn we realized we weren't moving. A hot-tempered passenger leapt up and beat the boatman and the mule with a stick. When at last we disembarked, it was almost ten o'clock. With due reverence and ceremony we washed our hands and faces in the fountain of Feronia.

After lunch we "crawled" the three miles to Anxur, which is perched on rocks that shine white in the distance. There our very good friend Maecenas was due to meet us. As my eyes were giving me trouble, I smeared black ointment on them. Meanwhile, Maecenas arrived with that perfect gentleman, Fonteius Capito. We were glad to leave Fundi behind, with its self-appointed "praetor" Aufidius Luscus. How we laughed at the official get-up of the ambition-crazy clerk, his toga praetexta and the tunic with the broad stripe. At last, tired out, we stayed in the city of Formiae, where Murena provided accommodation and Capito a meal.

The next day we reached Sinuessa and were met by Varius, Plotius, and Vergil—friends to whom I was most attached. Then a small villa next to the Campanian bridge gave us shelter, and the official purveyors, as they were obliged to do, provided us with wood and salt. After we left here, our pack-mules were unsaddled early at Capua. Maecenas went to play ball, Vergil and I to sleep; for ball games are bad for a man with sore eyes and an upset stomach. After Capua, Cocceius received us in a house with ample provisions built above the inns of Caudium.

From here we made our way right on to Beneventum, where the overworked innkeeper nearly burned the place down while roasting lean thrushes on a spit. Soon after leaving Beneventum, I saw again the familiar mountains of my native Apulia. We would never have struggled over those mountains if we had not found lodgings at Trivicum. There the smoke made our eyes water, for they put green branches on the fire, leaves and all. There also I waited until midnight for a deceitful girl who never showed up. What a fool I was!

From here we sped on twenty-four miles in carriages, intending to lodge in a small town, the name of which I cannot fit into the rhythm of my verse. Here they charge for the cheapest of all commodities—water. The bread, however, is very good indeed, so that the experienced traveler usually takes some away in his bag; for the bread at Canusium is as hard as a stone, and the water supply is no better.

From here we arrived at Rubi, tired out—as was to be expected—for the stage was long and the road conditions difficult because of heavy rain. After this the weather was better, but the road worse as far as Barium, a fishing town. Then Gnatia provided us with laughter and amusement: the people tried to convince us that in the temple there frankincense melts without a flame. I don't believe it!

Brundisium is the end of my long account and of my long journey.

Horace, *Satires* I.5 (abridged)

1. Explain the origin of the saying "All roads lead to Rome" in light of the reading and the map on page 154. To what degree is the saying accurate?
2. What do you think Horace enjoyed the most on his journey? What the least?

CHANCE ENCOUNTER

Ubi Cornēlia et māter cubitum iērunt, Mārcus et Sextus cum Cornēliō mānsērunt. Cum Cornēliō cēnāre et post cēnam ad mediam noctem vigilāre in animō habuērunt, nam omnia vidēre et omnia audīre voluērunt.

Mārcus, "Ēsuriō, pater," inquit. "Ēsurīsne tū quoque, Sexte?"

"Ita vērō!" respondit Sextus.   5

"Semper ēsurītis, tū et Mārcus!" exclāmāvit Cornēlius.

"Licetne nōbīs," inquit Mārcus, "hīc cēnāre?"

Paulisper tacēbat pater, sed tandem, "Estō!" inquit. "Tibi et Sextō licet hīc cēnāre. Post cēnam tamen necesse est statim cubitum īre."

Rīsērunt puerī quod laetī erant. "Gaudēmus, pater," inquit Mārcus, "quod nōs in   10
cubiculum nōn statim mīsistī. Voluimus enim hīc manēre et aliōs viātōrēs spectāre."

Tum Cornēlius caupōnem iussit cibum parāre. Brevī tempore servus cibum ad eōs portāvit. Dum puerī cibum dēvorant, subitō intrāvit mīles quīdam. Cornēlium attentē spectāvit. "Salvē, vir optime!" inquit. "Salvēte, puerī! Cūr vōs in hanc caupōnam intrā-vistis? Cūr nōn ad vīllam hospitis īstis? Nōnne tū es senātor Rōmānus?"   15

(continued)

1	**mānsērunt**, *(they) stayed*	
2	**post**, prep. + acc., *after*	
	medius, -a, -um, *mid-, middle of*	
	media nox, *midnight*	
7	**Licetne nōbīs…?** *Is it allowed for us…? May we…?*	
8	**paulisper**, adv., *for a short time*	
	Estō! *All right!*	
11	**mīsistī**, *you have sent*	
	voluimus, *we wanted*	

enim, conj., *for*

13 Dum…dēvorant, *While…were devouring*

mīles, mīlitis m., *soldier*

14 vir optime, *sir*

optimus, -a, -um, *best, very good*

in hanc caupōnam, *into this inn*

15 Cūr nōn…īstis? *Why didn't you go?*

EXERCISE 20a

Respondē Latīnē:

1. Quid Mārcus et Sextus facere voluērunt?
2. Ēsuriuntne puerī?
3. Licetne Mārcō et Sextō in caupōnā cēnāre?
4. Cūr puerī laetī sunt?
5. Quis intrāvit dum puerī cibum dēvorant?

Go Online
PHSchool.com
Web Code: jfd-0020

"Senātor Rōmānus sum," respondit Cornēlius. "Nōs in hanc caupōnam intrāvimus quod raeda nostra in fossā haeret immōbilis. In agrīs nocte manēre nōlēbāmus, sed numquam anteā in caupōnā pernoctāvimus. Certē in agrīs pernoctāre est perīculōsum."

Tum mīles, "Etiam in caupōnā pernoctāre saepe est perīculōsum."

"Cūr hoc nōbīs dīcis?" rogāvit Cornēlius. "Estne hic caupō homō scelestus? Dē Apollodōrō quid audīvistī?"

"Dē Apollodōrō nihil audīvī, sed semper est perīculōsum in caupōnā pernoctāre. Vōsne audīvistis illam fābulam dē caupōne nārrātam? Ille caupō hospitem necāvit."

"Minimē!" inquit Cornēlius. "Illam fābulam nōn audīvī. Cūr igitur nōbīs illam nōn nārrās dum cēnāmus?"

20

25

18 **numquam**, adv., *never*	**nārrātus, -a, -um**, *told*
anteā, adv., *before*	**necō, necāre**, *to kill*
20 **dīcō, dīcere**, *to say, tell*	25 **nārrō, nārrāre**, *to tell (a story)*
23 **fābula, -ae**, f., *story*	

Respondē Latīnē:

6. Cūr Cornēlius in agrīs pernoctāre nōlēbat?
7. Quid mīles dē Apollodōrō audīvit?
8. Quid fēcit caupō in fābulā?

FORMS

Go Online
PHSchool.com
Web Code: jfd-0020

Verbs: Perfect Tense II

You have now met all the endings of the perfect tense:

Singular			Plural		
1	*-ī*		1	*-imus*	
2	*-istī*		2	*-istis*	
3	*-it*		3	*-ērunt*	

These are the endings of the perfect tense of *all* Latin verbs, e.g.:

Singular			Plural		
1	mīs*ī*		1	mīs*imus*	
2	mīs*istī*		2	mīs*istis*	
3	mīs*it*		3	mīs*ērunt*	

EXERCISE 20b

Read each incomplete sentence to yourself. Identify all subjects and use the chart above to supply the correct perfect tense endings for the verbs. Then read aloud and translate:

1. Ego līberōs in hortō petīv_____; tū eōs in silvā invēn_____.
2. Ubi tunica Sextī in rāmīs haerēbat, nōs omnēs rīs_____.

3. Quō iit Cornēlia? Ego et Mārcus patrem hoc rogāv_____, sed ille nihil respond_____.
4. Quamquam Sextus fuit molestus, servī eum nōn verberāv_____.
5. Ubi heri fu_____, Mārce et Cornēlia? Pater et māter nōs iuss_____ hīc manēre.
6. Postquam vōs cēnāv_____, cubitum īre volu_____.
7. Heri nōs in urbe erāmus, sed mātrem ibi nōn vīd_____.
8. "Unde vēn_____, amīcī?" rogāv_____ caupō. "Quō nunc ītis?"
9. Tūne Cornēlium vīd_____, ubi tū Rōmam advēn_____? Ego certē eum nōn vīd_____.
10. Ille, postquam haec audīv_____, ē caupōnā sē praecipitāv_____.

ille, *he*　　　　　　　　　**postquam,** conj., *after*
fuit, (*he/she/it*) *was*　　　**haec,** *these things, this*
heri, adv., *yesterday*

BUILDING THE MEANING

Subordinate Clauses with the Conjunction *dum*

Look at the following sentences, in which subordinate clauses are introduced by the conjunction **dum**:

> **Dum** Cornēliī **cēnant**, mīles fābulam **nārrat**.
> *While/As long as the Cornelii **eat dinner**, the soldier **tells** a story.*

> **Dum** Cornēliī **cēnābant**, mīles fābulam **nārrābat**.
> *While/As long as the Cornelii **were eating dinner**, the soldier **was telling** a story.*

In the first sentence, the verb in each clause is in the present tense, and the sentence describes two actions that are taking place at the same time.

In the second sentence, the verb in each clause is in the imperfect tense, and the sentence describes two actions that were taking place over the same period of time in the past.

Now look at the following sentence:

> **Dum** puerī cibum **dēvorant**, subitō **intrāvit** mīles quīdam. (20:13)
> *While the boys **were devouring** their food, a certain soldier suddenly **entered**.*

Here the verb in the subordinate clause is in the present tense (**dēvorant**), and the verb of the main clause is in the perfect tense (**intrāvit**). The subordinate clause, introduced by **dum**, describes an action that was continuing over a period of time in the past when suddenly a single, simple action occurred, namely a soldier entered. Contrary to expectation, Latin uses the present tense and not the imperfect in subordinate clauses introduced by **dum** when the verb of the main clause is in the perfect tense. Translate as above: *While the boys **were devouring** their food. . . .*

Uses of the Infinitive (Consolidation)

You have met the following uses of the infinitive in your reading:

a. Complementary infinitive:

> Mārcus arborēs **ascendere** <u>nōn vult</u>.
> *Marcus <u>does not want</u> **to climb** trees.*

> Multī viātōrēs ad meam caupōnam **venīre** <u>solent</u>.
> *Many travelers <u>are accustomed</u> **to come** to my inn.*
> *Many travelers are in the habit of coming to my inn.*

In addition to **nōlle** and **solēre**, the verbs **parāre**, **posse**, **timēre**, and **velle** and the phrase **in animō habēre** are commonly accompanied by complementary infinitives.

b. Infinitive with impersonals:

> Nōbīs <u>necesse est</u> statim **discēdere**. (9:13–14)
> *<u>It is necessary</u> for us **to leave** immediately.*
> *We must leave immediately.*

> Vōbīs <u>licet</u> hīc **cēnāre**.
> *<u>It is allowed</u> for you **to dine** here.*
> *You may dine here.*

The verbal phrase **necesse est** and the verb **licet** are said to be *impersonal*, because we may supply a subject, *it*, and translate them with the impersonal phrases *it is necessary* and *it is allowed*. The infinitives, however, are actually the grammatical subjects, and we may translate very literally and rather awkwardly as follows:

> **To leave** immediately <u>is necessary</u> for us.
> **To dine** here <u>is allowed</u> for you.

c. Infinitive as subject of the verb **est**:

> Certē in agrīs **pernoctāre** <u>est</u> perīculōsum. (20:18)
> **To spend the night** in the fields <u>is</u> certainly dangerous.
> *It is certainly dangerous **to spend the night** in the fields.*

The infinitive is here being used as a *verbal noun*, and as such it is neuter in gender, hence the neuter complement **perīculōsum**.

d. Accusative and infinitive with verbs such as **docēre** and **iubēre**:

> Aurēlia **Cornēliam** <u>docet</u> vīllam **cūrāre**. (6:11)
> *Aurelia <u>teaches</u> **Cornelia** (how) **to take care of** the country house.*

> **Ancillam** <u>iubet</u> aliās tunicās et stolās et pallās in cistam **pōnere**. (10:2)
> *She orders **a slave-woman to put** other tunics and stolas and pallas into a chest.*

EXERCISE 20c

In the story at the beginning of this chapter, locate all infinitives and explain their uses.

EXERCISE 20d

Read aloud and translate. Explain uses of **dum** and of infinitives:

1. Cūr, Mārce et Sexte, ad mediam noctem vigilāre in animō habētis?
2. Omnia vidēre et audīre volumus quod numquam anteā in caupōnā pernoctāvimus.
3. Dum puerī in caupōnā erant, dormīre nōlēbant.
4. Cūr voluistī hīc pernoctāre, Mārce?
5. Cūr in caupōnā pernoctāvistis, puerī? Licetne fīliō senātōris in caupōnam intrāre?
6. Cornēlius servum in cubiculum īre iussit.
7. In viā pernoctāre perīculōsum est.
8. Dum Cornēlius et puerī cēnant, intrāvit mīles quīdam.
9. Vōbīs in caupōnā cēnāre licet.
10. Ego et tū cubitum īre nōluimus.

EXERCISE 20e

Using story 20 and the charts of forms showing perfect tense endings as guides, give the Latin for:

1. Cornelia: "I wanted to go to bed."
2. Boys: "We stayed with Cornelius."
3. Boys: "We intended to stay awake until midnight."
4. Cornelius: "Why did you laugh, boys?"
5. Soldier: "Why, sir, did you enter this inn?"
6. Cornelius: "I entered this inn because my carriage is stuck in a ditch."

Wine and other liquids, such as olive oil, were transported in large clay jars called *amphorae*, each capable of holding several gallons of liquid.

Go Online
PHSchool.com
Web Code: jfd-0020

ROMAN HOSPITALITY

Because inns were dirty and often dangerous, well-to-do Romans tried to avoid staying in them. Instead, they tried to plan their journeys so that they could stay at the **vīlla** of a **hospes**. This word means "host" or "guest," but it is also translated as "friend," although in this special sense it has no exact equivalent in English. It describes a relationship of friendship and trust between two men that could be continued by their descendants. As a result of such a relationship, a traveler could go to the house of his **hospes**—whom in some cases he personally might never have met—and claim **hospitium** for the night, producing, if need be, some token such as a coin that had been halved as proof of the link between the two men. The relationship could extend to other situations. For instance, if a Roman had business interests in one of the provinces, someone residing there might look after them for him. In return, he might have some service done for him in Rome. Cornelius, you may remember, is taking care of Sextus while his father is in Asia.

This open-air dining area of the so-called House of Neptune at Herculaneum is adorned with mosaic-covered niches for statues.
Open-air trīclīnium of House of Neptune at Herculaneum, first century A.D.

FORMS

Verbs: Principal Parts

A dictionary entry for a Latin verb normally gives the four principal parts, from which all forms of that verb may be derived. Since Chapter 10 you have been seeing the first two principal parts of verbs in vocabulary lists. All four principal parts of the verb **parō** are:

parō: 1st person singular, present tense = *I prepare, I am preparing, I do prepare*

parāre: present infinitive = *to prepare, to be preparing*

parāvī: 1st person singular, perfect tense = *I prepared, I did prepare, I have prepared*

parātus, -a, -um: perfect passive participle (verbal adjective) = *having been prepared, prepared, ready*

	Present	Infinitive	Perfect	Perfect Passive Participle	Meaning of the Verb
1st Conj.	párō	parā́re	parā́vī	parā́tus	*to prepare*
2nd Conj.	hábeō	habḗre	hábuī	hábitus	*to have*
3rd Conj.	míttō	míttere	mī́sī	míssus	*to send*
-iō	iáciō	iácere	iḗcī	iáctus	*to throw*
4th Conj.	aúdiō	audī́re	audī́vī	audī́tus	*to hear*

NOTES

1. The perfect stem is found by dropping the *-ī* from the end of the third principal part of the verb. The perfect endings are then added directly to this stem.

2. The fourth principal part of a Latin verb will usually be the *perfect passive participle*, which has the forms of a 1st and 2nd declension adjective. Sometimes perfect passive participles function as simple adjectives as in the following sentence from Chapter 10:

   Gāius ipse ascendere est **parātus.** (10:13)
   *Gaius himself is **ready** to climb [into the carriage].*

   Other examples are: **perterritus, -a, -um,** *frightened, terrified* (5:9); **commōtus, -a, -um,** *moved* (14:17); and **nārrātus, -a, -um,** *told* (20:23). You will study the perfect passive participle more fully later in the course.

3. Intransitive verbs do not have perfect passive participles, and the *future active participle* will be given as the fourth principal part instead:

   veniō, venīre, vēnī, ventūrus, *to come*

The future active participle **ventūrus** may be translated *being about to come* or simply *about to come*. You will study this form later.

4. The principal parts of most verbs of the 1st, 2nd, and 4th conjugations are predictable and follow the patterns on the previous page.

5. In future vocabulary lists, the principal parts of verbs of the 1st, 2nd, and 4th conjugations that follow the set patterns will appear as follows:

> **parō, -āre, -āvī, -ātus,** *to prepare*
> **habeō, -ēre, -uī, -itus,** *to have, hold*
> **audiō, -īre, -īvī, -ītus,** *to hear*

6. When verbs of the 1st, 2nd, and 4th conjugations do not follow the set patterns, their principal parts will be given in full, so that you can see how the stems change and note any irregularities:

> **lavō, lavāre, lāvī, lautus,** *to wash*

7. There is no set pattern for 3rd conjugation verbs. Their principal parts will be given in vocabulary lists in full:

> **dūcō, dūcere, dūxī, ductus,** *to lead*

8. The principal parts of irregular verbs will be given in full with the notation *irreg.*:

> **sum, esse, fuī, futūrus,** irreg., *to be*
> **eō, īre, iī** or **īvī, itūrus,** irreg., *to go*

9. The perfect tense of irregular verbs is formed by adding the perfect endings to the perfect stem in the same way as for all other verbs, e.g., **fuī, fuistī, fuit,** etc. Note, however, that in the perfect tense forms of the verb **īre,** formed from the stem **i-,** the double **i**'s become **ī** before **s**:

	Sing.	Pl.
1	íī	íimus
2	ī́stī	ī́stis
3	íit	iérunt

This verb also has forms from the stem **īv-:** īvī, īvistī, īvit, īvimus, īvistis, īvērunt.

10. It is very important that you learn the principal parts of Latin verbs.

To help you do this, the principal parts of new verbs that do not follow the set patterns or are irregular will be given in separate verb lists following the stories in which they first appear from this point on.

The principal parts of verbs that you have already met that do not follow the set patterns or are irregular will also be given in these separate verb lists following the stories in which they first reappear from this point on.

New verbs that follow the set patterns in the 1st, 2nd, and 4th conjugations will be given with their principal parts abbreviated in the regular vocabulary lists.

EXERCISE 20f

Read aloud and translate each verb form given at the left below. Then deduce and give the first three principal parts for each verb. Note that there are no 3rd conjugation **-iō** verbs in this list.

	1st Sing. Present	Present Infinitive	1st Sing. Perfect
necāmus, necāvimus intrant, intrāvērunt errās, errāvistī tenēs, tenuistī mittunt, mīsērunt manēmus, mānsimus iubet, iussit discēdimus, discessimus haeret, haesit dormiunt, dormīvērunt petunt, petīvērunt custōdīmus, custōdīvimus gemitis, gemuistis	necō	necāre	necāvī

Can you give the first three principal parts for the following?

estis, fuistis			

Go Online
PHSchool.com
Web Code: jfd-0020

THE EARLY REPUBLIC

The Roman Republic grew steadily from 509 B.C., when the election of Lucius Junius Brutus and Lucius Tarquinius Collatinus as its first consuls signaled its birth, until 264 B.C., the start of the First Punic War. Rome expanded physically, until through military conquests she gained control of all of Italy south of the Rubicon River. Political growth came about through the adaptation of the constitution to meet the changing needs of society and circumstances. This constitution was not a formal, written document but a set of practices and policies. A major cause of change was the long, yet successful, struggle of the common people, the plebs, to acquire legal and political equality with the upper-class patricians.

The Consuls and the Magistrates

The two consuls, essentially co-presidents, were both heads of the civil government and generals of the Roman army. The election of two leaders to a one-year term of office was a consciously dramatic change from the installation of a single king for life, and it assured that no one person could have unlimited power.

As time went on, to assist the consuls in managing the affairs of state, other officers were named: praetors, who directed the judicial system; aediles, who supervised commerce and public works; tribunes, who championed the lower classes; and quaestors, who handled financial matters. These magistrates, like the consuls, were elected annually. To maintain the balance of power, two or more individuals generally bore the same title and either shared the same duties or performed matching roles in the government. As Rome grew and the Roman government had greater responsibilities to fulfill, the number of quaestors, aediles, and praetors was increased. Censors, moreover, were chosen every five years to revise the list of members of the Senate and carry out the census that assigned citizens to specific classes. In times of crisis, a dictator could be appointed to take over the government for a period of no more than six months, as did Cincinnatus. An ambitious Roman's political career might carry him up the steps of a series of offices, the **cursus honōrum:** election as quaestor, followed by appointment to the Senate, then terms as praetor, consul, and censor. After being quaestor, one might become an aedile before becoming a praetor.

The Centuriate assembly (**comitia centuriāta**) had its origin in the army, which was originally divided into centuries or groups of a hundred men. It passed laws, ratified treaties, issued declarations of war, and elected consuls, praetors, aediles, the censors, and the priests of the state religion. A citizen was assigned to his century or voting block in the Centuriate assembly according to his wealth, originally equalling the amount of military equipment he could afford. The cavalry or horsemen, **equitēs**, made up the eighteen richest of the 193 centuries. The next richest class made up eighty centuries of infantry or foot soldiers. At the bottom of the ranking were the citizens who owned no property, the proletariat, all heaped into one century. Each century cast a single vote, determined by the majority of the entire group, like the American electoral college. Since the ninety-eight votes of the two wealthiest classes could constitute the majority when the entire assembly voted, and since clients in the lower ranks usually voted according to the wishes of their richer patrons, it is easy to guess how the voting went.

The Tribal assembly (**comitia tribūta**), an outgrowth of the Council of Plebeians, issued plebiscites, which eventually were as binding as laws passed by the Centuriate assembly. It also elected aediles and the tribunes, who, with their power of veto, could intercede in the passage of laws and in practices that were unjust to the plebeians.

The Senate, an advisory council whose members were former magistrates, controlled finances and foreign policy. In practice, they were the major influence in the government, for the magistrates followed the senators' advice and matters were brought before the assemblies only after the Senate had voiced its approval.

A Roman triumphal procession
A Roman Triumph, *oil on canvas, ca. 1630, Peter Paul Rubens*

The Citizen Army

For Rome to survive its continual battles with her neighboring states, especially those in the hills, a larger citizen army was needed. The plebeian class provided that human resource, and once they had assumed the burden of military duty, they began to demand full equality as citizens. Military successes brought spoils of war and property grants and made the lower class more prosperous and ambitious. The wealthier plebeians especially were eager to attain equality with the patricians. By organizing a mass strike and refusing to perform their military service, the plebeians could force changes. Their leadership came from the tribunes, originally military officers, who gained acceptance as plebeian representatives before the Senate. As a first step, existing legal practices were codified and written down on bronze tablets. This first collection of Roman law, the Laws of the Twelve Tables, guaranteed every Roman citizen the right to justice. The Tribal assembly became an official body, with formal powers to pass plebiscites and elect aediles and tribunes. Then the right to hold office, including the consulship, allowed the plebeians to become senators. And once the plebiscites of the Tribal assembly came to be equal to laws passed by the Centuriate assembly, Rome achieved a fairly representative form of government, in which a senatorial aristocracy of patricians and wealthy plebeians formed the new ruling class of citizens.

The Conquest of Italy

The progress of the Roman military conquest of Italy is not a simple story, since the conquered did not always stay conquered. A new generation was likely to bring a new war with an old foe. The first victories came in the struggle to survive against the threats of neighbors: the Sabines, Aequi, and Volsci from the mountains inland; the Etruscans, pushing across the Tiber from the north; the Latins to the south. When the Gauls invaded Italy from the north in 390 B.C., going so far as to occupy all of Rome except the Capitoline Hill, the Romans, under the command of the legendary Camillus, led a unified Italian force that chased out the invaders, who were interested more in plunder than conquest. The Romans then revamped their military operations. A standing army was formed. The legions, now armed with spears and short swords, arranged in units or maniples that could maneuver quickly and attack in three waves, proved more effective than the old phalanx formation. The practice of establishing a camp with a fixed plan, even when the army was on the move over the growing network of Roman roads, provided a safety-measure of defense.

Following the military conquest of their neighbors and the Gallic invaders, the Romans faced new opponents. They confronted the Samnites and the Greek cities in southern Italy. When Pyrrhus, king of the Greek nation of Epirus, was invited to assist his fellow Greeks in repelling the Romans, he brought such novelties as elephants to Italy, but could win battles only at the expense of great losses to his manpower. After one of his famous Pyrrhic victories such as those at Heraclea in 280 B.C. and at Ausculum in 279 B.C., the king reckoned the human cost and made his legendary remark, "One more victory like this, and we shall be truly ruined." After Pyrrhus went home to Greece, Rome was left master of Italy. From the time of the Gallic invasion, moreover, Rome ceased to be simply a vengeful conqueror and adopted the policy of forming an alliance with each city she won. These allies gave Rome military allegiance and control of foreign policy, but they retained home rule in the governing of their own states. To many neighbors, too, Rome offered Roman citizenship. Elsewhere throughout Italy, she planted colonies that provided a Roman presence. Thus Rome became not simply a strong city-state, but the head of a confederacy of cities in Italy.

---

1. What groups of people have been totally omitted from this discussion, and why?
2. In what ways did the plebs gain greater power during this period?
3. What were the main offices of the **cursus honōrum**, and what do you learn about them in the reading?

MURDER

Mīles hanc fābulam nārrāvit:

"Duo amīcī, Aulus et Septimus, dum iter in Graeciā faciunt, ad urbem Megaram vēnērunt. Aulus in caupōnā pernoctāvit, in vīllā hospitis Septimus. Mediā nocte, dum Septimus dormit, Aulus in somnō eī appāruit et clāmāvit. 'Age, Septime! Fer mihi auxilium! Caupō mē necāre parat.'   5

"Septimus, somniō perterritus, statim surrēxit et, postquam animum recuperāvit, 'Nihil malī,' inquit. 'Somnium modo fuit.'

"Deinde iterum obdormīvit. Iterum tamen in somnō Aulus suō amīcō appāruit; iterum Septimō clāmāvit, 'Ubi ego auxilium petīvī, tū nōn vēnistī. Nēmō mē adiuvāre nunc potest. Caupō enim mē necāvit. Postquam hoc fēcit, corpus meum in plaustrō   10
posuit et stercus suprā coniēcit. In animō habet plaustrum ex urbe crās movēre. Necesse est igitur crās māne plaustrum petere et caupōnem pūnīre.'   (*continued*)

4 **somnus, -ī,** m., *sleep* **eī,** *to him*	8 obdormiō, -īre, -īvī, -ītūrus, *to go to sleep*
6 **somnium, -ī,** n., *dream* **animum recuperāre,** *to regain one's senses, wake up*	10 **corpus, corporis,** n., *body*
7 nihil malī, *nothing of a bad thing, there is nothing wrong* **malus, -a, -um,** *bad*	11 stercus, stercoris, n., *dung, manure* **suprā,** adv., *above, on top*
	12 **māne,** adv., *early in the day, in the morning* **pūniō, -īre, -īvī, -ītus,** *to punish*

6 **surgō, surgere, surrēxī, surrēctūrus,** *to get up, rise*
7 **sum, esse, fuī, futūrus,** irreg., *to be*
9 **adiuvō, adiuvāre, adiūvī, adiūtus,** *to help*
11 **pōnō, pōnere, posuī, positus,** *to place, put*
   coniciō, conicere, coniēcī, coniectus, *to throw*

EXERCISE 21a

Respondē Latīnē:

Go Online
PHSchool.com
Web Code: jfd-0021

1. Ubi est Megara?
2. Ubi pernoctāvit Aulus? Ubi erat amīcus Aulī?
3. Quandō Aulus Septimō appāruit?   **Quandō…?** *When…?*
4. Quid fēcit Septimus postquam animum recuperāvit?
5. Ubi caupō corpus Aulī posuit? Quid in animō habuit?

"Iterum surrēxit Septimus. Prīmā lūce ad caupōnam iit et plaustrum petīvit. Ubi plaustrum invēnit, stercus remōvit et corpus extrāxit. Septimus, ubi amīcum mortuum vīdit, lacrimāvit. Caupō scelestus quoque lacrimāvit, nam innocentiam simulābat. Septimus tamen caupōnem statim accūsāvit. Mox cīvēs eum pūnīvērunt." 15

Postquam mīles fābulam fīnīvit, silentium fuit. Subitō Cornēlius exclāmāvit, "Agite, puerī! Nōnne vōs iussī post cēnam cubitum īre? Cūr ad cubiculum nōn īstis?"

Sed Sextus, "Nōs quoque fābulam mīlitis audīre voluimus. Nōn dēfessī sumus. Nōn sērō est." 20

Hoc tamen dīxit Sextus quod cubitum īre timēbat. Dum enim fābulam mīlitis audiēbat, caupōnem spectābat. Cōgitābat, "Quam scelestus ille caupō vidētur! Certē in animō habet mediā nocte mē necāre. Necesse est vigilāre."

Etiam Mārcus timēbat. Cōgitābat tamen, "Sī hic caupō est scelestus, gaudeō quod mīles in caupōnā pernoctat. Eucleidēs certē nōs adiuvāre nōn potest." 25

Invītī tandem puerī cubitum iērunt, vigilāre parātī. Mox tamen sēmisomnī fuērunt. Brevī tempore obdormīvit Mārcus.

13	**prīmus, -a, -um,** *first*	17	**finiō, -īre, –īvī, -ītus,** *to finish*
	lūx, lūcis, f., *light*	20	**sērō** adv., *late*
	prīmā lūce, *at dawn*	22	**cōgitō, -āre, -āvī, -ātus,** *to think*
14	**mortuus, -a, -um,** *dead*		**vidētur,** (*he*) *seems*
15	**simulō, -āre, -āvī, -ātus,** *to pretend*	26	**invītus, -a, -um,** *unwilling*

13 **eō, īre, iī** or **īvī, itūrus,** irreg., *to go*
   petō, petere, petīvī, petītus, *to look for, seek, head for, aim at, attack*
14 **inveniō, invenīre, invēnī, inventus,** *to come upon, find*
   removeō, removēre, remōvī, remōtus, *to remove, move aside*
   extrahō, extrahere, extrāxī, extractus, *to drag out, take out*
15 **videō, vidēre, vīdī, vīsus,** *to see*
18 **iubeō, iubēre, iussī, iussus,** *to order, bid*
19 **volō, velle, voluī,** irreg., *to wish, want, be willing*
21 **dīcō, dīcere, dīxī, dictus,** *to say, tell*
25 **possum, posse, potuī,** irreg., *to be able; I can*

Respondē Latīnē:

6. Quid Septimus prīmā lūce fēcit?
7. Quandō lacrimāvit Septimus?
8. Cūr lacrimāvit caupō?
9. Quid cīvēs fēcērunt?
10. Quid Sextus facere timēbat?
11. Cūr Mārcus gaudet?
12. Quōmodo puerī cubitum iērunt?
13. Quid Mārcus et Sextus facere in animō habuērunt?

EXERCISE 21b

The following sentences contain errors of fact in the light of the last story you read. Explain these errors and give new Latin sentences that correct them:

1. Duo amīcī, Aulus et Septimus, urbem Rōmam intrāvērunt.
2. Aulus et Septimus frātrēs Mārcī erant.
3. Septimus mediā nocte surrēxit quod ēsuriēbat.
4. Aulus auxilium petīvit quod lectus sordidus erat.
5. Cīvēs, postquam Septimum necāvērunt, corpus sub stercore cēlāvērunt.
6. Caupō Septimum accūsāvit postquam cīvem mortuum invēnit.
7. Septimus cīvēs pūnīre in animō habuit quod scelestī erant.
8. Cīvēs corpus in caupōnā sub lectō invēnērunt.
9. Mārcus cubitum īre timēbat quod silentium erat.
10. Cornēlius caupōnem pūnīvit quod Mārcus eum accūsāvit.

———

Vēnī, vīdī, vīcī. *I came, I saw, I conquered.* (Julius Caesar, after the battle of Zela, 47 B.C.; reported in Suetonius, *Julius Caesar* XXXVII)

Nihil sub sōle novum. *There's nothing new under the sun.* (Vulgate, *Ecclesiastes* I.10)

Mēns sāna in corpore sānō. *A sound mind in a sound body.* (Juvenal X.356)

———

EXERCISE 21c

Using the lists of principal parts given in the vocabularies on pages 173 and 174, give the Latin for:

1. What did you want, boys?
2. They got up suddenly.
3. The boys went to bed at last.
4. Septimus looked for the wagon.
5. What have you seen, girls?
6. We went to the inn.
7. What did you say, Marcus?
8. We ordered Cornelia to go to sleep.
9. What have they found?
10. He placed the body in the wagon.

EXERCISE 21d

Read aloud and translate. Identify the tense of each verb:

1. Mārcus sub arbore sedēbat sed subitō surrēxit.
2. Iam advesperāscēbat et viātōrēs aedificia urbis cōnspexērunt.
3. Dāvus in hortō saepe labōrābat.
4. Servī cēnam parāvērunt et nunc cēnāre possumus.
5. Aurēlia in caupōnā pernoctāre nōluit.
6. "Ego," Cornēlius inquit, "in caupōnā numquam pernoctāvī."
7. Cornēlia manum ad canem identidem extendēbat.
8. Sextus ā cane fūgit.
9. Quamquam Mārcus dormiēbat, Sextus obdormīre nōn potuit.

   nōlō, nōlle, nōluī, irreg., *not to wish, not to want, to be unwilling*

EXERCISE 21e

Read aloud, paying special attention to tenses of verbs. Then translate:

SEXTUS CAN'T SLEEP

Sextus tamen nōn obdormīvit, nam dē mīlitis fābulā cōgitābat. Itaque diū vigilābat et dē Aulō mortuō cōgitābat. Tandem, "Mārce!" inquit. "Tūne timēbās ubi illam fābulam audīvistī?"

Sed Mārcus nihil respondit. Iterum, "Mārce!" inquit. "Tūne caupōnem spectābās?" Iterum silentium! Deinde Sextus, iam timidus, "Mārce! Mārce!" 5 inquit. "Cūr tū obdormīvistī? Cūr tū nōn vigilāvistī?"

Subitō sonitum in cubiculō audīvit Sextus. "Ō mē miserum! Audīvitne sonitum Aulus ille miser ubi caupō eum necāre parābat? Quālis sonitus fuit?"

Sonitum Sextus iterum audīvit. "Ō Eucleidēs!" inquit. "Cūr ad cubiculum nōndum vēnistī? Ō pater! Cūr mē in Italiā relīquistī? Voluistīne ita mē ad mortem 10 mittere? In Asiam ad tē īre volō. Ibi enim nūllum est perīculum, sed perīculōsum est hīc in Italiā habitāre."

Multa sē rogābat Sextus, nam, quamquam puer temerārius esse solēbat, nunc mediā nocte in cubiculō tremēbat.

Itaque Sextus, per tōtam noctem vigilāre parātus, diū ibi sedēbat. "Quōmodo   15
iam ē manibus caupōnis scelestī effugere possum? Suntne omnēs caupōnēs
scelestī? Fortasse caupō mē, fīlium cīvis praeclārī, necāre in animō habet.
Quamquam Aulus aurum habuit, ego nihil habeō, neque aurum neque pecūniam."

Ita cōgitābat Sextus. Iterum sonitum audīvit. Timēbat sed tandem surrēxit
invītus, nam omnēs cubiculī partēs īnspicere volēbat. Mox tamen rīsit. Ecce! Sub   20
lectō erat fēlēs, obēsa et sēmisomna. Prope fēlem Sextus mūrem mortuum vīdit.
Mussāvit Sextus, "Nōn necesse est hoc corpus sub stercore cēlāre!"

7	**sonitum,** *sound*	15	**tōtus, -a, -um,** *all, the whole*
10	**ita,** adv., *thus, so, in this way*	18	**aurum, -ī,** n., *gold*
	ad mortem, *to my death*		**pecūnia, -ae,** f., *money*
	mors, mortis, gen. pl.,	21	**fēlēs, fēlis,** gen. pl., **fēlium,** f., *cat*
	mortium, f., *death*		**mūs, mūris,** m., *mouse*

4 **respondeō, respondēre, respondī, respōnsūrus,** *to reply*
10 **relinquō, relinquere, relīquī, relictus,** *to leave behind*
14 **tremō, tremere, tremuī,** *to tremble*
15 **sedeō, sedēre, sēdī, sessūrus,** *to sit*
16 **effugiō, effugere, effūgī,** *to run away, escape*
20 **īnspiciō, īnspicere, īnspexī, īnspectus,** *to examine*
   rīdeō, rīdēre, rīsī, rīsus, *to laugh (at), smile*

EXERCISE 21f

In the first twelve lines of the passage on page 42, locate the following in sequence:

1. All verbs in the present tense.
2. All verbs in the imperfect tense.
3. All verbs in the perfect tense.
4. All infinitives.

ADDITIONAL READING:
The Romans Speak for Themselves: Book I: "Ghosts," pages 59–64.

Go Online
PHSchool.com
Web Code: jfd-0021

EAVESDROPPING

It was quite dark. Cornelia was still wide awake. All kinds of exciting sounds were floating up from the inn downstairs, inviting her to go down and have a look. She slipped out of bed, put a shawl around her shoulders, and tiptoed into the corridor where Eucleides was on guard.

"Take me downstairs, Eucleides," she wheedled. "I've never seen the inside of an inn before." This was quite true, because an upper-class Roman away from home preferred to stay in a friend's villa and avoided inns if possible.

Eucleides took a lot of persuading, but Cornelia could always get around him; he soon found himself downstairs, looking into the main room, with Cornelia peering from behind his arm.

It was pretty dark inside, despite the lamps. The atmosphere was thick with smoke and reeked of garlic. On the far side Cornelia could see her father; and nearer were other customers seated on stools at rough tables, and an evil-looking group they were.

"Stay away from them, Cornelia," whispered Eucleides. "Those rogues would murder their own mothers for a silver **dēnārius**."

But Eucleides needn't have worried because they were all absorbed in what was going on at the far end of the low room, where a girl was dancing. Above the hum of conversation her singing could be heard to the accompaniment of a rhythmic clacking noise she seemed to be making with her fingers. "Makes that noise with castanets," whispered Eucleides. "Dancing girl from Spain, probably Gades."

But one person was not paying much attention to the entertainment—the **tabellārius**, whose reckless driving had forced their **raeda** into the ditch. He had not come out of the incident unscathed. One of his horses had gone lame, and he was making the most of the enforced delay, drinking the innkeeper's best Falernian wine.

As Cornelia and Eucleides entered, the innkeeper was bringing forward a young man to introduce him to the courier. "This is Decimus Junius Juvenalis, sir, a soldier like yourself." The **tabellārius**, unbending slightly as a rather haggard young man came forward wearing the insignia of a junior officer, dismissed the innkeeper with a look and said pleasantly enough, "Greetings, young man! Where are you from?"

"I'm on my way back from service in Britain, sir. What a place! They don't have any climate there, just bad weather! Mist, rain, hail, snow—the lot! Hardly a blink of sunshine!"

"Let me see!" said the **tabellārius**. "Who's governor of Britain these days? A chap called Agricola, I hear."

"That's right!" replied Juvenalis. "A madman, if you ask me. He's not content with conquering the bit of Britain that's near Gaul, where you can get something profitable, like silver or wool or hides or those huge hunting dogs. Before I left, he had gone to the

From silver mined in places like Britain and Spain, the Romans fashioned beautiful pieces such as this cavalry officer's mask.

very edge of the world where the Caledonii live. They say that there, in the middle of winter, the sun doesn't shine at all! But I can't vouch for that myself!"

"I've been to Britain too," said the **tabellārius**, much interested. "I'm not an ordinary **tabellārius**, you know. I personally carry dispatches only if they are confidential messages from—"

And here he whispered something in Juvenalis's ear, which Cornelia could not catch.

The innkeeper sidled up again with some more wine.

"We get lots of interesting people stopping here on the Via Appia," he confided. "Not only military gentlemen like yourselves, or that scum of humanity there"—jerking his thumb toward the dancer's audience—"but special envoys to the Emperor himself. When Nero was Emperor, we had one of this new Jewish religious sect who lodged here on a journey all the way from Judaea, to be tried by the Emperor himself no less! He was called Paul or something—"

Suddenly Cornelia felt her ear seized between finger and thumb and looked around into the eyes of a very angry Aurelia. She found herself upstairs and back in bed before she knew what had happened.

Take parts, read aloud, and translate:

EARLY THE NEXT MORNING

Nōndum lūcēbat, sed Cornēlia, ut solēbat, iam surgēbat. Tunicam induit et tacitē ē cubiculō exiit, quod mātrem excitāre nōlēbat. Ē cubiculīs caupōnae nihil nisi silentium. Omnēs adhūc dormiēbant, sed Cornēlia audīre poterat vōcem ancillae quae iam in culīnā labōrābat. Cornēlia igitur ad culīnam appropinquāvit et fēminam cōnspexit. Dum Cornēlia spectat, fēmina cibum coquit et cantat. 5
Cornēlia intrat.

CORNĒLIA: Nōnne tū es fēmina quae saltat? Quid tibi nōmen est?

ANCILLA: Ita vērō! Saltātrīx sum. Mē appellant Ēlissam. Quis es tū?

CORNĒLIA: Ego sum Cornēlia. Quis tē saltāre docuit?

ANCILLA: (*cum rīsū*) Ubi in urbe Gādibus habitābam cum parentibus, māter mē 10
    cum crotalīs saltāre, cantāre, multa alia facere docuit.

CORNĒLIA: Sī tū saltātrīx es, cūr cibum coquis?

ANCILLA: Quamquam sum saltātrīx, ancilla tamen sum.

CORNĒLIA: Tū ancilla es? Quōmodo ad Italiam vēnistī?

ANCILLA: Pīrātae mē in Hispāniā cēpērunt et ad Italiam tulērunt. Apollōdorus 15
    mē in urbe Rōmā ēmit.

CORNĒLIA: Cūr nōn effugis et ad Hispāniam redīs?

ANCILLA: Quōmodo effugere possum? Nūllōs amīcōs in Italiā habeō et ad
    Hispāniam sōla redīre nōn possum. Praetereā Apollōdorus dominus bonus
    est quod ipse servus fuit. Mē numquam verberat et omnia dat quae volō. 20

CORNĒLIA: Praeter lībertātem.

ANCILLA: Ita vērō! Praeter lībertātem.

  4 **culīna, -ae,** f., *kitchen*
  5 cantō, -āre, -āvī, -ātus, *to sing*
  7 saltō, -āre, -āvī, -ātūrus, *to dance*
  8 saltātrīx, saltātrīcis, f., *dancer*
    appellō, -āre, -āvī, -ātus, *to call, name*
 10 Gādēs, Gādium, f. pl., *Gades (Cadiz, a town in Spain)*
 11 crotalum, -ī, n., *castanet*
 15 pīrāta, -ae, m., *pirate*
 21 **praeter,** prep. + acc., *except*
    lībertās, lībertātis, f., *freedom*

    5 **cōnspiciō, cōnspicere, cōnspexī, cōnspectus,**
       to catch sight of
  11 **doceō, docēre, docuī, doctus,** *to teach*
  15 **capiō, capere, cēpī, captus,** *to take, capture*
    ferō, ferre, tulī, lātus, irreg., *to bring, carry*
  16 **emō, emere, ēmī, ēmptus,** *to buy*
  20 **dō, dare, dedī, datus,** *to give*

The seven-stringed cithara is one of the forerunners of today's guitar.
Second style fresco, Villa of P. Fannius Synistor, Boscoreale, ca. 40–30 B.C.

Web Code: jfd-0021

Exercise IVa: Agreement of Adjectives and Nouns pp. 4–5

Complete the following sentences with 3rd declension adjectives to match
the English cues. Make the adjective agree with the underlined noun. Read
aloud and translate:

1. Cornēliī ē raedā dēscendērunt _____. (unhurt)
2. Pater filiam _____ laudāvit. (brave)
3. Puer _____ lupum repellit. (brave)
4. In _____ caupōnā lectī sunt sordidī. (every)
5. Nōn _____ caupōnēs sunt scelestī. (all)
6. Puella _____ stat et manum ad canem extendit. (motionless)
7. Prīnceps _____ senātōrēs Rōmam redīre iussit. (all)
8. _____ Cornēliī Rōmam rediēbant. (all)
9. Servī per agrōs cum canibus _____ currunt. (brave)
10. Cornēlia et Flāvia sunt puellae strēnuae et _____. (brave)

Review the present, imperfect, and perfect tenses of regular verbs and of the
irregular verbs **esse, velle, nōlle,** and **īre** in the charts on pages 271–273
before doing exercises IVb–IVd.

Exercise IVb: Identification of Verb Forms; 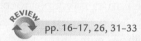 pp. 16–17, 26, 31–33
Principal Parts

Identify the tense, person, and number of each of the following verb forms.
Then give the principal parts of each verb:

	Tense	Person	Number
1. veniēbātis	_____	_____	_____
	_____	_____	_____
2. cōgitāvistis	_____	_____	_____
	_____	_____	_____
3. coniciēbam	_____	_____	_____
	_____	_____	_____
4. iussērunt	_____	_____	_____
	_____	_____	_____
5. surrēxī	_____	_____	_____
	_____	_____	_____
6. removēbās	_____	_____	_____
	_____	_____	_____
7. clāmāvistī	_____	_____	_____
	_____	_____	_____
8. obdormiēbāmus	_____	_____	_____
	_____	_____	_____

Exercise IVc: Imperfect, Present, and Perfect Tenses pp. 16–17, 26, 32

Change the following irregular verbs to the present tense and then to the perfect tense. Keep the same person and number:

	Present	Perfect
1. volēbam	_____	_____
2. erāmus	_____	_____
3. volēbās	_____	_____
4. ībant	_____	_____
5. erās	_____	_____
6. ībās	_____	_____
7. nōlēbat	_____	_____
8. ībātis	_____	_____
9. erant	_____	_____
10. nōlēbātis	_____	_____

Exercise IVd: Uses of *Dum* and of Infinitives pp. 27, 28

Read aloud and translate. Explain the tenses used with **dum,** and explain uses of infinitives:

1. Dum Cornēliī ad caupōnam appropinquant, subitō canis appāruit.
2. Cornēliī in caupōnā pernoctāre in animō habuērunt.
3. Perīculōsum nōn est in hāc caupōnā pernoctāre.
4. Cornēliōs caupō intrāre iussit.
5. Aurēlia et Cornēlia in caupōnā cēnāre nōluērunt.
6. Puerīs licet vigilāre et mīlitis fābulam audīre.
7. Dum mīles fābulam nārrābat, puerī vigilābant et audiēbant.
8. "Hic lectus est sordidus," inquit Aurēlia. "Necesse est alium lectum petere."
9. Aurēlia et Cornēlia in cubiculō manent, dum servī alium lectum petunt.
10. Aurēlia in lectō sordidō dormīre nōluit.
11. Dum Aurēlia et Cornēlia in cubiculō manent, servī alium lectum in cubiculum portāvērunt.

Exercise IVe: Reading Comprehension

Read aloud and translate:

MUCIUS GIVES A LESSON IN ROMAN VIRTUE

Porsenna, rēx Clūsīnōrum, urbem Rōmam iam diū obsidēbat. Rōmānī igitur, quod cibum in urbem ferre nōn poterant, famē perībant. Tum mīles quīdam Rōmānus, Gāius Mūcius nōmine, quī cīvēs patriamque servāre volēbat, Porsennam necāre cōnstituit.

Itaque Mūcius ad senātōrēs Rōmānōs iit et, "Tiberim trānsīre," inquit, "et 5 castra hostium intrāre in animō habeō. Ibi rēgem Porsennam necāre volō."

Respondērunt senātōrēs, "Sī hoc temptāre vīs, tibi licet." Laetus domum rediit Mūcius. Gladium arripuit et sub tunicā cēlāvit. Trāns Tiberim festīnāvit et castra hostium fūrtim intrāvit. Ibi magnam multitūdinem mīlitum vīdit. Ad mēnsam ante mīlitēs sedēbant duo hominēs. Alter pecūniam mīlitibus dabat, alter 10 eōs spectābat. Cōgitābat Mūcius, "Uter est rēx? Nōnne ille est, quī omnia facit? Necesse est illum necāre!"

Mūcius ad mēnsam appropinquāvit et virum gladiō necāvit. Stupuērunt omnēs mīlitēs. Ē castrīs effugiēbat Mūcius, sed mīlitēs eum cēpērunt.

"Ō sceleste!" inquiunt. "Cūr scrībam rēgis necāvistī?" 15

"Rēgem, nōn scrībam, necāre volēbam," respondit Mūcius.

Rēx, ubi haec audīvit, īrātus erat et mīlitēs iussit Mūcium pūnīre. Superbē respondit Mūcius: "Cīvis Rōmānus sum. Mē Gāium Mūcium vocant. Castra intrāvī quod urbem Rōmam servāre in animō habēbam. Mē cēpistī sed poenās nōn timeō." 20

Eō ipsō tempore stābat Mūcius prope āram et ignem. Subitō dextram manum in ignem iniēcit. Rēx statim surrēxit et mīlitēs iussit virum ab igne trahere. "Quamquam," inquit, "hostis es, tē ad cīvēs tuōs iam remittō quod vir fortissimus es."

Postquam Mūcius Rōmam rediit, rem tōtam nārrāvit. Cīvēs Mūcium nōn 25 modo laudābant sed, quod iam sinistram modo manum habēbat, eum appellāvērunt Scaevolam.

1 rēx, rēgis, m., *king*
Clūsīnī, -ōrum, m. pl., *the people of Clusium*
2 famē perīre, *to die of hunger*
3 patria, -ae, f., *native land*
-que, enclitic conj., *and*
servō, -āre, -āvī, -ātus, *to save*
5 Tiberis, Tiberis, m., *the Tiber River*
6 castra, -ōrum, n. pl., *camp*
hostēs, hostium, m. pl., *the enemy*
8 gladius, -ī, m., *sword*
trāns, prep. + acc., *across*
9 multitūdō, multitūdinis, f., *crowd*
10 mēnsa, -ae, f., *table*
ante, prep. + acc., *in front of*
mīlitibus, *to the soldiers*

11 Uter...? *Which (of the two)...?*
ille, *that one*
13 stupeō, -ēre, -uī, *to be amazed*
15 scrība, -ae, m., *scribe*
17 superbē, adv., *proudly*
19 poenae, -ārum, f. pl., *punishment*
21 āra, -ae, f., *altar*
ignis, ignis, gen. pl., ignium, m., *fire*
dexter, dextra, dextrum, *right*
23 fortissimus, -a, -um, *very brave*
26 sinister, sinistra, sinistrum, *left*
27 Scaevola, -ae, m., *Scaevola (nickname derived from the adjective scaevus, -a, -um, left)*

1 obsideō, obsidēre, obsēdī, obsessus, *to besiege*
4 cōnstituō, cōnstituere, cōnstituī, cōnstitūtus, *to decide*
5 trānseō, trānsīre, trānsiī or trānsīvī, trānsitus, irreg., *to cross*
22 iniciō, inicere, iniēcī, iniectus, *to throw into, thrust into*
23 remittō, remittere, remīsī, remissus, *to send back*

FROM THE INN TO ROME

Iam diēs erat. Prīmā lūce raedārius auxiliō servōrum caupōnis raedam ē fossā extrāxit et ad caupōnam admōvit. Tum servī cistās Cornēliōrum raedāriō trādidērunt. Intereā in caupōnā, dum omnēs sē parābant, Sextus, iam immemor terrōris nocturnī, mīlitis fābulam Cornēliae nārrābat; Eucleidēs mandāta servīs dabat. Cornēlius ipse Aurēliae et līberīs clāmābat, "Agite, omnēs! Nōlīte cessāre! Tempus est discēdere." 5

Tandem cūnctī ē caupōnā vēnērunt et in raedam ascendērunt.

"Valē!" clāmāvērunt puerī.

"Valēte!" respondit caupō, quī in viā stābat. "Nōlīte in fossam iterum cadere! Nōn in omnibus caupōnīs bene dormīre potestis."

Tum raedārius habēnās sūmpsit et equōs verberāvit. Tandem Rōmam iterum petēbant. 10

In itinere Sextus omnia dē mūre mortuō Mārcō explicāvit; Cornēlius mīlitis fābulam uxōrī nārrāvit. Iam urbī appropinquābant, cum subitō puerī ingēns aedificium cōnspexērunt.

(continued)

1 **auxiliō,** *with the help*
2 **raedāriō,** *to the coachman*
3 **sē parāre,** *to prepare oneself, get ready*
  immemor, immemoris + gen., *forgetful*
  nocturnus, -a, -um, *happening during the night*

4 **Cornēliae,** *to Cornelia*
  mandātum, -ī, n., *order, instruction*
9 **bene,** adv., *well*
10 habēnae, -ārum, f. pl., *reins*
12 **uxōrī,** *to his wife*
  cum, conj., *when*
  ingēns, ingentis, *huge*

2 admoveō, admovēre, admōvī, admōtus, *to move toward*
  trādō, trādere, trādidī, trāditus, *to hand over*
5 **discēdō, discēdere, discessī, discessūrus,** *to go away, depart*
6 **ascendō, ascendere, ascendī, ascēnsus,** *to climb, climb into (a carriage)*
8 **stō, stāre, stetī, statūrus,** *to stand*
  cadō, cadere, cecidī, cāsūrus, *to fall*
10 **sūmō, sūmere, sūmpsī, sūmptus,** *to take, take up*

EXERCISE 22a

Respondē Latīnē:

1. Cui Sextus mīlitis fābulam nārrābat?
2. Quid Eucleidēs faciēbat?
3. Quid dīxit caupō ubi Cornēliī discēdēbant?
4. Quid fēcit raedārius?
5. Quid Sextus Mārcō explicāvit?
6. Quid puerī cōnspexērunt?

Go Online
PHSchool.com
Web Code: jfd-0022

Mārcus patrem, "Quid est illud?" rogāvit.

Atque Sextus, "Quis in illō aedificiō habitat?"   15

Cui Cornēlius, "Nēmō ibi habitat," cum rīsū respondit. "Est sepulcrum Messallae Corvīnī, quī erat ōrātor praeclārus. Hīc sunt sepulcra multōrum et praeclārōrum cīvium quod Rōmānīs nōn licet intrā urbem sepulcra habēre."

Mox alterum aedificium magnum vīdērunt.

"Estne id quoque sepulcrum, pater?" rogāvit Mārcus.   20

"Ita vērō!" Cornēlius respondit. "Est sepulcrum Caeciliae Metellae. Nōnne dē Caeciliā Metellā audīvistī?"

Sed Mārcus patrī nihil respondit. Iam enim urbem ipsam vidēre poterat. "Ecce Rōma!" clāmāvit.

"Ecce Rōma! Ecce Rōma!" clāmāvērunt Sextus et Cornēlia.   25

Tum Cornēlius, "Brevī tempore ad Portam Capēnam adveniēmus et Titum, patruum vestrum, ibi vidēbimus. Epistulam enim per servum mīsī et omnia eī explicāvī. Titus mox nōs prope Portam excipiet."

14 illud, *that*
15 **atque,** conj., *and, and also*
16 **sepulcrum, -ī,** n., *tomb*
18 **intrā,** prep. + acc., *inside*
26 **adveniēmus,** *we will come*

patruus, -ī, m., *uncle*
27 **vester, vestra, vestrum,** *your* (pl.)
   vidēbimus, *we will see*
28 **excipiet,** *he will welcome*

28 **excipiō, excipere, excēpī, exceptus,** *to welcome, receive*

Respondē Latīnē:

7. Cūr sepulcra nōn sunt intrā urbem?
8. Cuius est alterum sepulcrum?   **Cuius**…? Whose…?
9. Audīvitne Mārcus dē Caeciliā Metellā?
10. Quis Cornēliōs ad Portam Capēnam excipiet?

———

Amīcus omnibus amīcus nēminī. *A friend to everyone is a friend to no one.*

FORMS

Nouns: Cases and Declensions: Dative Case

Look at the following sentences:

1. Mandāta **servīs** dabat. (22:4)
   *He was giving orders **to the slaves**.*

2. Omnia **Mārcō** explicāvit. (22:11)
   *He explained everything **to Marcus**.*

3. Cornēlius fābulam **uxōrī** nārrāvit. (22:11–12)
   *Cornelius told the story **to his wife**.*

4. Servī meī bonam cēnam **vōbīs** parāre possunt. (19:2–3)
   *My slaves are able to prepare a good dinner **for you**.*

The Latin words in bold type are all in the *dative case* and may be translated using *to…* or *for….*

Here is a chart showing the groups of nouns and cases, including the dative:

Number Case	1st Declension Fem.	2nd Declension Masc.	Masc.	Masc.	Neut.	3rd Declension Masc.	Fem.	Neut.
Singular								
Nom.	puélla	sérv*us*	púer	áger	bácul*um*	páter	vōx	nōmen
Gen.	puéllae	sérv*ī*	púer*ī*	ágr*ī*	bácul*ī*	pátr*is*	vṓc*is*	nṓmin*is*
Dat.	**puéllae**	**sérv*ō***	**púer*ō***	**ágr*ō***	**bácul*ō***	**pátr*ī***	**vṓc*ī***	**nṓmin*ī***
Acc.	puéll*am*	sérv*um*	púer*um*	ágr*um*	bácul*um*	pátr*em*	vṓc*em*	nōmen
Abl.	puéll*ā*	sérv*ō*	púer*ō*	ágr*ō*	bácul*ō*	pátre	vṓce	nṓmine
Voc.	puélla	sérve	púer	áger	bácul*um*	páter	vōx	nōmen
Plural								
Nom.	puéllae	sérv*ī*	púer*ī*	ágr*ī*	bácula	pátr*ēs*	vṓc*ēs*	nṓmina
Gen.	puéll*ārum*	servṓ*rum*	puerṓ*rum*	agrṓ*rum*	baculṓ*rum*	pátr*um*	vṓc*um*	nṓmin*um*
Dat.	**puéll*īs***	**sérv*īs***	**púer*īs***	**ágr*īs***	**bácul*īs***	**pátr*ibus***	**vṓc*ibus***	**nōmín*ibus***
Acc.	puéll*ās*	sérv*ōs*	púer*ōs*	ágr*ōs*	bácula	pátr*ēs*	vṓc*ēs*	nṓmina
Abl.	puéll*īs*	sérv*īs*	púer*īs*	ágr*īs*	bácul*īs*	pátr*ibus*	vṓc*ibus*	nōmín*ibus*
Voc.	puéllae	sérv*ī*	púer*ī*	ágr*ī*	bácula	pátr*ēs*	vṓc*ēs*	nṓmina

Be sure to learn the new dative forms thoroughly.

NOTES

1. In each declension dative and ablative plurals have the same endings.
2. The datives of the pronouns are as follows:

Singular		Plural	
Nominative	*Dative*	*Nominative*	*Dative*
ego	**mihi**	**nōs**	**nōbīs**
tū	**tibi**	**vōs**	**vōbīs**
is, ea, id	**eī**	**eī, eae, ea**	**eīs**
Quis…?	**Cui…?**	**Quī…?**	**Quibus…?**

Here is a chart showing the adjectives, including the dative case:

Number Case	1st and 2nd Declensions			3rd Declension		
	Masc.	Fem.	Neut.	Masc.	Fem.	Neut.
Singular						
Nom.	mágn**us**	mágn**a**	mágn**um**	ómn**is**	ómn**is**	ómn**e**
Gen.	mágn**ī**	mágn**ae**	mágn**ī**	ómn**is**	ómn**is**	ómn**is**
Dat.	**mágnō**	**mágnae**	**mágnō**	**ómnī**	**ómnī**	**ómnī**
Acc.	mágn**um**	mágn**am**	mágn**um**	ómn**em**	ómn**em**	ómn**e**
Abl.	mágn**ō**	mágn**ā**	mágn**ō**	ómn**ī**	ómn**ī**	ómn**ī**
Voc.	mágn**e**	mágn**a**	mágn**um**	ómn**is**	ómn**is**	ómn**e**
Plural						
Nom.	mágn**ī**	mágn**ae**	mágn**a**	ómn**ēs**	ómn**ēs**	ómn**ia**
Gen.	magn**órum**	magn**árum**	magn**órum**	ómn**ium**	ómn**ium**	ómn**ium**
Dat.	**mágnīs**	**mágnīs**	**mágnīs**	**ómnibus**	**ómnibus**	**ómnibus**
Acc.	mágn**ōs**	mágn**ās**	mágn**a**	ómn**ēs**	ómn**ēs**	ómn**ia**
Abl.	mágn**īs**	mágn**īs**	mágn**īs**	ómn**ibus**	ómn**ibus**	ómn**ibus**
Voc.	mágn**ī**	mágn**ae**	mágn**a**	ómn**ēs**	ómn**ēs**	ómn**ia**

You should now have thoroughly learned all of the forms above and on the previous page.

3rd Declension Adjectives of One Termination

Most 3rd declension adjectives have two different endings in the nominative singular, one that is used when the adjective modifies masculine or feminine nouns (e.g., **omn**is **ager, omn**is **vīlla**) and a second ending that is used when the adjective modifies neuter nouns (e.g., **omn**e **sepulcrum**).

Some 3rd declension adjectives use the same form in the nominative when the adjective modifies masculine, feminine, *or* neuter nouns, as **immemor**, *forgetful*, and **ingēns**, *huge*. Thus, we can say **ingēns ager** (masculine), **ingēns vīlla** (feminine), and **ingēns sepulcrum** (neuter). Adjectives of this sort are called *adjectives of one termination*. The nominative and genitive are given in vocabulary entries for this type of adjective: **immemor, immemoris,** and **ingēns, ingentis.** The base is found by dropping the *-is* ending from the genitive singular, and to this base are added the same endings as for **omnis.** As always, the neuter nominative, accusative, and vocative are the same in the singular and in the plural.

EXERCISE 22b
Write out a full set of the forms of **immemor.**

BUILDING THE MEANING

The Dative Case

1. The sentence below illustrates a basic pattern with which you have been familiar since Chapter 4:

          S   DO   TV
   Cornēlius fābulam nārrāvit.
   Cornelius told the story.

   You will often find sentences of this type with a subject (S), direct object (DO), and a transitive verb (TV) expanded with a word or phrase in the *dative case* that will modify the verb. In the sentence below the word in the dative case tells *to whom* the story was told:

          S   DO   IO   TV
   Cornēlius fābulam **uxōrī** nārrāvit. (22:11–12)

   The word in the dative case, **uxōrī**, is called the *indirect object* (IO). Words or phrases in the dative case functioning as indirect objects will often be found with verbs of *giving* (e.g., **dare, trādere**), *showing* (e.g., **mōnstrāre**), and *telling* (e.g., **dīcere, nārrāre**). They answer the question "to whom…?"

   Note that sentences with indirect objects can often be translated two ways in English. For example, the sentence above can be translated:

   *Cornelius told the story **to his wife**.* or *Cornelius told **his wife** the story.*

2. Note also that sometimes a word or phrase in the dative case can best be translated *for…* instead of *to…*:

   Servī meī bonam cēnam **vōbīs** parāre possunt. (19:2–3)
   *My slaves are able to prepare a good dinner **for you**.*

3. The dative case may also be found in sentences in which the verb is intransitive and does not have a direct object:

   Aulus **Septimō** clāmāvit. (21:8–9)   Aulus in somnō **eī** appāruit. (21:4)
   *Aulus shouted **to Septimus**.*   *Aulus appeared **to him** in (his) sleep.*

4. The intransitive verb **appropinquāre**, *to approach*, is sometimes used with the preposition **ad** + acc.:

   Mox **ad caupōnam** appropinquābant.
   *Soon they were coming near **to the inn**/approaching **the inn**.*

   It may also be used with a word or phrase in the dative case:

   Iam **urbī** appropinquābant. (22:12)
   *Already they were coming near **to the city**/approaching **the city**.*

5. You have also seen the dative case used with the impersonal verbal phrase **necesse est**, *it is necessary*, and the impersonal verb **licet**, *it is allowed*, with infinitives as their subjects:

> Cūr **mihi** quoque necesse est ad urbem redīre? (8:13–14)
> *Why is to return to the city necessary **for me** too?*
> *Why is it necessary **for me** too to return to the city?*

> "Licetne **nōbīs**," inquit Mārcus, "hīc cēnāre?" (20:7)
> *"Is to eat dinner here allowed **for us**?" said Marcus.*
> *"Is it allowed **for us**," said Marcus, "to eat dinner here?"*
> *"May **we** eat dinner here?" said Marcus.*

EXERCISE 22c

Reword the sentence **Cornēlius fābulam uxōrī nārrāvit** to say that Cornelius told the story to each of the following in turn: **Septimus, Flāvia, puellae, mīles, puerī, raedārius, senātōrēs, caupō, viātōrēs**.

EXERCISE 22d

In each sentence identify the word or phrase in the dative case and the reason for its use. Then read the sentence aloud and translate it:

1. Patruus pecūniam puerīs dat.
2. Ancilla invīta caupōnī scelestō cibum trādit.
3. Omnia patrī meō semper dīcō.
4. Nihil lēgātō prīncipis dīxit.
5. Cornēlius epistulam ad Titum mīsit et omnia eī explicāvit.
6. Mārcus, "Tacē, Sexte!" inquit. "Nōbīs nōn licet hīc clāmāre."
7. In somnīs Aulus amīcō Septimō appāruit.
8. Dum Cornēliī urbī appropinquābant, Titus omnia eīs parābat.
9. Apollodōrus Cornēliīs cubicula mōnstrat.   **mōnstrō, -āre, -āvī, -ātus,** *to show*
10. Servī alium lectum Aurēliae parāvērunt.

EXERCISE 22e

Give the Latin for:

1. Suddenly a soldier appeared to them.
2. "May I stay awake and hear the soldier's story?" asked Marcus.
3. It was necessary for Aurelia and Cornelia to go to bed, for they were tired.
4. Sextus told the soldier's story to Cornelia.
5. They were approaching the tomb of Caecilia Metella.

Nouns: Dative or Ablative? How Do You Decide?

You will have noticed that the dative and ablative cases often have identical endings, e.g., **servō, puellīs, mīlitibus**. How are you to tell which case is used in a particular sentence? Ask yourself these two questions:

a. Is the noun preceded by a preposition? If it is, the noun will be in the ablative case because no preposition governs the dative case.

b. If there is no preposition, does the noun refer to a *person*? If it does, it will normally be in the dative because nouns referring to persons are usually governed by a preposition if they are in the ablative. If the noun refers to a *thing*, it is more likely to be ablative than dative (exception: a word in the dative case with the verb **appropinquāre** often refers to a thing).

Consider the following sentences, noting each word and each group of words as you meet it:

1. **Canem nostrum puerō dedit.**
   The words **canem nostrum** are obviously accusative. When we reach **puerō**, knowing that **puer** refers to a person, we can say that it must be in the dative case because it would be governed by a preposition if it were in the ablative case. A Roman reading as far as **puerō** would have known before he reached the verb that the sentence deals with giving or showing "our dog" in some way or other "to the boy."

2. **Puerō canem nostrum dedimus.**
   The fact that **puerō** comes first in the sentence does not alter the reasoning. Since it refers to a person and is not governed by a preposition, it must be in the dative case.

3. **Mārcus lupum baculō repellit.**
   When we come to **baculō**, knowing that **baculum** refers to a thing, we can be sure because of the sense that it is in the ablative case. A Roman would have understood as soon as he reached **baculō** that Marcus is "doing" something to the wolf *with* a stick.

4. **Baculō lupum repellit.**
   Again, the fact that **baculō** appears as the first word makes no difference. We again know that **baculō** must be in the ablative case because it refers to a thing, and when we come to **lupum** we know that someone is "doing" something to the wolf *with* a stick.

Remember that some 3rd declension nouns end in **-ō** in the nominative singular, e.g., **caupō, caupōnis**. In addition, do not mistake the 3rd declension dative singular ending **-ī**, e.g., **caupōnī**, for a 2nd declension genitive singular or nominative plural ending.

EXERCISE 22f

Use the reasoning given in the preceding discussion to help you with the words in boldface that could be dative or ablative in form. Identify each as dative or ablative and then translate the entire sentence:

1. Septimus omnia dē Aulō mortuō **cīvibus** explicāvit.
2. Mihi necesse est **equīs meīs** cibum dare.
3. Mārcus **rāmō** lupum repellit.
4. Sextus **raedāriō** clāmāvit, "Tenē equōs! Cavē fossam!"
5. Raedārius **habēnīs** equōs dēvertēbat.
6. Cūr tū **ancillīs** lībertātem nōn dedistī?
7. Raedārius habēnās **manibus** sūmpsit.
8. Nōs bonam cēnam **hospitibus** parāvimus, domine.
9. **Puerīs** quoque cibum date!
10. Ego in animō habeō corpus et stercus **plaustrō** ē caupōnā removēre.
11. Mediā nocte Aulus in somnō **amīcō suō** appāruit.
12. **Rūsticīs** necesse erat bovēs tardōs **clāmōribus** et **baculīs** incitāre.
13. Mercātōrēs togās et tunicās **cīvibus** mōnstrant.

   mercātor, mercātōris, m., *merchant*

EXERCISE 22g

Here is the inscription from the tomb of Caecilia Metella on the Appian Way. Which words in the inscription are in the dative case, and which are in the genitive?

CAECILIAE
Q·CRETICI·F
METELLAE·CRASSI

Caeciliae
Q(uīntī) Crēticī f(īliae)
Metellae Crassī

(the tomb dedicated) to
Caecilia Metella, daughter
of Quintus (Caecilius
Metellus) Creticus, (wife)
of Crassus

The tomb of Caecilia Metella is situated on the Appian Way. The crenelations on the top of the rotunda are a medieval addition. *Via Appia, Rome, 60 B.C.*

Go Online
PHSchool.com
Web Code: jfd-0022

ROME AND NORTHERN EUROPE

When we think of the Roman conquest of parts of northwestern Europe and the subsequent spread of Roman civilization to these areas, we most often visualize the Roman general Julius Caesar and his army subjugating what is now France, called **Gallia** by the Romans, from 58 to 51 B.C. and invading Britain in 55 and 54 B.C. Or we think of Agricola, legate of the Twentieth Legion in Britain (A.D. 71–73), who, when governor of Britain (A.D. 78–83), led Roman troops as far as the Scottish Highlands, where the Caledonii lived (Agricola was mentioned in "Eavesdropping" on pages 178–179).

These images of the northward expansion of Roman power and control are quite correct, but there were men, other than these commanders, who brought about the Romanization of the native peoples in these areas. Perhaps these men had greater influence

Germany ——
France ——

Vercingetorix surrendering to Caesar, who is seated on the red dais in the distance, 52 B.C.
Vercingetorix before Caesar, *oil-acrylic, 1886, Henri-Paul Motte*

than their commanders because they had closer contact with the ordinary people. These men were the **mīlitēs legiōnāriī**, the ordinary foot soldiers of the legions. What follows is an imaginary account of how a common soldier might have helped to bring about the Romanization process somewhere in **Gallia** or **Germānia** shortly after the Roman conquest of those areas.

Our soldier, whom we will call Lucius, is a man in the Twentieth Legion (**Legiō XX Valeria**). This legion was transferred from Illyricum to the site of the modern Cologne (called **Āra Ubiōrum**, "Altar of the Ubii," by the Romans) on the Rhine River (**Rhēnus**), a site inhabited by a German tribe known as the Ubii and protected since 38 B.C. by a permanent Roman camp (**castra**). The legion was transferred there to help defend the Roman frontier shortly after the destruction of three Roman legions by the Germans in the Teutoburg Forest in A.D. 9 during the reign of the first emperor, Augustus (emperor 27 B.C.– A.D. 14). Lucius falls in love with Helge, an Ubian girl. A number of years before,

Reconstruction of the Roman town of *Venta Icenōrum*, Britain
Sue White, artist

Helge's family had been given land by Marcus Vipsanius Agrippa, when he moved the Ubii at their request from the eastern to the western bank of the Rhine in 38 B.C.

When Lucius learns that Helge is carrying his child, he arranges to marry her, although Roman law stipulated that any marriage contracted by a Roman soldier below the rank of centurion was invalid. However, many of the legionaries held marriage ceremonies with local women who lived in the area near the **castra** or legionary camp. Thus, before his bunkmates (**contubernālēs**), Lucius placed a small gold ring on the third finger of Helge's left hand, and she, prompted by Lucius, recited the traditional marriage vow, **Ubi tū Gāius, ego Gāia**, "Where you are Gaius, I am Gaia." Although the girl knew only a few words of Latin, she understood that this stocky and swarthy man was now her "husband."

Before the marriage ceremony, Lucius and his comrades had built a small hut for Helge. However, instead of building the hut in any open space that suited them, as the Germans did in their villages, the men carefully selected a location in accordance with the plan of streets established by surveyors (**agrimēnsōrēs**) when the Roman settlement of Ara Ubiorum began to be transformed into an outpost town about 12 B.C. There were two main streets, the north-south axis or **cardō**, and the **decumānus**, the east-west axis, oriented to the sunrise on September 23, the birthday of Augustus Caesar. This plan provided locations for a **forum**, which included a marketplace with shops, a **tabulārium** for the keeping of records, a theater, temples with altars not only to the Roman gods but also to Helge's gods such as the Three Mothers, and houses for the town's inhabitants. This foresight and planning were very different from the haphazard way Helge's people built their settlements, and the girl felt new respect and admiration for her husband's people, the Romans.

---

1. If Roman law did not allow foot soldiers to marry, why would officers and officials have overlooked "marriages" such as that of Lucius to Helge?
2. Judging from this story, what facilitated Romanization on the frontier with Germany?

English Words from the Fourth Principal Part of Latin Verbs

The stem of the fourth principal part of a Latin verb may be the source of other Latin words and of English derivatives. This stem is found by dropping the *-us* or the *-ūrus* from the end of the fourth principal part, e.g., the stem of **vīsus** is **vīs-**. Here are some common types of words formed from the stem of the fourth principal part:

1. No suffix.
   The stem may form an English word with no change:
   invent (**invent-**) fact (**fact-**)

2. Silent *-e*.
   An English word may be formed by adding silent *-e* to the stem:
   narrate (**nārrāt-**) finite (**fīnīt-**)

3. Suffix *-or*.
   When added to the stem of the fourth principal part, the Latin suffix *-or* creates a 3rd declension, masculine noun, which means *one who does* the action of the verb. These nouns are often borrowed into English with no change in spelling, although there is sometimes a change in meaning:

	Latin Noun & Meaning	English Word
nārrātus (nārrāre)	**nārrātor, nārrātōris,** m., *storyteller*	narrator
spectātus (spectāre)	**spectātor, spectātōris,** m., *onlooker, observer*	spectator
āctus (agere)	**āctor, āctōris,** m., *driver, doer, actor*	actor

4. Suffix *-iō*.
   The Latin suffix *-iō*, when added to the stem of the fourth principal part, forms a 3rd declension, feminine noun, which means the *act of, state of,* or *result of* the action of the verb. The genitive singular of these nouns ends in *-iōnis*, and the base has *-iōn-*, which is the source of English words ending in *-sion* and *-tion*. The meaning of the English word is similar or identical to that of the Latin noun, which takes its meaning from the Latin verb:

	Latin Noun & Meaning	English Word
vīsus (vidēre)	**vīsiō, vīsiōnis,** f., *act of seeing, vision*	vision
nārrātus (nārrāre)	**nārrātiō, nārrātiōnis,** f., *act of telling (a story), narrative, narration*	narration

   Note that whether the English word ends in *-sion* or *-tion* depends on whether the word from which it is derived ends in *-sus* or *-tus*.

EXERCISE 1

Using the preceding information, create a 3rd declension Latin noun and an English derivative from each of the following. Check in a Latin dictionary to verify the existence of each noun and compare its meaning with that of its English derivative:

1. audītus (audīre)
2. cautus (cavēre)
3. exclāmātus (exclāmāre)
4. factus (facere)
5. mānsūrus (manēre)
6. missus (mittere)
7. petītus (petere)
8. positus (pōnere)

EXERCISE 2

Give the meaning of each English word below. Then give the fourth principal part, the infinitive, and the meaning of the Latin verb from which the English word is derived. You may have to find some of the fourth principal parts in the Vocabulary at the back of this book:

1. apparition
2. cogitate
3. diction
4. habitation
5. inventor
6. motor
7. session
8. state
9. tacit

Latin Expressions in English

Latin phrases and expressions are often used in English. Some are very familiar, such as et cetera (etc.), *and the rest.* Others are more specialized, such as ipso facto, *by the fact itself*, a legal expression used to describe an assumption that has obvious truth, e.g., "A slave, ipso facto, had no right to vote."

While Latin expressions may sometimes be used in English as mere affectations, there are occasions when they are very effective in summarizing an idea succinctly. For example, the term *de facto segregation* refers to a long history of racial segregation that occurred *in fact*, even though no legal measures were taken to achieve it. De jure segregation, on the other hand, was achieved *by law*. These two Latin phrases capsulize these notions in a minimum of words, thereby making communication more efficient.

EXERCISE 3

Look up the following Latin expressions in an English dictionary. Use each expression in a sentence that illustrates its special use in English:

1. ad hoc
2. ad infinitum
3. modus operandi
4. non sequitur
5. per capita
6. per se
7. quid pro quo
8. sine qua non
9. status quo

AT THE PORTA CAPENA

Interea Titus, patruus Mārcī et Cornēliae, eōs prope Portam Capēnam exspectābat. Cīvēs, mercātōrēs, servī per portam ībant atque hūc illūc currēbant. Titus tamen in lectīcā sedēbat. Ubi Cornēliōs cōnspexit, ē lectīcā dēscendit. Ē raedā dēscendērunt Cornēliī. Interdiū enim raedās intrā urbem agere Rōmānīs nōn licēbat.

Stupuit Sextus ubi multitūdinem cīvium, servōrum turbam vīdit. Undique erat 5 strepitus plaustrōrum, undique clāmor mercātōrum, viātōrum, raedāriōrum.

Titus Cornēlium et Aurēliam et līberōs maximō cum gaudiō salūtāvit. "Quam laetus," inquit, "vōs omnēs excipiō! Nōnne estis itinere dēfessī?"

"Valdē dēfessī," respondit Cornēlius. "Mihi necesse est celeriter ad Cūriam īre, sed prīmum Aurēliam et Cornēliam domum dūcam." 10

"Ita vērō!" inquit Titus. "Ecce! Lectīcāriī, quōs vōbīs condūxī, vōs domum ferent. Ego puerōs cūrābō. Multa et mīra vidēbunt puerī, atque ego omnia eīs explicābō."

(continued)

2 **hūc illūc,** adv., *this way and that*	10 **prīmum,** adv., *first*
3 **lectīca, -ae,** f., *litter*	**domum,** *homeward, home*
4 interdiū, adv., *during the day*	**dūcam,** *I will take*
5 **stupeō, -ēre, -uī,** to be amazed, gape	11 **ferent,** *(they) will carry*
turba, -ae, f., *crowd, mob*	12 **cūrābō,** *I will take care of*
undique, adv., *on all sides*	multa et mīra, *many wonderful things*
6 strepitus, *noise, clattering*	**mīrus, -a, -um,** *wonderful,*
7 **maximus, -a, -um,** *greatest, very great*	*marvelous*
gaudium, -ī, n., *joy*	**vidēbunt,** *(they) will see*
9 Cūria, -ae, f., *Senate House*	

2 **currō, currere, cucurrī, cursūrus,** *to run*
3 **dēscendō, dēscendere, dēscendī, dēscēnsūrus,** *to come/go down, climb down*
4 **agō, agere, ēgī, āctus,** *to do, drive*
11 condūcō, condūcere, condūxī, conductus, *to hire*

EXERCISE 23a

Respondē Latīnē:

1. Quis Cornēliōs exspectābat?
2. Quī hūc illūc currēbant per portam?
3. Ubi sedēbat Titus?
4. Cūr Cornēliī ē raedā dēscendērunt?
5. Quid Sextus prope portam vīdit?
6. Quid Sextus prope portam audīvit?
7. Quōmodo Titus Cornēliōs salūtāvit?
8. Quō necesse est Cornēliō īre?
9. Quis lectīcāriōs condūxit?
10. Quis puerīs multa et mīra explicābit?

Itaque per viās urbis lectīcāriī patrem, mātrem, fīliam celeriter domum tulērunt. Postquam eō advēnērunt, Aurēlia et Cornēlia, itinere dēfessae, sē quiētī dedērunt. Cornēlius tamen sē lāvit, aliam togam praetextam induit, iterum in lectīcā cōnsēdit.

"Ad Cūriam celeriter!" inquit.

15

14 **eō** adv., *there, to that place*
sē quiētī dare, *to rest*
 quiēs, quiētis, f., *rest*

14 **adveniō, advenīre, advēnī, adventūrus,** *to reach, arrive (at)*
15 **induō, induere, induī, indūtus,** *to put on*
 cōnsīdō, cōnsīdere, cōnsēdī, *to sit down*

Respondē Latīnē:

11. Quō lectīcāriī Cornēlium et Aurēliam et Cornēliam tulērunt?
12. Quid Aurēlia et Cornēlia ibi fēcērunt?
13. Quid fēcit Cornēlius postquam domum advēnit?

BUILDING THE MEANING

Go Online
PHSchool.com
Web Code: jfd-0023

Adjectives as Substantives

In the sentence in line 12 of the story, **Multa et mīra vidēbunt puerī, atque ego omnia eīs explicābō,** the words **multa, mīra,** and **omnia** are adjectives, but they are here used with no nouns for them to modify. The adjectives themselves are used as *substantives*, i.e., as words that function as nouns.

The neuter gender and plural number of these particular substantives (**multa, mīra,** and **omnia**) imply the idea of *things*, and you may therefore translate *many and wonderful things* and *all things*. Note that Latin uses a conjunction between **multa** and **mīra**, while we would say merely "many wonderful things." Note also that we normally say "everything" instead of "all things," the literal translation of **omnia**.

You have also seen adjectives in the masculine or feminine used as substantives, e.g., **Cūnctī in caupōnam intrāvērunt** (19:1). Masculine adjectives so used, as here, refer to people in general, and **cūnctī** may be translated *everybody*. You have seen **omnēs** used in this way a number of times. A feminine adjective would refer to women, e.g., **bonae,** *good women*. We often use adjectives as substantives in English as well, e.g., "the good," "the brave," "the wise."

FORMS

Verbs: Future Tense I

Look at these sentences:

Ego omnia eīs **explicābō.**   *I will explain* everything to them.
Multa et mīra **vidēbunt** puerī.   *The boys **will see** many wonderful things.*

Ego Cornēliam domum **dūcam.**   *I will take* Cornelia home.
Brevī tempore ad Portam Capēnam   *In a short time **we will arrive** at the*
adveniēmus.   *Porta Capena.*

The words in boldface are examples of the *future tense*. The endings of the future tense are shown in the chart below:

		1st and 2nd Conjugations	3rd and 4th Conjugations
Singular	1	*-bō*	*-am*
	2	*-bis*	*-ēs*
	3	*-bit*	*-et*
Plural	1	*-bimus*	*-ēmus*
	2	*-bitis*	*-ētis*
	3	*-bunt*	*-ent*

Note that in the future tense the endings of verbs in the 3rd and 4th conjugations are quite different from the endings of verbs in the 1st and 2nd conjugations.

Note also that the *-e-* of the ending in the 3rd and 4th conjugations is short before final *-t* and *-nt*.

Note in the chart below that the letter *i* precedes the endings *-am, -ēs, -et,* etc., in 3rd conjugation **-iō** verbs (**iaciam, iaciēs, iaciet,** etc.) and in 4th conjugation verbs (**audiam, audiēs, audiet,** etc.).

		1st Conjugation	2nd Conjugation	3rd Conjugation		4th Conjugation
Infinitive		par*áre*	hab*ére*	mítt*ere*	iác*ere* (-iō)	aud*íre*
Singular	1	par*ábō*	hab*ébō*	mítt*am*	iáci*am*	aúdi*am*
	2	par*ábis*	hab*ébis*	mítt*ēs*	iáci*ēs*	aúdi*ēs*
	3	par*ábit*	hab*ébit*	mítt*et*	iáci*et*	aúdi*et*
Plural	1	par*ábimus*	hab*ébimus*	mitt*émus*	iaci*émus*	audi*émus*
	2	par*ábitis*	hab*ébitis*	mitt*étis*	iaci*étis*	audi*étis*
	3	par*ábunt*	hab*ébunt*	mítt*ent*	iáci*ent*	aúdi*ent*

Be sure to learn these forms thoroughly.

EXERCISE 23b

Read aloud, identify all verbs in the future tense, and translate:

1. Titus nōs prope Portam Capēnam exspectābit; omnēs maximō cum gaudiō salūtābit.
2. Hodiē magna sepulcra Rōmānōrum praeclārōrum vīdimus; crās Cūriam et alia aedificia Rōmāna vidēbimus.
3. Fortasse patruus noster nōs ad Cūriam dūcet.
4. Cornēliī omnēs sē parant; brevī tempore ad urbem iter facient.
5. Multa et mīra vident puerī; lectīcāriī eōs mox domum portābunt.
6. Cornēlius ē raedā dēscendet, nam raedam intrā urbem agere nōn licet.
7. Quam diū in urbe manēbis, pater?
8. Bene dormiētis, puerī. Longum enim iter hodiē fēcistis.
9. Cornēlia, itinere longō dēfessa, sē quiētī dabit.
10. Puerī multa rogābunt dē aedificiīs quae in urbis viīs vidēbunt.

faciō, facere, fēcī, factus, *to make, do*   **maneō, manēre, mānsī, mānsus,** *to remain, stay, wait (for)*

EXERCISE 23c

Using story 23, its verb list, and the charts of the future tense as guides, give the Latin for:

1. Will you run home, boys?
2. We will sit near the Porta Capena.
3. When will the Cornelii climb down out of the carriage?
4. Cornelius, will you drive your carriage inside the city during the day?
5. Who will hire the litter-bearers?
6. Litter-bearers, will you carry us home?
7. Where will Cornelius wash himself?
8. What will you put on, Cornelius?
9. We will all sit down in two litters.

Detail of a reconstructed view of the *Forum Rōmānum,* early third century A.D. Clockwise from the upper left-hand corner: Temple of Concord, Arch of Septimius Severus, Curia Julia, Basilica Aemilia, Temple of Antoninus and Faustina, Regia (Temple of the Divine Julius in front of it), Temple of Castor (roof only), and Basilica Julia.

Watercolor, Peter Connolly

BUILDING THE MEANING

Present or Future Tense? How Do You Decide?

Look at these sentences:

Cornēlius multōs servōs hab**et**.	*Cornelius **has** many slaves.*
Scelestōs servōs ad vīllam rūsticam mitt**et**.	*He **will send** the wicked slaves to the country house and farm.*
Hodiē in caupōnā man**ēmus**.	*Today we **remain** in the inn.*
Crās Rōmam advenī**ēmus**.	*Tomorrow we **will reach** Rome.*

It is important to know to which conjugation a verb belongs in order to determine its tense.

The endings *-ēs, -et, -ēmus, -ētis, -ent* can denote the present tense of verbs of the 2nd conjugation or the future tense of verbs of the 3rd and 4th conjugations. If there is an *i* before the *e*, the verb will be the future tense of a 3rd conjugation **-iō** verb or the future tense of a 4th conjugation verb.

EXERCISE 23d

Following the examples, identify and translate the remainder of the verb forms below:

Verb	Conjugation	Tense	Meaning
habent	2	present	they have
mittent	3	future	they will send
vident			
iubent			
ascendent			
admovent			
timent			
dūcent			
rīdent			
facient			

EXERCISE 23e

Look carefully at the verbs in the following sentences. Decide the conjugation number first (this will help you get the tense right). Then read aloud and translate:

1. Puerī Eucleidem nōn vident sed vōcem eius audient.
2. Vidēsne senātōrēs in viīs? Quandō Cornēlius veniet?
3. Servī celeriter current, nam Cornēlium timent.
4. Sextus māne surget; in animō habet exīre.
5. Ego et Cornēlia tacēmus; patrem timēmus.

EXERCISE 23f

Read the dialogue below to yourself, mentally noting all verbs in the imperfect, perfect, and future tenses. Then take parts and read the dialogue aloud:

Intereā Eucleidēs et puerī cum Titō extrā Portam Capēnam stābant.

TITUS: Salvēte, puerī! Quid in itinere vīdistis? Vīdistisne rūsticōs in agrīs? Agrōsne colēbant?

SEXTUS: Rūsticōs vīdimus. Agrōs nōn colēbant, sed sub arboribus quiēscēbant. At caupōnam vīdimus; nostra raeda in fossā haerēbat et nōbīs necesse erat in 5 caupōnā pernoctāre.

MĀRCUS: Ita vērō! Gaudēbam quod pater meus in illā caupōnā pernoctāre cōnstituit. Caupō erat vir Graecus, amīcus Eucleidis.

SEXTUS: Ego quoque gaudēbam, nam mīles bonam fābulam nōbīs nārrāvit. In illā fābulā caupō quīdam hospitem necāvit. Tālēs fābulās amō. Sed quid nunc 10 faciēmus? Ego volō Circum Maximum vīsitāre. Ecce! Nōnne Circum Maximum suprā mūrōs urbis exstantem vidēre possum?

MĀRCUS: Ita vērō! Est Circus Maximus. Nōn procul abest.

TITUS: Nōn possumus omnia hodiē vidēre. Crās satis temporis habēbimus.

SEXTUS: Sed quid est illud aedificium? Nōnne pontem ingentem suprā portam videō? 15

MĀRCUS: Nōn pontem hīc vidēs, ō stulte! Est aquaeductus, Aqua Mārcia. Per illum aquaeductum Rōmānī aquam in urbem ferunt. Cavē imbrem, Sexte!

SEXTUS: Sed nōn pluit.

TITUS: Semper hīc pluit, Sexte. Rīmōsa enim est Aqua Mārcia.

1 **extrā**, prep. + acc., *outside*
4 **at**, conj., *but*
10 **tālis, -is, -e**, *such*
11 Circus Maximus, *the Circus Maximus (a stadium in Rome)*
12 **suprā**, prep. + acc., *above*
mūrus, -ī, m., *wall*
exstantem, *standing out, towering*
14 satis temporis, *enough of time, enough time*

15 **pōns, pontis**, gen. pl., **pontium**, m., *bridge*
16 **stultus, -a, -um**, *stupid, foolish*
17 Cavē imbrem! *Watch out for the rain!*
imber, imbris, gen. pl., **imbrium**, m., *rain*
19 rīmōsus, -a, -um, *full of cracks, leaky*

3 **colō, colere, coluī, cultus**, *to cultivate*
4 **quiēscō, quiēscere, quiēvī, quiētūrus**, *to rest, keep quiet*
7 **cōnstituō, cōnstituere, cōnstituī, cōnstitūtus**, *to decide*
18 **pluit, pluere, pluit**, usually found only in 3rd person singular, *it rains, is raining*

Verbs: Future Tense II

The following are the future tenses of the irregular verbs you have met:

Infinitive		ésse	pósse	vélle	nólle	férre	íre
Singular	1	érō	póterō	vólam	nólam	féram	íbō
	2	éris	póteris	vólēs	nólēs	férēs	íbis
	3	érit	póterit	vólet	nólet	féret	íbit
Plural	1	érimus	potérimus	volémus	nōlémus	ferémus	íbimus
	2	éritis	potéritis	volétis	nōlétis	ferétis	íbitis
	3	érunt	póterunt	vólent	nólent	férent	íbunt

Note that **velle, nōlle, ferre,** and **īre** have future tense endings like those of regular verbs. Note also where long vowels occur in the endings of these verbs. The tenses of the compounds of irregular verbs are formed in the same way as those of the uncompounded verbs, e.g., the future tense of **exeō** is **exībō**.

Cistern

Water wheel

Spring-fed watering channel

EXERCISE 23g

Read aloud, identify all verbs in the future tense, and translate:

1. Ībisne ad Cūriam, pater? Ita vērō! Ad Cūriam celeriter ībō.
2. Quandō domum redībis, pater? Nesciō.
3. Fortasse Cornēlius domum redīre brevī tempore poterit.
4. Eucleidēs et puerī in urbem māne exiērunt.
5. Necesse erat diū in urbe manēre.
6. Nocte vehicula magna onera in urbem ferent.

> **redeō, redīre, rediī** or **redīvī, reditūrus,** irreg., *to return, go back*
> **exeō, exīre, exiī** or **exīvī, exitūrus,** irreg., *to go out*

(continued)

7. Puerī Circum Maximum crās vidēre volent.
8. Ubi līberī māne erunt? Tū līberōs nōn vidēbis, nam ē domō nostrō mox exībunt.
9. Sī equī strēnuē labōrābunt, raedam ē fossā extrahere poterunt.
10. Sī pluet, ad silvam ambulāre nōlam.
11. Ferēsne cistam meam in caupōnam? Minimē! Tū ipse eam fer!
12. Redībitisne ad vīllam rūsticam? Fortasse redīre poterimus.
13. Volētisne crās ad Circum Maximum īre? Ita vērō! Crās illūc īre volēmus.
14. "Ego īre nōlam," inquit Aurēlia.
15. Post cēnam puerī cubitum īre nōlēbant.

ē domō nostrō, *out of our house*   **illūc,** adv., *there, to that place*

Note that in sentences 9 and 10 the verbs in both clauses are in the future tense because the actions in both clauses are conceived of as taking place at the same time in the future. English, however, normally uses the present tense in the *if* clause in this type of conditional sentence.

Go Online
PHSchool.com
Web Code: jfd-0023

AQUEDUCTS

One feature of the city that the Cornelii would notice as they approached Rome was the evidence of the Romans' passion for water. Abundant water for baths and fountains and pools was a vital necessity to the Romans, and water was brought in by aqueducts, whose arches strode into Rome from all directions. By A.D. 80, nine aqueducts were in use, carrying water across the plains to Rome from sources up to fifty-six miles or ninety kilometers distant.

The drawing on page 75 shows the arches supporting the water channel and a cross-section of the channel itself. To maintain the downhill flow, experts recommended a fall of six inches or fifteen centimeters in every ninety-eight feet or thirty meters. Tunnels, with inspection shafts built into them, were driven through those hills that were impossible to bypass. Sometimes, by using the principle that water rises to its own level, a U-shaped arrangement of the tunnel allowed an uphill flow.

The first aqueduct, named the Aqua Appia after its builder Appius Claudius, was built in 312 B.C. and ran underground for much of its route in order to speed its construction

France

A Roman aqueduct in southern France, called the Pont du Gard

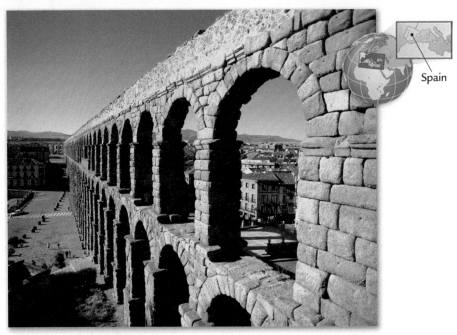

Spain

This 8.5 mile long Roman aqueduct brought water to the city of Segovia into the twentieth century.
Roman aqueduct, Segovia, Spain

and to hide its presence from Rome's enemies. Its waters supported the growth in Rome's population during the fourth century B.C. Appius's pride in its construction was commemorated in his epitaph, which lists this accomplishment on a par with his victories in war.

Later aqueducts had to supply water to the more hilly and elevated districts of Rome. Since the Romans used a gravity system to propel the flow of water, sources higher in the Sabine and Alban Hills had to be found.

The Romans then hit on the idea of using arches to support the water channel. The arches turned out to be beautiful structures in themselves, but the Romans had adopted them for quite different reasons. The arches required less brick and stone than a solid wall and allowed people and animals to pass through easily. An arched structure could be easily repaired, as workmen could take the building materials from one side to the other.

Admiring comments about the aqueducts abound from native and foreigner alike. "Just as impressive," says one writer, "as the pyramids, but how much more useful!" Not only so, but we also have an astonishing book, *De aquis urbis Romae*, by Frontinus, Superintendent of Aqueducts, written about A.D. 97, describing the system in detail and the difficulties of organizing and maintaining it. He reports that, through bribery of watermen, supplies were sometimes diverted into private estates and never reached Rome at all. Householders in Rome itself often succeeded in bribing inspectors (who were, after all, slaves) to replace a narrow pipe by one of wider bore, while they continued to pay at the old rate!

The emperor appointed the Superintendent of Aqueducts, who, with his staff, had responsibility for maintaining and cleaning the whole vast system. Concern for the health of the immense population of Rome made the emperors keenly aware of the importance of maintaining a supply of clean water. In his official statement of his accomplishments, Augustus took justifiable pride in his improvement of the water supply of Rome:

> In many places I rebuilt the channels of the aqueducts that had collapsed due to old age, and the aqueduct which is called the Marcia I doubled in quantity, by means of a new source flowing into its channel.

Augustus, *Res gestae* 20

According to the latest available figures, the daily consumption of water in a large city today is about 120 gallons or 455 liters per person. According to Frontinus, in his day the Roman aqueducts could deliver over 264 million gallons or one billion liters in twenty-four hours, providing a daily allowance of about 240 gallons or 900 liters per person! The aqueducts leaked dreadfully, as the Cornelii found at the Porta Capena, and what with water thieves and corrupt inspectors, all this water did not actually reach Rome. For all that, the Roman citizen still had a lot of water at his disposal. Did he use it all? The answer is "Yes," because as one Roman writer put it, "The waters, having provided the city with the life-giving element, passed on into the sewers." The Roman, you see, hardly ever turned the tap off. For him, running water was quite literally running water!

1. Appius Claudius was responsible for both the first aqueduct and the first great Roman road, the Via Appia used by our characters. Both these projects took place in 312 B.C. What does this construction boom tell us about the Roman world of that year?
2. From the eassays that have appeared so far in this book, how would you characterize the Romans? What does this essay on aqueducts add to your characterization of the Romans?

Sketch of the Pont du Gard showing the water channel

ADDITIONAL READING:
The Romans Speak for Themselves: Book I: "The Aqueducts of Ancient Rome," pages 65–74.

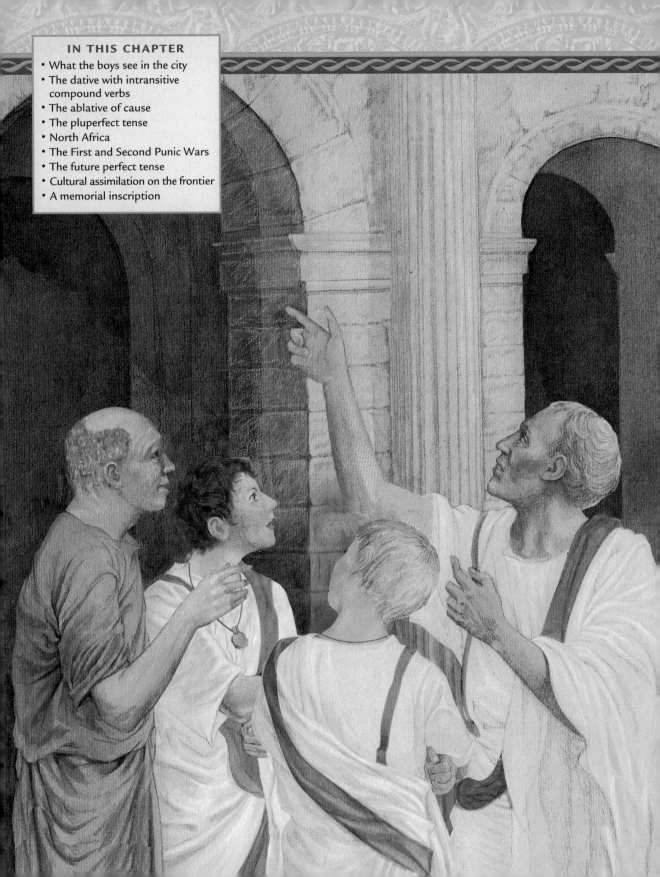

ALWAYS TOMORROW

Simulac Titus et puerī et Eucleidēs urbem per Portam Capēnam intrāvērunt, clāmāvit Sextus, "Quid nōs prīmum faciēmus? Quō ībimus? Vīsitābimusne— ?"

"Quō tū nōs dūcēs, patrue?" interpellāvit Mārcus. "Vidēbimusne Cūriam et Forum? Sextus multa dē Rōmā lēgit et audīvit et nunc, patrue, omnia vidēre vult."

Titus, "Tacēte! Tacēte!" inquit. "Forum crās vīsitābimus. Crās, Eucleidēs, tibi licēbit puerōs eō dūcere. Tum erit satis temporis. Hodiē tamen, puerī, vōs domum per urbem dūcam et omnia in itinere vōbīs dēmōnstrābō." 5

Iam advēnerant ad Circum Maximum, quī nōn procul aberat. Stupuit Sextus ubi mōlem Circī Maximī vīdit. Mārcus quoque stupuit, quamquam Circum anteā vīderat. Stupuit Titus, attonitus nōn mōle, sed silentiō Circī. 10

"Ēheu! Ēheu!" inquit Titus. "Hodiē Circus est clausus. Tribus diēbus tamen prīnceps ipse, Titus Flāvius Vespasiānus, lūdōs magnificōs faciet."

"Nōnne tū nōs eō dūcēs?" rogāvit Mārcus.

"Ēheu! Ego nōn poterō vōs dūcere," inquit Titus. "Fortasse Eucleidēs vōs dūcet."

(continued)

1 **simulac,** conj., *as soon as*
8 **advēnerant,** *they had arrived*
9 mōlēs, mōlis, gen. pl., mōlium, f., *mass, huge bulk*
vīderat, *he had seen*

10 **attonitus, -a, -um,** *astonished, astounded*
11 **clausus, -a, -um,** *shut, closed*
12 **lūdī, -ōrum,** m. pl., *games*

4 **legō, legere, lēgī, lēctus,** *to read*
5 **licet, licēre, licuit** + dat., usually found only in 3rd person singular and infinitive, *it is allowed*

EXERCISE 24a

Respondē Latīnē:

Go Online
PHSchool.com
Web Code: jfd-0024

1. Quis puerōs crās ad Forum dūcet?
2. Vīderatne Sextus anteā Circum Maximum?
3. Eratne Titus attonitus mōle Circī?
4. Cūr Circum hodiē puerī nōn intrant?
5. Quid faciet prīnceps tribus diēbus?
6. Dūcetne Titus puerōs ad lūdōs?

"Minimē!" respondit Sextus. "Librōs, nōn lūdōs amat Eucleidēs." 15

"Agite, puerī!" interpellāvit Titus. "Nunc circumībimus Montem Palātīnum et Forum intrābimus ad arcum Tiberiī. Ibi fortasse patrī tuō occurrēmus, Mārce. Mox senātōrēs ē Cūriā exībunt."

Itaque Circum relīquērunt et Palātīnum circumiērunt. Titus in itinere mōnstrāvit puerīs mīra aedificia quae prīncipēs in Palātīnō aedificāverant. Tandem ad arcum Tiberiī 20 advēnērunt, iam labōre et aestū dēfessī.

"Hic est arcus," inquit Titus, "quem— "

"Omnia vidēre poteritis crās," interpellāvit Cornēlius, quī eō ipsō tempore ad arcum ē Cūriā advēnerat. "Cum ad Forum crās redieritis, Eucleidēs omnia vōbīs explicābit. Iam sērō est. Agite! Iam domum ībimus." 25

15 **liber, librī,** m., *book*	21 aestū, *from the heat*
16 Mōns Palātīnus, Montis Palātīnī,	22 quem, acc., *which*
m., *the Palatine Hill*	24 **redieritis,** *you* (pl.) *will have returned,*
17 **arcus,** *arch*	*you return*
20 **aedificō, -āre, -āvī, -ātus,** *to build*	

16 **circumeō, circumīre, circumiī** or **circumīvī, circumitus,**
irreg., *to go around*

17 **occurrō, occurrere, occurrī, occursūrus** + dat., *to meet, encounter*

Respondē Latīnē:

7. Quid amat Eucleidēs?
8. Quī mīra aedificia in Palātīnō aedificāverant?
9. Quis puerīs prope arcum Tiberiī occurrit?
10. Quō Cornēlius puerōs hodiē dūcet?

BUILDING THE MEANING

Go Online
PHSchool.com
Web Code: jfd-0024

Dative with Intransitive Compound Verbs

Look at the following sentence:

Ibi fortasse **patrī tuō** occurrēmus. (24:17) *Perhaps we will meet **your father** there.*

The verb **occurrere** is a compound verb, that is, it consists of the intransitive verb **currere** plus the prefix **ob-** *against,* which becomes **oc-** by assimilation to the initial consonant of the verb. The compound verb is still intransitive, and its meaning (*to run against, to meet*) is completed not by a direct object in the accusative case but by a word or phrase in the *dative case,* here **patrī tuō**.

You have also seen the intransitive compound verb **appropinquāre** (= the prefix **ad-** + **propinquāre**) used with the dative:

Iam **urbī** appropinquābant. (22:12)
*Already they were coming near **to the city**/approaching **the city**.*

Sentences with compound verbs and the dative such as these give us another basic pattern of Latin sentences (see pages 8 and 21).

Ablative of Cause

You have met words or phrases in the ablative case assigning blame for something that has happened or stating the cause of someone's being in a certain state:

> **Tuā culpā** raeda est in fossā. (14:7)
> *Because of your fault the carriage is in the ditch.*
> *It's your fault that the carriage is in the ditch.*
>
> **magnā īrā** commōtus (14:17)   *moved because of/by great anger*
>
> **itinere** dēfessī (23:8)   *tired because of/from the journey*
>
> attonitus nōn **mōle**... (24:10)   *astonished not because of/by the mass...*

This is called the *ablative of cause*; note that no preposition is used in Latin.

FORMS

Go Online
PHSchool.com
Web Code: jfd-0024

Verbs: Pluperfect Tense

Look at this sentence:

> Mārcus quoque stupuit, quamquam Circum anteā **vīderat.** (24:9)
> *Marcus too was amazed, although **he had seen** the Circus before.*

The verb in the subordinate clause in this sentence is in the *pluperfect tense*. A verb in the pluperfect tense describes an action that was completed *before* some other action in the past took place. Thus, Marcus had seen the Circus *before* the occasion when he saw it in our story.

Verbs in the pluperfect tense can nearly always be translated with *had...* in English.

The endings of the pluperfect tense are the same for *all* Latin verbs. They look like the imperfect tense of **esse:**

Singular		Plural	
1	*-eram*	1	*-erāmus*
2	*-erās*	2	*-erātis*
3	*-erat*	3	*-erant*

These endings are added to the perfect stem, which is found by dropping the **-ī** from the end of the third principal part, e.g., **relinquō, relinquere, relīquī,** perfect stem **relīqu-.**

Singular		Plural	
1	relīqu*eram*	1	relīqu*erāmus*
2	relīqu*erās*	2	relīqu*erātis*
3	relīqu*erat*	3	relīqu*erant*

EXERCISE 24b

Read each sentence aloud. Identify each pluperfect verb and explain how the action it describes was completed before the action of the other verb took place. Then translate:

1. Eucleidēs puerōs ad urbem māne dūxerat et omnia eīs dēmōnstrābat.
2. Aurēlia laeta erat quod servī cēnam bonam iam parāverant.
3. Hodiē librum diū legēbam quem mihi heri dederās.
4. Dēfessus eram quod multās epistulās iam scrīpseram.
5. Vix domum advēnerant puerī, cum Eucleidēs in hortum intrāvit.

   scrībō, scrībere, scrīpsī, scrīptus, *to write*   **vix**, adv., *scarcely*

EXERCISE 24c

Substitute the corresponding pluperfect form for each verb in parentheses (all present tense), read the sentence aloud, and translate:

1. Tantum sonitum numquam anteā (audīmus) _____.
2. Mārcus laetus erat quod patrī prope Cūriam (occurrit) _____.
3. Via erat plēna hominum quī ad urbem (veniunt) _____.
4. Lectīcāriī, quī Cornēlium per urbis viās (ferunt) _____, extrā Cūriam eum exspectābant.
5. Titus, quod Circum (invenit) _____ clausum, puerōs domum dūcēbat.
6. Sextus, ubi ad urbem advēnit, laetus erat quod numquam anteā in urbe Rōmā (est) _____.
7. Arcus, quem Tiberius (aedificat) _____, erat ingēns.
8. Senātōrēs iam ē Cūriā (exeunt) _____, cum puerī ad Forum advēnērunt.
9. Mārcus multa aedificia quae iam (videt) _____ iterum vīsitābat.
10. Sextus, quod multa dē Rōmā (audit) _____ et (legit) _____, omnia vidēre volēbat.

    tantus, -a, -um, *so great, such a big*

Go Online
PHSchool.com
Web Code: jfd-0024

NORTH AFRICA

Egypt

Cornelius has been recalled to Rome due to urgent messages the emperor and consuls have received from the governor of the province of Africa (who is appointed by the Senate) and the prefect (administrator) of Numidia (see map, page 110). One of the fierce nomadic tribes of Africa, the Nasamones, has made several attacks on two of the colonies lately established in the province of Africa. The agricultural territory given to these colonies was seized from the Nasamones, who were consequently restricted to pasturing their flocks on poorer ground. Because these colonies contributed to the large supply of

Mummy portraits such as these reflect the multicultural, multiethnic society of Roman Africa.
Funerary portraits from Roman Egypt, first to third centuries A.D.

grain sent from Africa to Rome for free distribution to its inhabitants, the emperor asked the consuls to summon an extraordinary session of the Senate to consider what should be done to end the raids.

Cornelius's opinions and advice will be of particular interest to the emperor and Senate in their deliberations. At age seventeen Cornelius began his political career by serving as military tribune in the army stationed in Numidia and came to know some young men who are now leaders of the Nasamones. His subsequent experience in government offices has given him a good understanding of the potential danger posed by these raids. His first post after the army was on the Board of Twenty (**Vīgintīvirī**), where he and two others were placed in charge of the state mint. At age twenty-seven, elected as one of forty quaestors, he was in charge of the grain supply from Africa at Rome's port city, Ostia. As an ex-quaestor, Cornelius automatically became a member of the Senate and has attended its meetings regularly. At age thirty-two, he was elected curule aedile and was in charge of regulating the grain supply at Rome. Two years ago as the officer in charge of lawsuits involving foreigners (**praetor peregrīnus**) he adjudicated lawsuits of non-Roman citizens; because of his prior stay in Africa, he specialized in suits of non-Roman citizens of Africa. His friends in the Senate think he will be elected consul in a few years and that the Senate will probably appoint him governor of Africa after his year in that office.

Go Online
PHSchool.com
Web Code: jfd-0024

THE FIRST AND SECOND PUNIC WARS

As we learned in the essay on North Africa on page 81, Cornelius was recalled to Rome to take part in senatorial deliberations over attacks by native tribesmen on recently founded Roman colonies in Africa. Rome's involvement with North Africa already spanned hundreds of years—going back as far, in fact, as the Punic Wars of the third and second centuries B.C.

Rome, the great land power of Italy, engaged Carthage, the great sea power of North Africa, in a long struggle for control of Sicily and the western Mediterranean Sea that lasted through three wars and spanned more than a century (264–146 B.C.) A strong navy protected

the flourishing commercial center of Carthage, colonized as an outpost centuries earlier by the Phoenicians, whom the Romans called **Pūnicī**. In the First Punic War (264–241 B.C.), the Romans were quick to realize that if they wanted to win they too must take to the sea. Roman marines shocked the Carthaginians when they dropped gangways with sharp metal points on one end, called "crows" (**corvī**), onto their decks; these held the enemy ships fast while the Romans boarded them with their superior soldiers. The birth of the Roman fleet ultimately led to a Roman victory.

Just as significant was the hatred between the two nations that the war produced. Roman legend confidently reports that Hannibal Barca, when he was a boy of nine years old, stood before an altar with his father, Hamilcar, and swore his undying hatred of the Romans. When Hannibal was twenty-six, troops loyal to Hamilcar, who had been slain in battle in Spain,

Hamilcar invites his son Hannibal to swear eternal enmity to Rome. Hamilcar points his sword at the she-wolf nursing Romulus and Remus, and Roman legionary standards lie on the ground.
Hannibal Swearing Eternal Enmity to Rome, *oil on canvas*, Jacopo Amigoni

were quick to pledge allegiance to Hannibal. Determined to fulfill his father's dreams of revenge on the Roman conquerors and of a new Carthaginian empire, Hannibal set out for Italy to ignite the Second Punic War (218–201 B.C.).

With an army of Carthaginians and mercenaries, Hannibal left Spain, crossed the Pyrenees, proceeded up the coast of France, and arrived at the great barrier into northern Italy, the Alps. Thirty-seven elephants, including Hannibal's pet, Syrus, were the most memorable members of the forces that Hannibal led up the Alps.

Fending off the attacks of mountain tribesmen, battling against snow and cold and slippery paths, the fiercely loyal troops reached a promontory high in the Alps where Hannibal, pointing to the vista of Italy far below his troops, proclaimed: "Now you are crossing not only the walls of Italy, but those of Rome." When a rockslide blocked their way down, Hannibal ordered his men to build fires that heated the rocks; according to the Roman historian Livy, the rocks split apart when sour wine was poured on them, clearing a path that the Carthaginian army descended, elephants and all.

Employing clever tactics, Hannibal dealt the Romans crushing defeats as he swept southward through Italy. The worst occurred at Lake Trasimene, where mist rising off the water prevented the Romans from realizing that they were heading into an ambush until the trap had already been sprung. At Cannae, a year later, Hannibal led the center of his line in a planned retreat, luring the Romans into a trap again. Hannibal's cavalry closed in from the flanks and dealt a crippling blow to the Roman army.

Hannibal did not have a large enough force at his command to march on the city of Rome, however. He waited, expecting that Rome's Italian allies would revolt and come

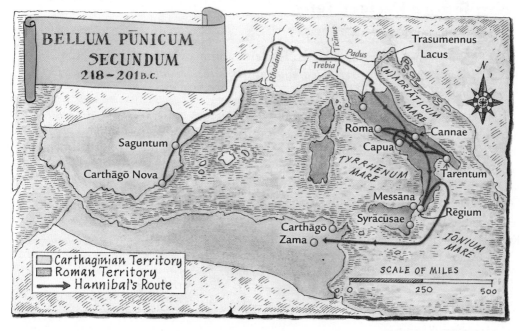

over to his side. They did not. For years Hannibal and the wary Romans played cat and mouse. In 207 B.C., Hasdrubal, Hannibal's brother, crossed the Alps with a relief force but was intercepted by the Romans—a disaster Hannibal learned about when a Roman cavalryman tossed Hasdrubal's head into his camp.

Publius Cornelius Scipio, the Roman commander, after victories over Carthaginian forces in Spain, returned to Italy and convinced the Roman Senate to send him to Africa with a Roman army. Scipio achieved so much success there that Hannibal, after fifteen years of fighting in Italy, was summoned to return home and defend Carthage. On the plain of Zama, Scipio, employing Hannibalic tactics against his foe, claimed the decisive victory of the war. Scipio received the title (**cognōmen**) **Africānus.** Hannibal, Rome's most memorable enemy, was forced into exile.

1. Summarize the three famous military encounters of the Second Punic War: Trasimene, Cannae, and Zama.
2. In Vergil's *Aeneid*, Dido, Queen of Carthage, when abandoned by Aeneas, curses the Trojans. With her dying breath, she calls upon **aliquis ultor** (*some avenger*) to arise from her bones. How would Vergil's Roman audience have interpreted this curse?
3. What are some ways in which the course of Western history might have been different if Hannibal and his Carthaginians had defeated Rome?

FORMS

Verbs: Future Perfect Tense

Look at this sentence:

"Cum ad Forum crās **redieritis**, Eucleidēs omnia vōbīs explicābit." (24:24)
"*When **you will have returned/you return** to the Forum tomorrow, Eucleides will explain everything to you.*"

The verb in the subordinate clause in this sentence is in the *future perfect tense*. A verb in the future perfect tense describes an action that will have been completed *before* some other action in future time begins. Thus, the boys will have returned to the Forum *before* Eucleides will explain everything to them. Note that Latin verbs in the future perfect tense are often best translated by the present tense in English as in the example above, *When you return...* The literal translation is *When you will have returned....*

The endings of the future perfect tense are the same for *all* Latin verbs. They look like the future tense of **esse,** except for the 3rd person plural:

Singular		Plural	
1	-erō	1	-erimus
2	-eris	2	-eritis
3	-erit	3	-erint

These endings are added to the perfect stem, which is found by dropping the *-ī* from the end of the third principal part, e.g., **redeō, redīre, rediī,** perfect stem **redi-.**

Singular			Plural		
	1	redí*erō*		1	redí*erimus*
	2	redí*eris*		2	redí*eritis*
	3	redí*erit*		3	redí*erint*

EXERCISE 24d

Read each sentence aloud. Identify each verb in the future perfect tense and explain how the action it describes will have been completed before the action of the other verb takes place. Then translate:

1. Sī baculum coniēceris, canēs ferōciter lātrābunt.
2. Cum ad Portam Capēnam advēnerimus, ē raedā dēscendēmus.
3. Sī equī raedam ē fossā extrāxerint, Cornēliī ad urbem iter facere poterunt.
4. Nisi caupō alium lectum in cubiculum mōverit, Aurēlia ibi dormīre nōlet.
5. Crās puerī, cum surrēxerint, strepitum plaustrōrum audient.
6. Eucleidēs et puerī, ubi Circum relīquērunt et Palātīnum circumiērunt, Forum intrāvērunt.
7. Cum ad arcum Tiberiī advēnerint, Cornēliō occurrent.
8. Crās puerī dēfessī erunt, sī omnia aedificia in forō vīsitāverint.
9. Aurēlia et Cornēlia, cum domum advēnerint, sē quiētī dabunt.
10. Aurēlia et Cornēlia, cum ē lectīs surrēxerint, lānam trahent.

   moveō, movēre, mōvī, mōtus, *to move*

EXERCISE 24e

Using the sentences in Exercise 24d and the charts of pluperfect and future perfect forms as guides, give the Latin for:

1. The boys had already thrown the stick.
2. We had already arrived at the Porta Capena.
3. The horses had not yet dragged the carriage out of the ditch.
4. Unless you will have moved/you move another bed into the bedroom, we will not be willing to sleep here.
5. Tomorrow when you will have gotten up/you get up, Sextus, you will hear the noise of wagons.
6. Eucleides and the boys had already left the Circus and had gone around the Palatine.
7. When we will have arrived/we arrive at the Arch of Tiberius, we will meet Cornelius.
8. Yesterday the boys had visited all the buildings in the forum. At night they were tired from their exertion/labor and the heat.
9. Aurelia and Cornelia had already rested.
10. What will you do when you will have gotten up/you get up, Aurelia and Cornelia?

Go Online
PHSchool.com
Web Code: jfd-0024

CULTURAL ASSIMILATION

In "Rome and Northern Europe" on pages 59–61, you were introduced to the Ubian girl Helge and her Roman legionary husband Lucius. Their story continues here.

One day, shortly before Helge's child was born, an officer of the **Legiō XX Valeria** came to Helge's hut and saw that she was weaving a colorful tartan for her husband. The men of the legion needed new tunics and cloaks, and the officer decided that the legionaries' women (**focāriae**) could weave and make tunics and cloaks for the legion. When Helge finished the tartan, she then wove cloth for legionary tunics and cloaks. Afterward, whenever she and the other Ubian legionary wives saw their men wearing the tunics and cloaks they had made, she and her friends felt pride in their work.

Helge bore a son, and when he was nine days old Lucius, the proud father, gave the baby his name and placed a **bulla** containing good luck charms around the child's neck in accordance with the Roman custom. Because Helge was not the daughter of a Roman citizen, little Lucius did not inherit Roman citizenship from his father. Lucius the legionary, however, knew that if his son served in a Roman auxiliary unit, he would be given citizenship upon discharge after twenty-five years of service. Helge knew that Roman citizenship brought certain privileges: exemption from taxation, the right to run for public office, and rights of appeal in cases of litigation in the Roman court.

As little Lucius grew from child to young man, the Romanization process continued. Lucius grew up speaking both Latin and the language of his mother's people. When the boy was seven years old, his father enrolled him in a school run by a Greek freedman. Helge learned that while the customs of her people allowed only the priests to know how to read and write, the Romans permitted literacy to everyone.

The population of the Roman settlement increased, and to meet its needs the men of the **Legiō XX Valeria** and the **Legiō I Germānica** built an underground aqueduct to bring water to the city from springs in the nearby hills. The legionaries also built a head-quarters (**praetōrium**) for the Roman governor of Lower Germany and a wall to enclose and protect the inhabitants. In addition, a road and a dock alongside the Rhine were built.

The years passed and Helge and Lucius were now the parents of four children. In addition to the first son, a daughter and two other sons had been born to them. Their first son joined the auxiliaries and looked forward to receiving the coveted Roman citizenship. Although years earlier Helge had been reluctant to accept Roman ways, she now had grown to appreciate the advantages of Roman civilization, especially after she

Roman parents enjoyed providing their children with toys such as this toddler's pull-toy in the form of a Roman cavalry soldier.

Wheeled toy, Romano-German, Cologne, first to third centuries A.D.

and a merchant were involved in a dispute over a price and the matter was settled in the court before a Roman magistrate (**praetor**) with both sides satisfied, instead of by a fight in which someone might have been killed. When she went shopping, she used Roman coin, which was acceptable to all the tradesmen instead of the complicated system of barter used by her own people and the clans on the other side of the Rhine.

Finally, Lucius received his honorable discharge (**missiō honesta**) from the legion, and, using his mustering-out pay of 3000 sesterces, he opened up a small tavern where he and his old comrades and other legionaries met to drink, spin tales of past campaigns, and play at **latrunculī** (a game like chess). His two younger sons also joined the auxiliaries and along with their older brother participated in the invasion of Britain in A.D. 43.

And so we see how a common foot soldier peaceably helped spread Roman civilization and its benefits. Not all of Rome's conquests were military! The most enduring aspects of its civilization—its laws, its customs, and its architectural and engineering accomplishments—are still embodied in our present-day civilization.

1. List some distinct advantages of Romanization.
2. What disadvantages might the advance of Roman culture bring to the frontier?
3. If you had been Lucius, would you have stayed on the frontier after your discharge from the army or would you have returned to your native Italy? Explain your decision.

Go Online
PHSchool.com
Web Code: jfd-0024

MEMORIAL INSCRIPTION

T he following inscription on a tombstone found in Colchester, England, commemorates a centurion of the **Legiō XX Valeria**, named Marcus Favonius Facilis:

M·FAVON·M·F·POL·FACI
LIS>LEG XX VERECVND
VS·ET·NOVICIUS·LIB·POSV
ERUNT·H·S·E

M(ārcus) Favōn(ius), M(ārcī) f(īlius) Pol(liā)(tribū), Facilis (centurio) leg(iōnis) XX. Verēcund-
us et Novīcius līb(ertī) posu-
ērunt. H(īc) s(itus) e(st).

Marcus Favonius Facilis, son of Marcus, of the Pollia tribe, centurion of the Twentieth legion. Verecundus and Novicius his freedmen set up this tomb. Here he lies buried.

Write a possible epitaph in English or Latin for Lucius or Helge based on the readings in Frontier Life I and II.

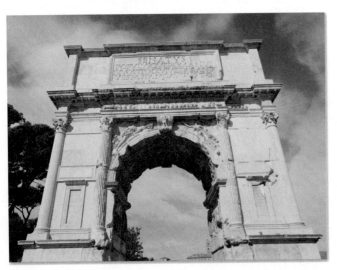

The emperor Domitian built the Arch of Titus in A.D. 81–82 to celebrate Titus's triumphs and his deification.
Rome

Go Online
PHSchool.com
Web Code: jfd-0024

Exercise Va: Dative Case pp. 52–54, 55–56, 57, 78

Supply Latin words to match the English cues. Be sure to use the right endings. Explain the reason for each use of the dative case. Then read each sentence aloud and translate it:

1. Sextus fābulam dē caupōne scelestō _____ nārrābat. (to Cornelia)
2. Eucleidēs mandāta _____ et _____ dabat. (to the slaves) (to the slave-women)
3. Dum Cornēlius fābulam _____ nārrābat, _____ appropinquābant. (to his wife) (the city)
4. Interdiū raedās intrā urbem agere _____ nōn licēbat. (to *or* for the Romans)
5. "_____ necesse est ad Cūriam īre." (For me)
6. Titus respondet, "_____ lectīcāriōs condūxī." (For you, *pl.*)
7. "Ego multa et mīra _____ et _____ explicābō," inquit Titus. (to you, *sing.*) (to Sextus)
8. "_____ in caupōnā pernoctāre necesse erat," inquit Sextus. (for us)
9. Crās Forum vīsitāre _____ licēbit. (to *or* for the boys)
10. Hodiē māne _____ dormīre licet. (to *or* for Cornelia)
11. Cornēlius ē Cūriā mox exībit. _____ Mārcus et Sextus occurrent. (Him)
12. Titus mīra aedificia _____ mōnstrāvit. (to the boys)
13. Crās multa alia aedificia _____ mōnstrābit. (to them)

Exercise Vb: Future, Pluperfect, and Future Perfect Tenses pp. 67, 68, 69, 71, 79, 84

Read aloud, identify the tenses of the verbs, and translate:

1. "Sī ego ad Cūriam sērō advēnerō, senātōrēs īrātī erunt," cōgitābat Cornēlius.
2. Sextus numquam aedificia tam magnifica vīderat.
3. Crās Eucleidēs puerōs ad Forum dūcet.
4. Ībisne cum puerīs, Cornēlia?
5. Crās puerī in Forō aderunt et aedificia vidēbunt.
6. Cornēlius fābulam dē caupōne scelestō nārrātam nōn audīverat.
7. "Sī fābulam mīlitis audīverimus, pater, statim cubitum ībimus," inquit Mārcus.
8. Crās Cornēlius fābulam Aurēliae nārrāre poterit.
9. Nēmō caupōnam Apollodōrī anteā reprehenderat.
10. Cum pater manūs lāverit et aliam togam induerit, ad Cūriam statim ībit.

tam, adv., *so, such*

Exercise Vc: Verb Forms REVIEW pp. 16–17, 26, 67, 71, 79, 84

Give the requested forms of the following verbs in the present, imperfect, future, perfect, pluperfect, and future perfect tenses:

	Present	Imperfect	Future	Perfect	Pluperfect	Future Perfect
1. circumīre (3rd pl.)						
2. dēscendere (2nd sing.)						
3. ferre (2nd pl.)						
4. dare (1st pl.)						
5. esse (3rd sing.)						
6. respondēre (1st sing.)						
7. surgere (3rd pl.)						
8. cōgitāre (2nd sing.)						
9. conicere (1st sing.)						
10. venīre (1st pl.)						

Exercise Vd: Reading Comprehension

Read the following passage and answer the questions below with full sentences in Latin:

ROME'S FIERCEST ENEMY

Ubi Hannibal puer novem annōrum erat, pater eius, nōmine Hamilcar, ad Hispāniam multīs cum mīlitibus nāvigāre parābat. Multīs ante annīs Rōmānī Hamilcarem in bellō vīcerant; ab Carthāginiēnsibus īnsulās Siciliam Sardiniam-que cēperant. Nunc in animō habēbat Hamilcar ad Hispāniam trānsīre et ibi imperium novum condere. In Āfricā manēre nōlēbat puer Hannibal, itaque patrī 5 appropinquāvit.

"Pater, pater!" clāmāvit Hannibal. "Dūc mē tēcum ad Hispāniam! Nōlī mē in Āfricā cum puerīs relinquere!"

"Sed tū puer es," respondit pater, quī eō ipsō tempore ōmina ad āram cōnsulere parābat. "Virī Carthāginiēnsēs, nōn puerī, hostēs Rōmānīs sunt." 10

"Puer nōn sum," inquit Hannibal. "Sī tū hostis Rōmānīs es, ego quoque Rōmānīs hostis sum."

"Sī ita cōgitās," inquit Hamilcar, "necesse tibi erit id iūre iūrandō affirmāre." Manum filiī in capite victimae posuit.

Hannibal, "Ego semper hostis Rōmānīs erō," inquit. "Semper contrā 15 Rōmānōs pugnābō. Nōn quiēscam nisi urbem Rōmam cēperō."

Itaque Hamilcar sēcum ad Hispāniam filium Hannibalem dūxit. Multīs post annīs Hannibal, ubi dux Carthāginiēnsium erat, ingentem exercitum contrā Rōmānōs dūxit; multa et mīra perfēcit. Contrā Rōmānōs diū pugnābat et eōs multīs in proeliīs vīcit. Numquam habuērunt Rōmānī hostem ferōciōrem. 20

1 annus, -ī, m., *year*
2 Hispānia, -ae, f., *Spain*
   nāvigō, -āre, -āvī, -ātūrus, *to sail*
   multīs ante annīs, *many years before*
3 bellum, -ī, n., *war*
   Carthāginiēnsēs, Carthāginiēnsium,
      m. pl., *the Carthaginians*
   īnsula, -ae, f., *island*
4 -que, enclitic conj., *and*
5 imperium, -ī, n., *empire*
9 ōmen, ōminis, n., *omen*
   āra, -ae, f., *altar*
10 hostis, hostis, gen. pl., hostium, m.,
      enemy

13 id, *it*
   iūre iūrandō affirmāre, *to affirm by
      swearing an oath*
14 caput, capitis, n., *head*
   victima, -ae, f., *sacrificial victim*
15 contrā, prep. + acc., *against*
16 pugnō, -āre, -āvī, -ātūrus, *to fight*
17 multīs post annīs, *many years later*
18 exercitus, *army*
20 proelium, -ī, n., *battle*
   ferōciōrem, *fiercer*

3 vincō, vincere, vīcī, victus, *to conquer*
4 trānseō, trānsīre, trānsiī or trānsīvī, trānsitus, irreg., *to go across*
5 condō, condere, condidī, conditus, *to found*
19 perficiō, perficere, perfēcī, perfectus, *to accomplish*

1. How old was Hannibal when his father prepared
   to sail to Spain?
2. What had the Romans done many years before?
3. What did Hamilcar intend to do?
4. What did Hannibal not want to do?
5. Why did Hamilcar want to leave Hannibal
   in Africa?
6. What did Hannibal want to be?
7. Where did Hamilcar place Hannibal's hand?
8. Hannibal will never rest unless he does what?
9. How did Hannibal go about trying to fulfill
   his oath?
10. Did the Romans ever have a fiercer enemy?

Roman battle ship

EXERCISE Ve

1. In lines 1–6 of the passage on page 90, identify two verbs in the pluperfect tense and
   explain why this tense is used in each instance.
2. In lines 13–16 of the passage on page 90, identify five verbs in the future or future
   perfect tense, and explain why the tense is used in each instance.

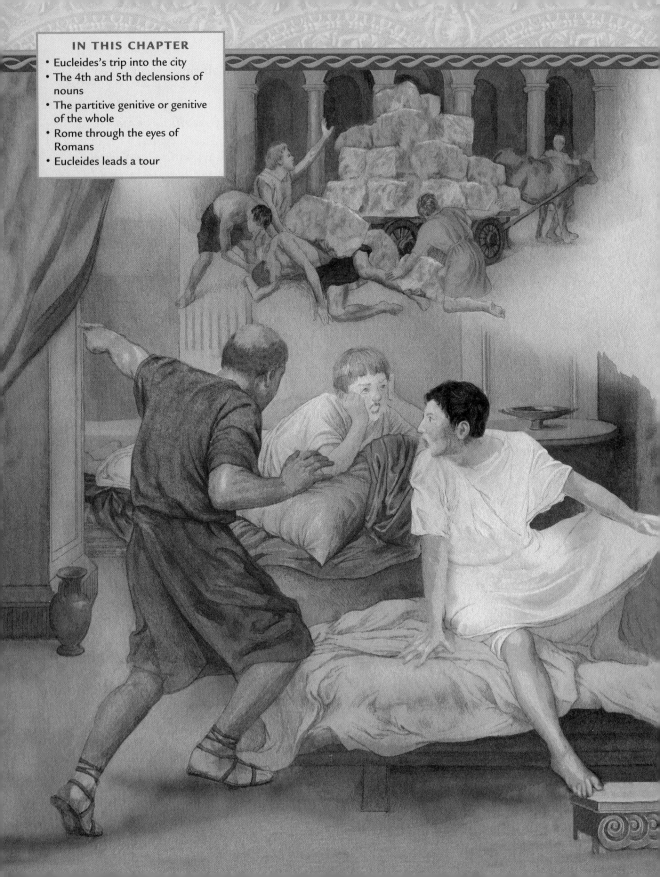

FIRST MORNING IN ROME

Iam diēs erat. Magnus erat clāmor in urbe. Servī ad Forum magnō tumultū onera ferēbant. Undique clāmor et strepitus! Sed nihil clāmōris, nihil strepitūs ad Mārcum pervēnit. In lectō stertēbat, nam dēfessus erat. Sextus quoque in lectō manēbat sed dormīre nōn poterat. Clāmōribus et strepitū excitātus, iam cōgitābat dē omnibus rēbus quās Titus heri nārrāverat. "Quid hodiē vidēbimus? Cornēliusne nōs in Forum dūcet? 5 Ego certē Forum et Cūriam et senātōrēs vidēre volō."

Intereā Eucleidēs, quī prīmā lūce exierat, iam domum redierat. Statim cubiculum puerōrum petīvit et, "Eho, puerī!" inquit. "Cūr nōndum surrēxistis? Abhinc duās hōrās ego surrēxī. Quod novum librum emere volēbam, in Argīlētum māne dēscendī ad tabernam quandam ubi in postibus nōmina multōrum poētārum vidēre potes. 10 Catullus, Flaccus—"

At puerī celeriter interpellāvērunt quod Eucleidēs, ut bene sciēbant, semper aliquid novī docēre volēbat. "Quid in viīs vīdistī?"

Eucleidēs, "Nihil," inquit, "nisi miserum hominem lapidibus oppressum. Bovēs lapidēs quadrātōs in plaustrō trahēbant ad novum aedificium quod Caesar prope 15 Domum Auream cōnficit. Illud aedificium est ingēns amphitheātrum et mox prīnceps lūdōs ibi faciet. Sī bonī puerī fueritis, fortasse ad lūdōs ībitis."

1 **tumultus,** *uproar, commotion*
4 **excitātus, -a, -um,** *wakened, aroused*
   dē omnibus rēbus, *about everything*
8 Eho! interj., *Hey!*
   abhinc duās hōrās, *two hours ago*
   abhinc, adv., *ago, previously*
10 ad tabernam quandam, *to a certain shop*
   taberna, -ae, f., *shop*

postis, postis, gen. pl., postium, m., *doorpost*
   poēta, -ae, m., *poet*
12 aliquid, *something*
14 **lapis, lapidis,** m., *stone*
   oppressus, -a, -um, *crushed*
15 quadrātus, -a, -um, *squared*
   quod, *which, that*
16 Domus Aurea, *(Nero's) Golden House*

3 **perveniō, pervenīre, pervēnī, perventūrus,** *to arrive (at), reach*
   stertō, stertere, stertuī, *to snore*
15 **trahō, trahere, trāxī, tractus,** *to drag, pull*
16 **cōnficiō, cōnficere, cōnfēcī, cōnfectus,** *to finish*

EXERCISE 25a

Respondē Latīnē:

1. Cūr Sextus dormīre nōn poterat?
2. Quid Sextus facere et vidēre vult?
3. Cūr Eucleidēs in Argīlētum dēscendit?
4. Quid in postibus tabernae vīdit?
5. Quid Eucleidēs in viīs vīdit?
6. Quid prīnceps mox faciet?

Nouns: 4th and 5th Declensions

Most Latin nouns belong to the 1st, 2nd, or 3rd declensions. There are two other declensions, to which a few nouns belong. Most 4th declension nouns are masculine, and most 5th declension nouns are feminine. Note, however, that **diēs** is usually masculine. Be sure to learn these forms thoroughly.

Note endings that could be more than one case and those that could be more than one case and number.

Number Case	4th Declension	5th Declension	
Singular			
Nominative	árcus	díēs	rēs
Genitive	árcūs	diḗī	réī
Dative	árcuī	diḗī	réī
Accusative	árcum	díem	rem
Ablative	árcū	díē	rē
Vocative	árcus	díēs	rēs
Plural			
Nominative	árcūs	díēs	rēs
Genitive	árcuum	diḗrum	rḗrum
Dative	árcibus	diḗbus	rḗbus
Accusative	árcūs	díēs	rēs
Ablative	árcibus	diḗbus	rḗbus
Vocative	árcūs	díēs	rēs

Nouns of the 4th and 5th declensions will appear in vocabularies as follows:

4th Declension

aestus, -ūs, m., *heat*
aquaeductus, -ūs, m., *aqueduct*
arcus, -ūs, m., *arch*
complexus, -ūs, m., *embrace*
domus, -ūs, f., *house, home*
manus, -ūs, f., *hand*

rīsus, -ūs, m., *smile, laugh*
senātus, -ūs, m., *Senate*
sonitus, -ūs, m., *sound*
strepitus, -ūs, m., *noise, clattering*
tumultus, -ūs, m., *uproar, commotion*

5th Declension

diēs, diēī, m., *day*

rēs, reī, f., *thing, matter, situation*

EXERCISE 25b

Identify the case and number of each of the following nouns (give all possibilities):

1. sonitūs	4. arcuum	7. reī	10. sonituum	13. tumultibus
2. diēbus	5. diēs	8. diērum	11. rīsū	14. rēs
3. arcum	6. senātuī	9. rem	12. aestus	15. domus

ante meridiem, *before noon*	in medias res, *into the middle of things*
post meridiem, *after noon*	
per diem, *a daily allowance for expenses*	in situ, *in its original place*

EXERCISE 25c

Read aloud, mentally noting the case and number of each 4th and 5th declension noun, paying special attention to each ending that could be more than one case. Then translate:

1. Mediā nocte tumultum magnum audīvī. Quae erat causa huius tumultūs? Magnō cum strepitū bovēs plaustra per viās trahēbant. Prīmum strepitus procul aberat; deinde in viā nostrā erat tumultus.
   causa, -ae, f., *reason*   huius, *of this*
   absum, abesse, āfuī, āfutūrus, irreg., *to be away, be absent, be distant*

2. Multās rēs manibus nostrīs facimus. Eucleidēs manū stilum tenēbat, nam puerōs scrībere docēbat. Puerī arborēs manibus et pedibus anteā ascenderant. Manūs igitur eōrum sordidae erant. Eucleidēs eōs iussit manūs statim lavāre.
   stilus, -ī, m., *pen*   **eōrum,** *of them,* *their*

3. Multōs diēs in vīllā manēbāmus. Vēnit tamen diēs reditūs. Necesse erat iter trium diērum facere quod ad urbem celerrimē redīre volēbāmus. Eō diē discessimus. Duōs diēs per Viam Appiam iter faciēbāmus. Tertiō diē Rōmam pervēnimus.
   reditus, -ūs, m., *return*   eō diē, *on that day*   tertius, -a, -um, *third*

4. Titus rem mīram nōbīs nārrāvit. Servus, quī nocte per viās urbis ambulābat, subitō fūgit perterritus. Quae erat causa huius reī? In viā occurrerat canī quī, ut ipse dīxit, tria capita habēbat. Dē tālibus rēbus in librīs saepe legimus sed numquam tālem rem ipsī vīdimus. Dē hāc rē omnēs cīvēs multās fābulās nārrant.
   fugiō, fugere, fūgī, fugitūrus, *to flee*   **caput, capitis,** n., *head*

BUILDING THE MEANING

Go Online
PHSchool.com
Web Code: jfd-0025

The Partitive Genitive or Genitive of the Whole

Look at the following sentence:

> Eucleidēs semper **aliquid novī** docēre volēbat. (25:12–13)
> *Eucleides always wanted to teach **something new**.*

The Latin words in boldface literally mean *something of the new*. The word **novī** is an adjective in the neuter genitive singular used as a substantive (see page 200). A better English translation is simply *something new*.

The word in the genitive case refers to a larger whole (*the new*) of which only a part (**aliquid,** *something*) is under consideration. This is called the *partitive genitive* or *genitive of the whole*.

Here are other examples that you have seen in the stories:

> Nihil **malī.** (21:7)   satis **temporis** (24:6)
> *Nothing **of a bad thing**. = There is nothing wrong.*   *enough **of time** = enough time*

Find two examples in line 2 of the story on page 93. For more on the partitive genitive, see page 147.

ROME

Impressions of Rome

What nation is so far distant, Caesar, or so barbarous that it does not have a representative at the games here in your city? Here come farmers from the Balkans, natives of South Russia nurtured on horse's blood, people from the banks of the Nile, as well as those from the Atlantic's farthest shores. Here too are Arabs, men from Southern Turkey, German tribesmen, and Ethiopians—all so different in dress and in appearance. Their speech too sounds all different; yet it is all one when you are hailed, Caesar, as the true father of our country.

Martial, *De spectaculis* III

Caecilius, in your own eyes you are a polished gentleman, but take my word for it, you are not. What are you then? A clown! You are like the hawker from across the Tiber who trades pale brimstone matches for broken glass or the man

Tunisia

Rome imported grains, wines, and other kinds of food from all over the empire, including North Africa.
Mosaic, Tunisia, second-third centuries A.D.

This terra cotta plaque from the bustling port and commercial center of Ostia shows a shopfront with (far left) the shopkeeper and a customer haggling over the price of a hare; fresh-killed poultry hanging from a rack; an aged customer buying fruit from the shopkeeper's wife; hutches containing hares beneath the counter; and two monkeys on the counter to attract the attention of passers-by.
Funerary stele from Ostia, third century A.D.

who sells to the idle bystanders soggy pease-pudding; like the keeper and trainer of snakes or the cheap slaves of the salt-sellers; like the hoarse-voiced seller of smoking sausages with his hot trays or a third-class street poet.

Martial, *Epigrams* I.41

If duty calls, the crowd gives way and the rich man is borne along rapidly over their heads by stout Liburnian bearers. On the way he will read, write, or sleep, for with the windows shut the litter induces sleep. Even so, he will get there before us. Though we hurry, the sea of humanity in front hinders us, and the great throng following jostles our backs. One man strikes us with his elbow, another with a hard pole; one knocks a beam against our heads, another a barrel. Our legs are plastered with mud, we are trampled on all sides by great feet, a soldier's hob-nailed boot crushes my toe. Newly patched togas are torn. A tall fir tree sways as the wagon rumbles on. Other carts carry pine trees, a nodding menace over the heads of the crowd. If the cart carrying Ligurian stone tilts forward and pours its overturned pile on the crowds, what remains of their bodies?

Juvenal, *Satires* III.239

The Streets of Rome

Roman houses were neither named nor numbered. Hence the very complicated instructions given to those wishing to reach a certain "address":

> Every time you meet me, Lupercus, you ask, "May I send a slave to fetch your book of poems? I'll return it as soon as I've read it." Lupercus, it's not worth troubling your slave. It's a long journey to the Pear Tree, and I live up three flights of steep stairs. You can find what you want closer to home. No doubt you often go down to the Argiletum. There's a shop opposite Caesar's Forum with both door-posts covered with advertisements so that you can in a moment read the names of all the poets. Look for me there.

> Martial, *Epigrams* I.117

Domitian, who followed Titus as Emperor of Rome, issued an edict forbidding shopkeepers to display their wares on the streets. This, according to Martial, was a vast improvement:

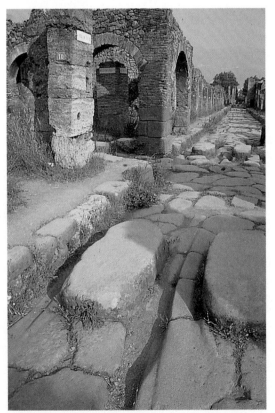

> The aggressive shopkeepers had taken the whole city away from us and never kept to the limits of their thresholds. But you, Domitian, ordered our narrowed streets to expand and what had been but a path has now become a street. No longer do they chain wine bottles to the pillars in front of their shops, and no longer are officials forced to walk in the middle of the mud. No longer does the barber blindly draw his razor in a dense crowd, and no longer do the greasy fast-food shops take up the whole street. The barbers, bartenders, cooks, and butchers now keep to their own thresholds. Now Rome is a city again, whereas before it was just one big shop.

> Martial, *Epigrams* VII.61

Streets had raised stepping stones that allowed pedestrians to cross when the street was flooded with rainwater.
Pompeiian street

Shopping malls are as old as Rome. Here, art lovers admire wares on display in an elaborate portico setting.
Roman Art Lover, oil on canvas, 1870, Sir Lawrence Alma-Tadema

Columns and Porticos

The column was one of the main features of Roman architecture. Sometimes a single column was used to support a statue; more often, columns were used to support the roofs or to form the entrance porches of temples and other buildings.

From the idea of the porch, there developed the portico or long covered walk, which afforded the citizens protection from sun and dust, while allowing them to enjoy the fresh air. In the shelter of the portico various activities took place. The Portico of Minucius was used as a corn exchange; in another a vegetable market was held. In the porticos, philosophers lectured, poets recited, schoolmasters held their classes, lawyers met their clients, entertainers performed, snacks were sold, and business deals were concluded. In fact, porticos became so common that it was eventually possible to walk from one end of the city to the other without coming out into the open at all!

According to one writer, porticos covered more than a quarter of the total area of the Campus Martius, the number of columns supporting them being about 2,000. Halls built in the shelter of these housed wall-maps of Rome and the Roman world, exhibitions of wonders from the Far East, natural marvels such as a snake 23 yards or 21 meters long, and, in the Portico of Philippus, a display of wigs and the latest in ladies' hairstyles.

---

1. Summarize Martial's and Juvenal's views of life in the metropolis of Rome.
2. If you had been Cornelius or Aurelia, would you have allowed your children to go out into the city without an escort? Why or why not?

ADDITIONAL READING:
The Romans Speak for Themselves: Book I: "Finding One's Way in Ancient Rome," pages 75–81.

EXERCISE 25d

Take parts, read aloud, and translate:

SEXTUS: Quam dēfessus sum, Mārce! Nam hodiē māne dormīre nōn poteram. Tantus clāmor in viīs erat.

MĀRCUS: Quālem clāmōrem audīvistī? Ego certē nihil clāmōris audīvī.

SEXTUS: Quid? Nōnne audīvistī illōs canēs in viīs lātrantēs? Multās hōrās lātrābant. Numquam audīvī tantum strepitum. Audīvī etiam clāmōrem multōrum   5
hominum quī per viās currēbant.

MĀRCUS: Quid clāmābant?

SEXTUS: Id audīre nōn poteram, nam omnēs simul clāmābant. Certē tamen īrātī erant. Erat quoque strepitus plaustrōrum. Nōs in urbe herī plaustra nōn vīdimus. Unde vēnērunt plaustra?   10

MĀRCUS: Interdiū nōn licet plaustra intrā urbem agere. Nocte igitur necesse est labōrāre. Servī in urbem ferēbant cibum, vīnum, lapidēs—

SEXTUS: Cūr lapidēs in urbem tulērunt?

MĀRCUS: Caesar ingēns amphitheātrum in urbe cōnficit.

SEXTUS: Nōs illud aedificium vīdimus?   15

MĀRCUS: Herī illud cōnspexistī, ubi ad Forum cum patre meō dēscendēbāmus. Herī nōn satis temporis erat id īnspicere quod pater domum festīnābat. Sed mox amphitheātrum iterum vīsitābimus atque id īnspiciēmus. Fortasse Eucleidēs nōs dūcet.

SEXTUS: Dum hoc mihi dīcis, multī hominēs in domum nostram vēnērunt. Quī sunt?   20

MĀRCUS: Nōnne herī in urbe vīdistī multōs cīvēs post senātōrem sequentēs? Hic erat patrōnus, illī erant clientēs. Pater meus est patrōnus multōrum cīvium. Tū audīvistī clientēs domum intrantēs.

SEXTUS: Ēheu! Eucleidēs quoque intrāvit!

12 **vīnum, -ī,** n., *wine*   22 illī, *those men, the former*
21 sequentēs, *following*
    hic, *this man, the latter*

Patrōnī were wealthy men who gave food or money to their dependents (**clientēs**). The **clientēs** came to the patron's home early in the morning to receive this dole and then escorted him to the Forum and performed other services for him. Here is Juvenal's satirical comment:

> Now the meager dole sits on the outer edge of the threshold of the patron's house to be snatched up by the clients in their togas. But first the patron inspects each face, fearing that someone might come and claim his due under a false name. Once he recognizes you, you'll get your share.
>
> Juvenal, *Satires* I.95–99

Go Online
PHSchool.com
Web Code: jfd-0025

EUCLEIDES THE TOUR GUIDE

Marcus had always visualized himself showing Sextus around the city of Rome, but he should have realized that Cornelius would never allow Sextus and himself to wander around Rome unsupervised. If neither Cornelius nor Titus were free to act as guide, Eucleides was bound to be their companion. He certainly knew a lot; the trouble was, there was no stopping him.

"Rome," Eucleides was now saying in that pedagogical tone of his, "is built on seven hills, the most famous being the Capitoline and the Palatine. By now, of course, it has far outstripped these petty limits. Augustus divided it into fourteen regions, which are in turn subdivided into 265 **vīcī** or wards. At the last census the population numbered 1,284,602, living in 1,797 **domūs** and 46,602 **īnsulae**."

"I can't see any islands!" complained Sextus, in all seriousness.

"**Īnsulae**," explained Eucleides, "are those apartment buildings, some of them five stories high."

"And the **Īnsula Feliculae** is the biggest in the world," said Marcus.

"There are," said Eucleides, "64 miles of streets, using your Roman measurements."

"Not very wide, are they?" commented Sextus.

"The maximum width according to *The Twelve Tables* can be only 17 feet."

"And some of them are not even paved!" cried Sextus, peering along the dark tunnel they were now traversing between the **īnsulae**.

Reconstruction of an *īnsula* (center) in Ostia with shops on the ground floor and apartments on the floors above
Ostia, second century A.D.

"Watch out!" yelled Marcus, pulling Sextus and Eucleides close to the wall to dodge a deluge of slops from a third-floor window.

"We'll have the law on you for that!" shouted Marcus up at the unseen lawbreaker. But Eucleides, not anxious to linger bandying threats, hustled the boys off through the labyrinth of shadowy alleys.

Suddenly they emerged into the blinding sun of the open Forum.

"This," said Eucleides impressively, pointing to a massive column, "is the center of the universe, the *Golden Milestone*. Erected by Augustus, it bears upon it in letters of gilt bronze the distances to all the cities of the Empire."

But it was not the *Golden Milestone* the boys were looking at, nor was it the splendor of the temple of Jupiter Optimus Maximus on the Capitoline Hill behind them. They were gazing into the **Forum Rōmānum,** which glittered with marble and bronze and gold. Senators and businessmen with their slaves were hurrying in and out of the **basilicae** that flanked the Forum. The noise was deafening. Cries of sausage-sellers and pastry-vendors mingled with the uproar of every language under heaven. White toga and tunic jostled with colorful foreign garb of all kinds.

Eucleides, sensing their preoccupation, was just pursing his lips to launch into a lecture on the Forum; but Marcus and Sextus were off, scampering along the **Via Sacra.**

"Come and tell us what's going on here!" they shouted, running to the far end of the Forum where their attention had been caught by the feverish activity of an army of masons engaged, amidst mountains of rubble and building stone, in some mammoth task of demolition or construction—it was hard to tell which.

"The Emperor Nero—" began Eucleides breathlessly as he caught up with them.

"I know," said Marcus. "He's the one that set Rome on fire for fun."

"The Emperor Nero," Eucleides repeated, "on the space cleared of unsightly hovels by a quite accidental fire, built the wonderful **Domus Aurea.**"

"And they're still working at it by the look of it!" said Sextus, grinning.

"No, you idiot!" said Marcus. "Vespasian and Titus pulled down parts of Nero's folly and are putting up things for the citizens of Rome to enjoy, baths, for instance, and—"

"And that terrific statue over there?" pointed Sextus.

"That was a statue of Nero himself," Marcus went on, "but Vespasian put rays around its head and made it into a statue of the sun-god."

"It is 118 feet high," began Eucleides, but his hearers were gone again, toward an immense building nearing completion.

"What's this?" they asked, as an exhausted Eucleides caught up with them.

"This is the **Amphitheātrum Flāvium,**" he gasped. "The Emperor Titus is to dedicate it soon."

ADDITIONAL READING:
The Romans Speak for Themselves: Book I: "Domus Aurea Neronis," pages 82–88.

Forum Rōmānum Aetāte Augustī

Watercolor, Peter Connolly

1 Tabularium
2 Temple of Concord
3 Temple of Saturn
4 Basilica Julia
5 Rostra
6 Temple of Castor and Pollux
7 Temple of the Deified Julius Caesar
8 Temple of Vesta
9 Regia
10 Basilica Aemilia
11 Curia Julia
12 Forum of Julius Caesar
13 Temple of Venus Genetrix
14 Forum of Augustus
15 Temple of Mars Ultor

A GRIM LESSON

Eucleidēs et puerī iam domum redierant. Post cēnam Cornēlius et Mārcus et Sextus in ātriō sedēbant.

"Quid hodiē vīdistis, puerī?" inquit Cornēlius.

"Nihil nisi aedificia antīqua," respondit Mārcus. "Nōs in urbem exīre volumus sōlī. Cūr nōn licet?" 5

Cui Cornēlius, "Est perīculōsum sine custōde exīre in viās huius urbis. Sunt multī hominēs scelestī quī bona cīvium arripiunt. Nōnnumquam hī hominēs cīvēs ipsōs necant. Vōbīs igitur nōn licet sine custōde exīre. Iam sērō est. Nunc necesse est vōbīs cubitum īre. Nōlīte cessāre sed īte statim!"

Puerī, labōre diēī dēfessī, simulac cubitum iērunt, obdormīvērunt. 10

Postrīdiē māne Mārcus in lectō suō iacēbat et dē Circō Maximō ita cōgitābat: "Quandō Circum Maximum vīsitābimus? Cūr pater meus nōs exīre vetat? Herī nūllōs hominēs scelestōs in urbe vīdī. Interdiū certē praedōnēs nōbīs nōn nocēbunt. Meum patrem, quod est senātor Rōmānus, praedōnēs timent. Nihil perīculī est."

Brevī tempore, ut Mārcō vidēbātur, puerī ad Circum ībant. Mox mōlem ingentem 15 Circī Maximī Mārcus cōnspexit.

"Ecce!" clāmāvit Mārcus. "Est Circus. Cum intrāverimus, tandem aurīgās ipsōs spectābimus."

Subitō tamen in viam sē praecipitāvērunt trēs hominēs.

"Cavē illōs hominēs!" clāmāvit Sextus. "Illī certē nōs in domūs vīcīnās trahent et ibi 20 nōs necābunt."

Sed frūstrā, nam Mārcus, metū commōtus, postquam Sextum audīvit clāmantem, ad terram cecidit et iacēbat in lutō immōbilis. *(continued)*

2 **ātrium, -ī**, n., *atrium, main room*
4 **nisi**, conj., *unless, except*
6 **sine**, prep. + abl., *without*
   custōs, custōdis, m., *guard*
7 **bona, bonōrum**, n. pl., *goods, possessions*
   nōnnumquam, adv., *sometimes*
11 **postrīdiē**, adv., *on the following day*
   iaceō, -ēre, -uī, -itūrus, *to lie, be lying down*
   7 **arripiō, arripere, arripuī, arreptus**, *to grab hold of, snatch, seize*
   12 **vetō, vetāre, vetuī, vetitus**, *to forbid*

13 **praedō, praedōnis**, m., *robber*
   noceō, -ēre, -uī, -itūrus + dat., *to do harm (to), harm*
15 ut Mārcō vidēbātur, *as it seemed to Marcus, as Marcus thought*
22 **metus, -ūs**, m., *fear*
23 **terra, -ae**, f., *earth, ground*
   lutum, -ī, n., *mud*

Go Online
PHSchool.com
Web Code: jfd-0026

EXERCISE 26a Respondē Latīnē:

1. Cūr nōn licet puerīs exīre in urbem sōlīs?
2. Quōcum puerīs licet exīre in urbem?
3. Quō ībant puerī?
4. Quī sē in viam praecipitāvērunt?

"Eho!" clāmāvit ūnus ē praedōnibus. "Quō abīs, parvule? Quid est nōmen tuum? Nōnne tū fīlius es senātōris? Nōnne nōmen tuum est Mārcus Cornēlius?" 25

Cui Mārcus, "Quid vultis, scelestī? Nihil pecūniae habeō. Nōlīte mē verberāre! Sī mihi nocueritis, pater meus certē vōs pūniet."

Sed interpellāvit praedō, "Tacē, puer! Tū es captīvus noster neque ad patrem redībis. Nēmō nunc poterit tē servāre. Ipse enim tē necābō."

Tum praedō gladium strīnxit. Sextus stabat perterritus et, "Fer auxilium!" clāmāvit. 30 "Fer auxilium!" Sed nēmō clāmōrem audīvit. Nēmō auxilium tulit. Mārcus oculōs clausit et mortem exspectābat.

Nihil accidit. Oculōs aperuit. In lectō erat suō. Somnium modo fuerat. Hodiē tamen domī manēre cōnstituit Mārcus. Exīre nōluit.

24 parvulus, -a, -um, *small, little*
29 **servō, -āre, -āvī, -ātus,** *to save*
30 **gladius, -ī,** m., *sword*

31 **oculus, -ī,** m., *eye*
34 **domī,** *at home*

30 **stringō, stringere, strīnxī, strictus,** *to draw*
31 **claudō, claudere, clausī, clausus,** *to shut*
33 **accidit, accidere, accidit,** *(it) happens*
   aperiō, aperīre, aperuī, apertus, *to open*

Respondē Latīnē:

5. Quid fēcit Mārcus postquam Sextum clāmantem audīvit?
6. Cūr praedō gladium strīnxit?
7. Quis vēnit ubi Sextus clāmāvit?

Go Online
PHSchool.com
Web Code: jfd-0026

Demonstrative Adjectives and Pronouns: *hic* and *ille*

Look at the following sentences:

Ille tabellārius equōs vehementer incitāvit.	*That courier fiercely whipped the horses on.*
Quis in **illō** aedificiō habitat?	*Who lives in that building?*
Hī canēs lātrant modo.	*These dogs are only barking.*
Est perīculōsum in viās **huius** urbis exīre.	*It is dangerous to go out into the streets of this city.*
Sextus, **hīs** clāmōribus et **hōc** strepitū excitātus, dormīre nōn poterat.	*Roused by these shouts and this noise, Sextus could not sleep.*

You will see from the above examples that both **hic** and **ille** are used adjectivally with nouns to point out someone or something. **Hic** points to someone or something near at hand or near in time, while **ille** points to someone or something further away or distant in time or space. These are called *demonstrative adjectives*, from the Latin verb **dēmōn-strō, dēmōnstrāre,** *to point out, show.*

Here is a chart showing all the cases of **hic** (*this, these*) and **ille** (*that, those*) in masculine, feminine, and neuter genders:

Number Case	Masc.	Fem.	Neut.	Masc.	Fem.	Neut.
Singular						
Nominative	hic	haec	hoc	ílle	ílla	íllud
Genitive	húius	húius	húius	illíus	illíus	illíus
Dative	húic	húic	húic	íllī	íllī	íllī
Accusative	hunc	hanc	hoc	íllum	íllam	íllud
Ablative	hōc	hāc	hōc	íllō	íllā	íllō
Plural						
Nominative	hī	hae	haec	íllī	íllae	ílla
Genitive	hốrum	hắrum	hốrum	illốrum	illắrum	illốrum
Dative	hīs	hīs	hīs	íllīs	íllīs	íllīs
Accusative	hōs	hās	haec	íllōs	íllās	ílla
Ablative	hīs	hīs	hīs	íllīs	íllīs	íllīs

The Latin sentences on page 240 show these demonstrative words being used as *adjectives* modifying nouns; they may also be used without nouns as *pronouns* meaning *he, she, it, this, that,* etc.:

> **Ille**, postquam **haec** audīvit, ē caupōnā sē praecipitāvit.
> *He, after he heard **this** (lit., **these things**), rushed out of the inn.*

> Postquam **hoc** fecit,...   *After he did **this**,...*

> Mārcus patrem, "Quid est **illud**?" rogāvit. *Marcus asked his father, "What is **that**?"*

> "Cavē **illōs** hominēs!" clāmāvit Sextus. "**Illī** certē nōs in domūs vīcīnās trahent et ibi nōs necābunt." (26:20–21)
> *"Watch out for those men!" shouted Sextus. "**They** will certainly drag us into the neighboring houses and kill us there."*

Sometimes **hic** refers to a nearer noun and means *the latter*, while **ille** refers to a farther noun and means *the former*:

> Nōnne herī in urbe vīdistī multōs cīvēs post senātōrem sequentēs? **Hic** erat patrōnus, **illī** erant clientēs. (25d:21–22)
> *Didn't you see yesterday in the city many citizens following behind a senator?*
> ***The latter** (literally, **this one**, i.e., the one last mentioned) was a patron, **the former** (literally, **those men**, i.e., the ones first mentioned) were clients.*

Be careful to distinguish **hic**, the adjective or pronoun, from the adverb **hīc**, *here*:

> Quid tū **hīc**? (9:8)   *What (are) you (doing) **here**?*

EXERCISE 26b

Read aloud and translate:

1. Hic puer in hāc viā, ille in illā habitat.
2. Illa puella in hāc vīllā habitat; hī puerī in illā habitant.
3. Sī in hāc caupōnā pernoctābimus, hic caupō nōbīs certē nocēbit.
4. Illī praedōnēs illōs viātōrēs sub illīs arboribus petunt.
5. Quandō illī haec onera in vīllam portābunt?
6. Nōlī illud plaustrum in hanc urbem interdiū agere!
7. Huic puerō multa dabimus, illī nihil.
8. Hīs rūsticīs licēbit agrōs huius vīllae rūsticae colere.
9. Huic senātōrī ad Cūriam in lectīcā redīre necesse erat.
10. Illī aedificiō appropinquāre perīculōsum est, nam scelestī hominēs ibi habitant.
11. Ūnus ex hīs praedōnibus aliquid illī servō dīcēbat.

EXERCISE 26c

Choose the proper form of **hic** or **ille** to modify the noun in italics, and then read the sentence aloud and translate:

1. Cornēliī in _____ *vīllā* habitant.
2. "Spectāte _____ *arcum*, puerī!" clāmāvit Eucleidēs.
3. Ōlim _____ *puellae* in agrīs ambulābant.
4. Vīlicus cibum _____ *servō* nōn dabit.
5. "Vīdistīne _____ *aedificium*, Mārce?" inquit Sextus.
6. Raeda _____ *mercātōris* prope tabernam manet.
7. Māne _____ *canēs* ferōciter lātrābant.
8. Bona _____ *rūsticōrum* in raedā erant.
9. Ūnus ex _____ *praedōnibus* gladium strīnxit.
10. Nōbīs _____ *arborēs* ascendere nōn licet.
11. _____ *rem* explicāre nōn possum.
12. _____ *strepitus* Mārcum nōn excitāvit.

EXERCISE 26d

Using story 26 and the charts of demonstrative adjectives as guides, give the Latin for:

1. It is not dangerous to go out into the streets of that city.
2. Those wicked men seized the goods of these citizens.
3. Yesterday I saw this wicked man in that city.
4. Sextus had never seen this huge mass of the Circus Maximus.
5. Marcus will never give money to that robber.

Take parts, read aloud, and translate:

AURELIA'S CONCERN FOR SEXTUS

Quīnta hōra est. Domī in tablīnō Gāius Cornēlius strēnuē labōrat sōlus. Iam ā
Cūriā rediit et nunc ōrātiōnem scrībit, quam crās apud senātum habēbit. Aurēlia
iānuae tablīnī appropinquat et tacitē intrat, nam coniugem vexāre nōn vult.

AURĒLIA:	Salvē, Gāī! Esne occupātus?	
CORNĒLIUS:	Ita vērō! Paulisper tamen colloquium tēcum habēre possum.	5
	Quid agis, uxor?	
AURĒLIA:	Sollicita dē Sextō sum, coniūnx.	
CORNĒLIUS:	Dē Sextō? Cūr? Quid ille puer molestus iam fēcit?	
AURĒLIA:	Nihil malī fēcit Sextus. Sollicita sum quod hic puer numquam	
	anteā in urbe tantā adfuit. Puerī in urbe sine custōde exīre	10
	nōn dēbent. Necesse est igitur et Mārcō et Sextō custōdem habēre.	
CORNĒLIUS:	Titus frāter meus custōs cum illīs ībit. Eucleidēs quoque Sextum	
	custōdiet. Ille enim puerōs ad lūdum dūcet.	
AURĒLIA:	Frātrī Titō nōn cōnfīdō, et Sextus Eucleidem numquam audiet.	
	Nam Eucleidēs numquam tacet.	15
CORNĒLIUS:	(*īrātus*) Sī Sextus custōdem nōn audīverit, ego ipse eum pūniam!	
AURĒLIA:	Minimē, Gāī. Sextus nōn est puer scelestus. Est, ut bene scīs, puer	
	strēnuus. Mātrem tamen propter ēruptiōnem Montis Vesuviī nōn	
	iam habet Sextus. Certē eam valdē dēsīderat. Dēbēmus Sextum	
	dīligenter cūrāre.	20
CORNĒLIUS:	Ita vērō! Estō! Ubi nōn in Cūriā sum, ego ipse puerōs custōdiam.	
	Aliter aut patruus Titus aut Eucleidēs verbōsus eōs cūrābit.	
AURĒLIA:	Grātiās tibi agō, coniūnx!	
CORNĒLIUS:	Nunc, sī vīs, abī! Sōlus esse volō. Mihi necesse est hanc ōrātiōnem	
	cōnficere.	25

1 quīntus, -a, -um, *fifth*	18 **propter,** prep. + acc., *on account of,*
tablīnum, -ī, n., *study*	*because of*
2 **ōrātiō, ōrātiōnis,** f., *oration, speech*	Mōns Vesuvius, Montis Vesuviī,
quam...habēbit, *which he will deliver*	m., *Mount Vesuvius*
apud, prep. + acc., *in front of, before*	19 **dēsīderō, -āre, -āvī, -ātus,** *to long*
3 **coniūnx, coniugis,** m./f., *husband,*	*for, miss*
wife	22 aliter, adv., *otherwise*
5 colloquium, -ī, n., *conversation*	**aut...aut...,** conj., *either...or...*
11 **dēbeō, -ēre, -uī, -itūrus** + infin.,	23 **Grātiās tibi agō!** *I thank you! Thank*
ought	*you!*
13 **lūdus, -ī,** m., *school*	24 sī vīs, *if you wish, please*

10 **adsum, adesse, adfuī, adfutūrus,** irreg., *to be present*
14 **cōnfīdō, cōnfidere** + dat., *to give trust (to), trust*

201–146 B.C.

Go Online
PHSchool.com
Web Code: jfd-0026

ROME IN THE MEDITERRANEAN WORLD

Rome, the victor over Carthage, became an international power, the ruler of the western Mediterranean. Winning the war with Hannibal gave Rome secure control over Sicily, Spain, and Sardinia. Then, after subduing the Gauls in northern Italy, the Romans looked toward the East. Starting with Macedonia, the former ally of Carthage, Rome gradually took control of Greece and the Greek states in Asia Minor. In order to maintain a balance of power, the Romans established a permanent military presence all around the Mediterranean Sea.

The act that symbolized this age of control came in 146 B.C., when the consul Lucius Memmius demolished the city of Corinth and sold her inhabitants into slavery. In the same year, the Senate acceded to Marcus Cato's relentless pronouncement at the close of every speech he made to the Senate, **Carthāgō dēlenda est**, "Carthage must be destroyed." By razing that city, too, the Roman army ended the Third Punic War (149–146 B.C.). The Roman commander, Publius Cornelius Scipio Aemilianus Africanus, adoptive grandson of Hannibal's conqueror, had his troops sow the land with salt to assure its infertility and had them curse the site. The area around Carthage and to the south became the Roman province of Africa.

GALLIA TRANSALPĪNA
GALLIA CISALPĪNA
ILLYRICUM
HISPĀNIA
Numantia
ULTERIOR CITERIOR
CORSICA
(H)ADRIĀTICUM MARE
ITALIA
MACEDONIA
Rōma
Cynoscephalae
SARDINIA
TYRRHĒNUM MARE
Pydna
Epīrus
HIBĒRICUM MARE
INTERNUM MARE
SICILIA
IŌNIUM MARE
ACHAIA
Corinthus
MAURĒTĀNIA
NUMIDIA
Utica
Carthāgō
ĀFRICA

SCALE OF MILES
0   250   500

Roman Territory, 201 B.C.
Additions up to 133 B.C.

RŌMĀNĪ MULTĀS TERRĀS REGUNT

The Roman Senate emerged as the dominant power in the state during the years of conflict with Carthage and expansion into the eastern Mediterranean. Whereas new consuls, praetors, and other magistrates were elected every year, senators were appointed for life. This stable, more permanent voice of authority directed both foreign and domestic policies and administered finances. The **nōbilēs**, descended from the old families of patrician and plebeian stock, formed a ruling aristocracy, whose ranks supplied most of the consuls and exerted most of the influence on the way the Roman government operated. The Roman Senate organized the newly acquired foreign territories into provinces (**prōvinciae**), whose governors, taken from the pool of former magistrates, were responsible to that same body.

The Italian economy changed when Roman senators spent their share of war-booty and profits from the provinces on the purchase of large estates (**lātifundia**), and under

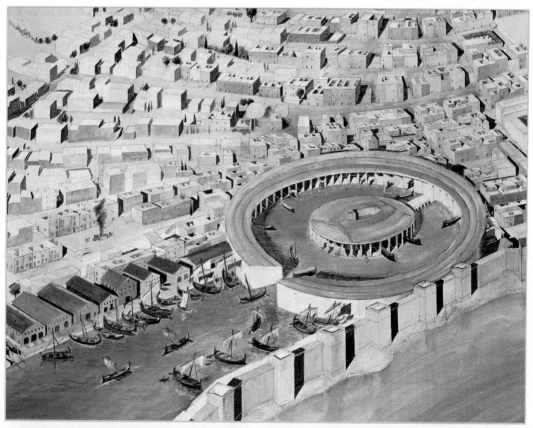

Carthage maintained her empire with ships from a large circular military harbor that could repair or build 220 ships at a time.

A reconstruction of Carthage's harbors, fourth—second century B.C.

this system there developed a more organized, more profitable type of agriculture that utilized slave labor. The model Roman of earlier times, a citizen-soldier who farmed his own fields, was pushed off his land and into the city. Deriving sufficient wealth from their **lātifundia**, senators chose not to venture into the new realm of international trade; this lucrative opportunity was seized instead by a growing middle class, the equestrian order, members of which emerged as leaders of Roman commerce.

Graecia capta ferum victōrem cēpit, said the poet Horace: "Captive Greece captivated her uncivilized conqueror." Roman life had already been changing during the century before Rome destroyed Corinth and Carthage, as the Romans had gotten to know the Greeks, their language, and their literature, partly through contact with the Greek cities of southern Italy and Sicily.

Both the family-based Roman worship of rustic spirits, who watched over farms, flocks, and storeroom, and the formal state religion began to incorporate Greek rituals, and the Roman gods became associated with the Greek Olympians, who were more human in appearance and personality. At the same time, the Stoic philosophy preached by many Greeks at this time, which offered an intellectual basis for a strong moral code, was welcomed by leading Romans.

Greece also taught Rome the value of literature. Livius Andronicus adapted a Greek play for the Roman stage in 240 B.C., the year after the First Punic War. Gnaeus Naevius composed the *Bellum Punicum*, an epic poem in which he combined the history of the

The nine Muses were among the goddesses of Greek origin that were embraced by the Romans.
Sarcophagus, Rome, second century A.D.

First Punic War with the myth of Queen Dido of Carthage and Aeneas, the Trojan hero and forefather of Rome. In another epic, the *Annales*, Quintus Ennius recounted the glorious history of Rome from its beginnings to his own day. More firmly based on Greek content and form were the comic plays of Plautus and Terence, in which Latin-speaking Italian characters with Greek names romped through Greek plots.

Marcus Cato, fiercely advocating that Romans retain the old standards of Italian independence, wrote the *Origines*, a Roman history book for his son, and the *De agricultura*, advice for Roman landholders. He lamented the appearance of Greek statues in Roman homes and condemned the new interest in barbers and Greek cooks.

Many more Romans, such as Scipio Aemilianus, rather enjoyed the new luxuries, became patrons of the arts, and welcomed the civilizing influence of Greek teachers, writers, and philosophers. Once Rome learned Greek literature and ideas, she evolved into a Hellenized civilization best labeled Greco-Roman. Roman culture and rule of earlier days had both outgrown Italy.

---

1. In what ways was the period discussed in this essay a turning point in Roman history?
2. How would a Cincinnatus have reacted to these changes in the Roman state and agriculture described in this essay?
3. Summarize the fusion of Greek and Roman culture that took place at this time.
4. Which side would you have taken in the "debate" between Marcus Cato and Scipio Aemilianus? Why?

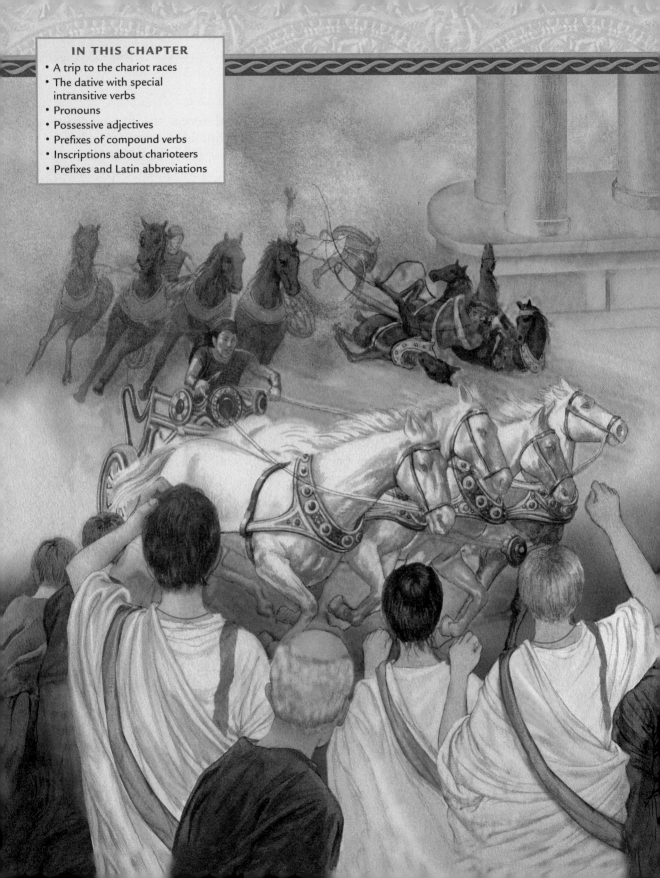

A VISIT TO THE RACES

Chariot races (**lūdī circēnsēs,** literally, *games in the Circus*) were perhaps the most popular spectacle in ancient Rome. It was held in the **Circus Maximus**, a huge open-air stadium in the valley between the Palatine and the Aventine hills. It could hold about 200,000 spectators, seated in tiers around the race track (**curriculum**).

It has been estimated that at one time some 90 holidays (**fēriae**) were given over to games at public expense. On these days the citizens were "celebrating a holiday" (**fēriātī**).

A barrier (**spīna**) ran down the center of the course, and the chariots (**quadrīgae**), each pulled by four horses, had to complete seven laps, about five miles or eight kilometers in all. Fouling was permitted, and collisions were frequent, especially at the turning posts (**mētae**). A race began when the Emperor (**Caesar**) or presiding official gave the signal (**signum**) by dropping a white cloth (**mappa**).

The charioteers, some of whom won great popularity and very high salaries, were employed by four companies (**factiōnēs**), each with its own color—the "Reds" (**russātī**), the "Whites" (**albātī**), the "Greens" (**prasinī**), and the "Blues" (**venetī**). Rival groups of spectators were accustomed to show their support (**favēre**) for each color vociferously.

One charioteer we hear about, Gaius Apuleius Diocles, drove chariots for the Red Stable for twenty-four years, ran 4,257 starts, and won 1,462 victories.

No wonder Marcus, Cornelia, and Sextus are eager to go to the races! As we return to our story, three days after the Cornelii arrived in Rome, Sextus is sitting alone when suddenly Marcus rushes in.

MĀRCUS: Sexte! Sexte! Hodiē nōbīs licet ad lūdōs circēnsēs īre. Eucleidēs mē et tē et Cornēliam ad Circum dūcet.

SEXTUS: Lūdōs circēnsēs amō. Sed nōnne Circus clausus erit?

MĀRCUS: Minimē! Circus nōn erit clausus, nam hodiē cīvēs omnēs fēriātī sunt. Viae erunt plēnae hominum. Virī, mulierēs, līberī Circum celerrimē petent.   5

SEXTUS: Sed cūr nōn nunc discēdimus? Ego sum iam parātus.

MĀRCUS: Simulac Cornēlia ē somnō surrēxerit, statim ībimus.

(*Much to the boys' disgust, Cornelia was rather late in waking up from her siesta, but soon they were all ready to leave.*)

EUCLEIDĒS: Agite! Iam tandem ad Circum īre tempus est. Estisne parātī, puerī? Esne   10 parāta, Cornēlia?

(*Eucleides takes Cornelia and the boys quickly through the streets; they can now hear the noise of the Circus crowds.*)

EUCLEIDĒS: Iam ā Circō nōn procul absumus. Nōnne strepitum audītis? Ecce! Omnēs ad Circum festīnant. Brevī tempore nōs ipsī intrābimus.   (*continued*)   15

5 **mulier, mulieris,** f., *woman*

(They enter the Circus.)

CORNĒLIA: Quam ingēns est turba hominum! Tōtus Circus est plēnus spectātōrum.

EUCLEIDĒS: Ita vērō! Semper multī spectātōrēs in Circō sunt. Hīc cōnsīdēmus?

MĀRCUS: Minimē! Prope curriculum sedēre necesse est quod ibi omnia vidēre   20
poterimus.

EUCLEIDĒS: At prope curriculum sedēre perīculōsum est. Pater vester multa dē perīculō
dīxit.

MĀRCUS: Nihil perīculī est, nam Titus, patruus meus, cum amīcīs prope curriculum
sedēre solet.

SEXTUS: Ecce! Caesar ipse iam surrēxit; signum dare parat. Ego russātīs favēbō.   25

MĀRCUS: Ego albātīs.

CORNĒLIA: Ego venetīs.

MĀRCUS: Ecce! Mappa! Signum est!

CORNĒLIA: Quam ferōciter equōs verberant illī aurīgae! Quam celeriter equōs agunt!
Quam temerāriī sunt! Nōnne mortem timent?   30

SEXTUS: Ecce! Russātus meus certē victor erit, nam equōs magnā arte agit.

25 **faveō, favēre, fāvī, fautūrus** + dat., *to give favor (to), support*

**This charioteer is approaching the dangerous turning posts where many collisions and
accidents occurred.**

Roman relief sculpture, Rome, first century A.D.

MĀRCUS: Ō mē miserum! Aurīga meus equōs dēvertit. Cavē mētam! Cavē mētam! Esne sēmisomnus, fatue? Cūr mētam nōn vītāvistī?

CORNĒLIA: Ēheu! Ille aurīga cecidit. Humī iacet. Estne mortuus?

SEXTUS: Minimē! Minimē! Ecce! Animum recuperāvit. Iam surgit. 35

CORNĒLIA: Audīvistisne clāmōrēs hōrum spectātōrum? Magnā vōce nōmina aurīgārum et equōrum semper clāmant! Undique ingēns est strepitus! Tantum strepitum ego numquam audīvī.

MĀRCUS: Russātī vīcērunt, sed mox etiam albātī vincent.

EUCLEIDĒS: Hoc fortasse accidet, sed Caligula ipse, ut dīcunt, prasinōs amābat. 40

(continued)

32 **dēvertō, dēvertere, dēvertī, dēversus,** *to turn aside*
34 **humī,** *on the ground*

39 **vincō, vincere, vīcī, victus,** *to conquer, win*

Charioteers bound their tunics to protect their chests and wore a stiff leather helmet to protect their heads.
Mosaic from villa in Baccano, Tuscany, third century A.D.

(They watch a few more races, but it is not Marcus's lucky day. Eucleides becomes a little anxious as it grows later. He had been caught once before in a crush at the gates.)

EUCLEIDĒS: Iam sērō est. Nunc domum redībimus.

SEXTUS: Nōndum tempus est domum redīre. Ecce! Aurīgae habēnās sūmpsērunt et signum exspectant.

EUCLEIDĒS: Nisi mox discēdēmus, turbam ingentem vītāre nōn poterimus. Agite! Domum!

45

ADDITIONAL READING:
The Romans Speak for Themselves: Book I: "Finding a Date in Ancient Rome or Why Some Men Went to the Chariot Races," pages 89–98; "Pliny's Views on the Chariot Races," pages 93–98.

BUILDING THE MEANING

Go Online
PHSchool.com
Web Code: jfd-0027

Dative with Special Intransitive Verbs

Look at the following sentences:

Sī **mihi** nocueritis, pater meus certē vōs pūniet. (26:26–27)
*If you do harm **to me**, my father will certainly punish you.*
*If you harm **me**, my father will certainly punish you.*

Frātrī Titō nōn cōnfīdō. (26e:14)   Ego **russātīs** favēbō. (27:25)
*I do not give trust **to (my) brother Titus**.*   *I will give favor **to the reds**.*
*I do not trust **(my) brother Titus**.*   *I will favor/support **the reds**.*

The verbs **nocēre**, *to do harm (to)*, **cōnfīdere**, *to give trust (to)*, and **favēre**, *to give favor (to)*, are intransitive and so do not take direct objects in the accusative case. Their meaning is completed by a word or phrase in the dative case. The meaning of the dative case in this type of sentence can be clearly seen in the literal translations of the sentences above: *If you do harm **to me**, I do not give trust **to (my) brother Titus***, and *I will give favor **to the reds***. In translating into idiomatic English, we usually use a direct object, as in the alternative translations above.

These sentences are similar in pattern to those discussed on page 78, Building the Meaning: "Dative with Intransitive Compound Verbs," and may be grouped with those as a basic pattern of Latin sentences.

Pronouns: 1st and 2nd Persons

From the early chapters of our story, you have seen many examples of 1st and 2nd person pronouns. They include the words for *I*, *me*, *you*, *we*, and *us*:

1st Person Singular:

Sed **ego** volō cōnsulere Mārcum! (8:16)	*nominative*
Mihi necesse est hīc manēre. (9:18–19)	*dative*
Nihil **mē** terret. (4:7) Multās epistulās ad **mē** mitte! (9:19)	*accusative*

1st Person Plural:

Nōs ad urbem redīre parāmus. (8:7)	*nominative*
Nōbīs necesse est statim discēdere. (8:13–14)	*dative*
Dāvus **nōs** verberāre potest. (11:8)	*accusative*
Vīsne **nōbīscum** lūdere, Cornēlia? (16:19)	*ablative*

2nd Person Singular:

Mārce, cūr **tū** arborem nōn ascendis? (4:5)	*nominative*
Servī meī alium lectum **tibi** parāvērunt. (19:17–18)	*dative*
Quid **tē** terret? (4:5–6)	*accusative*

2nd Person Plural:

Cūr **vōs** ibi sedētis? (8:3)	*nominative*
Servī meī bonam cēnam **vōbīs** statim parāre possunt. (19:2)	*dative*

The following chart includes every case of each of these pronouns:

These words are called *personal pronouns* because they show what person is involved in the action.

For **nōs** and **vōs**, two genitive forms are found, as shown. Their use is limited, as is the use of the genitives of **ego** and **tū**, and you will not meet any of these genitives until later in your study of Latin. They are *not* used to indicate possession (see page 121, "Adjectives: Possessive").

Notice how the preposition **cum** is attached to the end of **nōbīs** in the sentence above from Chapter 16. So also you will find **mēcum**, **tēcum**, and **vōbīscum**.

Number Case	1st	2nd
Singular		
Nominative	égo	tū
Genitive	méī	túī
Dative	míhi	tíbi
Accusative	mē	tē
Ablative	mē	tē
Plural		
Nominative	nōs	vōs
Genitive	nóstrī	véstrī
	nóstrum	véstrum
Dative	nốbīs	vốbīs
Accusative	nōs	vōs
Ablative	nốbīs	vốbīs

Pronouns: 3rd Person

Now look at these sentences, also from earlier chapters:

Sextus, quod lupus **eum** terret, arborem petit. (5:11)   *accusative, masc., sing.*
Nēmō **eam** cōnspicit. (9:2)   *accusative, fem., sing.*
Lupus **eōs** iam cōnspicit. (5:10)   *accusative, masc., pl.*

Latin 3rd person pronouns include the words for *he, him, she, her, it, they,* and *them.* The adjacent chart shows all cases, singular and plural.

The genitive can be used to indicate possession, e.g., **eius** can mean *his, her,* or *its,* and **eōrum, eārum, eōrum** can mean *their.*

The forms of **is** and **ea** can refer to things: **Flāvia epistulam scrībit; Cornēlia eam legit**, *Flavia writes a letter; Cornelia reads it.*

Number Case	Masc.	Fem.	Neut.
Singular			
Nominative	is	éa	id
Genitive	éius	éius	éius
Dative	éī	éī	éī
Accusative	éum	éam	id
Ablative	éō	éā	éō
Plural			
Nominative	éī	éae	éa
Genitive	eórum	eárum	eórum
Dative	éīs	éīs	éīs
Accusative	éos	éās	éa
Ablative	éīs	éīs	éīs

EXERCISE 27a

Select, read aloud, and translate:

1. Necesse erat _____ prope curriculum sedēre.
2. Eucleidēs _____ dēmonstrābat circum et aurīgās.
3. Nōn vult, Sexte, Cornēlia prope _____ sedēre.
4. Sextus saepe _____ vexat.
5. Cornēlius clāmābat et servī vōcem _____ audīvērunt.
6. Sepulcrum vīdimus, sed _____ nōn appropinquāvimus.
7. Canēs Getam invēnērunt quod tunicam _____ olfēcerant.
8. Caupō, "Novum lectum," inquit, "_____ parābō."
9. Equī mētam petunt. Ecce, nunc _____ praetereunt!
10. Aurīgae hodiē bene fēcērunt. _____ laudāre dēbētis.

eius/nōbīs
ego/mē/mihi
tū/tibi/tē
eī/eam/eius
eius/eum/eōrum
id/eum/eī
eō/eius/ea
is/vōs/tibi
id/eōs/eam
Eās/Eōs/Vōbīs

Pronouns: Reflexive

Look at these sentences:

Mē in piscīnā vīdī.   Ubi cecidistis, **vōbīs** nocuistis.
*I saw **myself** in the fishpond.*   *When you fell, you hurt **yourselves**.*

The words in boldface are being used as reflexive pronouns. A pronoun is reflexive when it refers to the subject of the sentence, as **mē** in the first sentence refers to the understood 1st person subject of the verb **vīdī**, just as in the translation *myself* refers to *I.*

While the genitive, dative, accusative, and ablative forms of the regular 1st and 2nd person pronouns may be used reflexively, as in the examples, there are special forms for the 3rd person reflexive pronoun, as in the following sentences:

Puellae, ubi cecidērunt, **sibi** nocuērunt.
*The girls hurt **themselves** when they fell.*

Mārcus **sē** in piscīnā cōnspexit.
*Marcus caught sight of **himself** in the fishpond.*

In the first example, **sibi** refers to **puellae**, just as in the translation *themselves* refers to *the girls*.

Here is the complete set of forms of the 3rd person reflexive pronoun:

There is no nominative form. The same forms are used for singular and plural and for masculine, feminine, and neuter. The dative, **sibi**, therefore can mean *to/for himself, to/for herself, to/for oneself, to/for itself,* or *to/for themselves.*

Case	m/f/n s/pl
Genitive	súī
Dative	síbi
Accusative	sē
Ablative	sē

EXERCISE 27b

Read each incomplete sentence to yourself. Select the correct pronoun, remembering that reflexives always refer to the subject. Then read aloud and translate:

1. Aurēlia _____ in aquā cōnspexit.   sibi/sē/suī
2. "Ego _____ in aquā cōnspexī," inquit Aurēlia.   sē/mē/sibi
3. Canēs ē iānuā caupōnae _____ praecipitant.   mē/sibi/sē
4. Nocuistīne _____, ubi cecidistī?   tē/tibi/sibi
5. Ego _____ nōn nocuī.   mihi/sibi/mē

Adjectives: Possessive

In your reading you will not find the genitive of the 1st and 2nd person pronouns or of the reflexive pronouns used to indicate possession. Rather, you will find a *possessive adjective*:

Librum **tuum** legō.
*I am reading **your** book.*

Librum **meum** legō.
*I am reading **my (own)** book.*

The possessive adjectives, corresponding to the personal and reflexive pronouns, are 1st and 2nd declension adjectives, as follows:

meus, -a, -um	*my, my own, mine*
tuus, -a, -um	*your, your own, yours* (singular)
suus, -a, -um	*his own, her own, its own*

noster, nostra, nostrum	*our, our own, ours*
vester, vestra, vestrum	*your, your own, yours* (plural)
suus, -a, -um	*their own*

Notice that just as the pronoun **sē** is used for both singular and plural, so also the adjective **suus, -a, -um** can be singular or plural and mean *his own, her own, its own,* or *their own.*

EXERCISE 27c

Select, read aloud, and translate:

1. Ad lūdōs circēnsēs cum amīcīs _____ ībitis.
2. Omnēs spectātōrēs factiōnibus _____ favent.
3. In somniō _____ appāruērunt praedōnēs scelestī.
4. In vīllā _____ sunt multī servī.
5. Puellae domī cum amīcīs _____ manēbant.

vestrī/vestrīs/vestrōs
suae/suīs/suum
meīs/meī/meō
nostrī/nostra/nostrā
suae/suīs/suō

factiō, factiōnis, f., *company (of charioteers)*

Note carefully the distinction in use between the adjective **suus, -a, -um** (which is always reflexive) *his own, her own, their own,* and the genitives of the 3rd person pronoun, namely, **eius,** *of him = his,* or *of her = her;* and **eōrum, eārum,** *of them = their:*

Mārcus librum **suum** habet.
*Marcus has **his own** book.*

Puellae librōs **suōs** habent.
*The girls have **their own** books.*

Mārcus librum **eius** habet.
*Marcus has **his** (e.g., Sextus's) book.*

Puellae librōs **eōrum** habent.
*The girls have **their** (e.g., the boys') books.*

EXERCISE 27d

Using the dialogue at the beginning of this chapter and the information on special intransitive verbs, pronouns, and adjectives as guides, give the Latin for the following. Be sure to use pronouns for the emphatic words in italics:

1. As soon as *she* has gotten up, we will go.
2. *We* want to sit near the race track.
3. *I* favor the whites. Do *you* favor them?
4. Look at the blue! *I* favor him.
5. Is your blue winning?
6. My white fell down. Did he hurt himself?
7. *He* is safe, but he harmed his own horses.
8. The horses of your blue are safe.
9. My charioteer did not harm his own horses.
10. It is time for us to return home.

Prefixes: Compound Verbs I

Compare the following sentences:

1. Equī raedam **trahunt**.
   *The horses **pull** the carriage.*
2. Servī lectum **ferēbant**.
   *The slaves **were carrying** the bed.*

1. Equī raedam **extrahunt**.
   *The horses **pull out** the carriage.*
2. Servī lectum **referēbant**.
   *The slaves **were carrying back** the bed.*

In the right-hand column a prefix has been added to the beginning of the verb to give it a more specific meaning. Verbs with prefixes attached to them are called *compound verbs*. Common prefixes are:

ab-, abs-, ā-, *away, from*
ad-, *toward, to*
circum-, *around*
con-, *along with, together*
    (or simply to emphasize)
dē-, *down, down from*
dis-, dī-, *apart, in different directions*
ex-, ē-, *out, out of*
in-, *into, in, on*

inter-, *between*
per-, *through* (or simply to emphasize)
prae-, *in front, ahead*
praeter-, *past, beyond*
pro-, prōd-, *forward*
re-, red-, *back, again*
sub-, *under, below*
trāns-, trā-, *across*

Note that many of these are common prepositions.
Be sure to learn these prefixes thoroughly.

EXERCISE 27e

Read each sentence aloud. Identify each compound verb and give the meaning of its prefix. You are to deduce the meanings of compound verbs that you have not met in the stories. Then translate:

1. Pater līberōs ē vīllā ēdūxit et trāns viam trādūxit.
2. Cornēlius Eucleidem iussit līberōs abdūcere.
3. Eucleidēs līberōs ad hortum redūxit.
4. Servī togās et tunicās in cistās repōnunt.
5. Ubi ad Portam Capēnam veniunt, servī onera dēpōnunt.
6. Ubi plaustrum invēnit, stercus remōvit et corpus extrāxit.
7. Cornēliī Rōmam herī advēnērunt.
8. Homō per viam it. Mox viam trānsībit et ad vīllam redībit.
9. Ubi urbem intrāmus, necesse est Aquam Mārciam subīre.
10. Puerī Circum relīquērunt et Palātīnum circumiērunt.
11. Nihil clāmōris, nihil strepitūs ad Mārcum pervēnerat.
12. Puerōs, quod praecurrēbant, identidem revocābat Cornēlius.

Go Online
PHSchool.com
Web Code: jfd–0027

INSCRIPTIONS ABOUT CHARIOTEERS

Honorary Inscription

P. Aelius, Marī Rogātī fīl(ius), Gutta Calpurniānus equīs hīs vīcī in factiōne venetā: Germinātōre n(igrō) Āf(rō) LXXXXII, Silvānō r(ūfō) Āf(rō) CV, Nitid(ō) gil(vō) Āf(rō) LII, Saxōne n(igrō) Āf(rō) LX, et vīcī praemia m(aiōra) L̄ I, X̄L̄ IX, X̄X̄X̄ XVII.

I, Publius Aelius Gutta Calpurnianus, son of Marius Rogatus, won for the Blue stable with the following horses: Germinator, African black, 92 (times); Silvanus, African chestnut, 105 (times); Glossy, African sorrel, 52 (times); Saxon, African black, 60 (times); and I won major purses of 50,000 sesterces (1), of 40,000 sesterces (9), and of 30,000 sesterces (17).

Sepulchral Inscription

D. M. Epaphrodītus, agitātor f(actiōnis) r(ussātae), vīc(it) CLXXVIII, et ad purpureum līber(ātus) vīc(it) VIII. Beia Felicula f(ēcit) coniugī suō merentī.

To the deified spirits. Epaphroditus, driver for the Red stable, won 178 (times), and after being manumitted to the Purples he won 8 (times). Beia Felicula made (this monument) for her deserving husband.

Curses against Charioteers and Their Horses

Adiūrō tē, daemōn, quīcumque es et dēmandō tibi ex hāc hōrā ex hāc diē ex hōc mōmentō, ut equōs Prasinī et Albī cruciēs occīdās, et agitātōrēs Clārum et Fēlīcem et Prīmulum et Rōmānum occīdās collīdās, neque spīritum illīs relinquās.

I adjure you, demon, whoever you are, and I ask of you from this hour, from this day, from this moment, that you torture and kill the horses of the Green and the White, and that you kill and smash their drivers Clarus and Felix and Primulus and Romanus, and leave no breath in them.

Word Study VII

Prefixes

Knowledge of Latin prefixes will help not only with the meanings of Latin compound verbs but also with the meanings of many English words derived from them. For example, when the Latin simple verb **portāre** is combined with various prefixes, the resulting compound verbs provide English with several words, e.g.:

deport (from **dēportāre**)   report (from **reportāre**)
export (from **exportāre**)   transport (from **trānsportāre**)

Relying on your knowledge of prefixes, can you tell the meaning of each of the English words above?

Some English words are derived from the infinitive base of the Latin compound verb, e.g., *transport* (from **trānsportāre**). Others are derived from the stem of the fourth principal part, e.g., *transportation* (from **trānsportātus**). (For the suffix *-tion*, see Word Study VI.)

EXERCISE 1

After each Latin simple verb below is a group of English verbs that are derived from Latin compounds of that simple verb. (The Latin compound verbs are in parentheses.) Give the meaning of each English verb:

dūcō, dūcere, dūxī, ductus, *to lead, bring*

1. to conduct (**condūcere**)   4. to reduce (**redūcere**)
2. to induct (**indūcere**)   5. to produce (**prōdūcere**)
3. to deduct (**dēdūcere**)   6. to adduce (**addūcere**)

pōnō, pōnere, posuī, positus, *to put, place*

1. to propose (**prōpōnere**)   4. to depose (**dēpōnere**)
2. to dispose (**dispōnere**)   5. to transpose (**trānspōnere**)
3. to expose (**expōnere**)   6. to deposit (**dēpōnere**)

cēdō, cēdere, cessī, cessūrus, *to go*

1. to precede (**praecēdere**)   *variant spelling:*
2. to recede (**recēdere**)   4. to proceed (**prōcēdere**)
3. to intercede (**intercēdere**)   5. to exceed (**excēdere**)

Note that **cēdere** can also mean *to yield*. From this meaning come the following English derivatives:

6. to cede (**cēdere**)   7. concede (**concēdere**)

ferō, ferre, tulī, lātus, irreg., *to bring, carry, bear*

1. to refer (**referre**)
2. to infer (**īnferre**)
3. to defer (**dēferre**)
4. to transfer (**trānsferre**)
5. to confer (**cōnferre**)
6. to relate (**referre**)

EXERCISE 2

Give the infinitive of the Latin compound verb from which each of the following English nouns is derived. Use each English noun in a sentence that illustrates its meaning:

1. disposition
2. proponent
3. recess
4. inference
5. product
6. exposition
7. relation
8. procession
9. conference
10. precedent
11. translator
12. concession
13. deduction
14. referee
15. reference

EXERCISE 3

Each adjective in the pool below is derived from a Latin compound verb. Choose an adjective to fill each blank and give the Latin compound verb from which it is derived:

1. Eucleides provided an atmosphere for the boys that would lead them to learn. The atmosphere was _____ to learning.
2. Although the horses tried to pull the carriage out, their efforts brought forth no results. Their efforts were not _____.
3. Some masters treat their slaves with violence that goes beyond reasonable limits. Their use of violence is _____.
4. Davus was not unhappy, but he was not as happy as he might have been if he were not a slave. Davus enjoyed _____ happiness.
5. When Cornelius entered a shop, the merchant left the other customers and helped him immediately. Cornelius received _____ treatment.
6. After he considered all of the evidence, the overseer was certain which slave stole the money. The overseer used _____ reasoning to come to his conclusion.
7. When the emperor went by, all the citizens bowed respectfully. The emperor was greeted in a _____ manner.

relative	deferential	conducive
productive	excessive	preferential
deductive		

Latin Abbreviations in English

Many abbreviations used in English are actually abbreviations of Latin words. For example, the common abbreviations for morning and afternoon, A.M. and P.M., stand for the Latin phrases **ante merīdiem** (*before noon*) and **post merīdiem** (*after noon*).

EXERCISE 4

With the aid of an English dictionary, give the full Latin words for the following abbreviations and explain how each is used in English:

1. etc.
2. A.D.
3. P.S.
4. i.e.
5. e.g.
6. N.B.
7. ad-lib
8. vs.
9. cf.
10. et al.
11. q.v.
12. Rx

EXERCISE 5

Replace the words in italics with abbreviations chosen from the list in Exercise 4 above:

1. The senators discussed the most critical problems first, *for example*, the revolt in Judea.
2. Titus was known for his ability to *speak off the cuff* on almost any subject.
3. The eruption of Vesuvius occurred in *the year of our Lord* 79.
4. Titus pointed out the Curia, the Arch of Tiberius, *and the rest*, as they passed them.
5. The announcement of the chariot race read, "Reds *against* Blues."
6. Eucleides said that they would return early, *that is*, before the eleventh hour.
7. At the bottom of the letter Cornelius added an *additional message*.
8. Cornelius had invited Titus, Messala, *and others*, to a dinner party.
9. The abbreviation "B.C." is used to give dates before the birth of Christ. (*Compare* the abbreviation "A.D.")
10. A sign near the Porta Capena read, "*Note well*: It is forbidden to drive wagons or carriages within the city during the day."
11. "*Take this*" was written at the bottom of the doctor's prescription.
12. "*Which see*" is written after a word or topic that needs further explanation, and it directs the reader to find such explanation elsewhere in the book.

Find examples of Latin abbreviations in textbooks, newspapers, or magazines and bring them to class.

Review VI: Chapters 25–27

Exercise VIa: Demonstrative Adjectives pp. 53, 94, 106, 107

Select the correct form first of **hic, haec, hoc** and then of **ille, illa, illud** to
modify each of the following nouns:

1. diem	(hōrum/hunc/hoc)	(illum/illōrum/illud)
2. arbore	(hōc/hae/hāc)	(illō/illā/illae)
3. lutum	(hoc/hunc/hōc)	(illum/illud/illō)
4. diēbus	(hās/hōs/hīs)	(illās/illīs/illōs)
5. fēminam	(hunc/hanc/hoc)	(illam/illum/illud)
6. terrās	(hōs/hāc/hās)	(illā/illōs/illās)
7. mandātō	(hōc/hoc/hāc)	(illā/illō/illud)
8. terra	(hae/hāc/haec)	(illā/illae/illa)
9. oculō	(hoc/huic/hic)	(illud/ille/illī)
10. arcuum	(hōrum/hārum/hunc)	(illārum/illōrum/illum)
11. somnia	(haec/hae/hanc)	(illā/illa/illam)
12. rīsū	(hāc/hī/hōc)	(illō/illā/illī)
13. vōcum	(hārum/hōrum/hunc)	(illārum/illum/illōrum)
14. diē	(hōc/hoc/haec)	(illud/illō/illa)
15. manūs	(huius/hōs/hī)	(illōs/illīus/illī)

Exercise VIb: Agreement of Adjectives pp. 53, 54, 94, 106, 107
and Nouns

From the pool of words below, choose an adjective to go with each noun in
Exercise VIa above. Give the noun with the adjective in its proper form to
modify the noun.

bonus, -a, -um	īrātus, -a, -um	parvulus, -a, -um
brevis, -is, -e	longus, -a, -um	pūrus, -a, -um
dēfessus, -a, -um	magnus, -a, -um	scelestus, -a, -um
prīmus, -a, -um	multī, -ae, -a	sēmisomnus, -a, -um
īnfirmus, -a, -um	novus, -a, -um	sordidus, -a, -um
ingēns, ingentis	omnis, -is, -e	vester, vestra, vestrum

Exercise VIc: Personal Pronouns pp. 119–120

Give the correct form of the appropriate Latin pronoun to translate the
English word or phrase in italics:

1. *I* heard nothing. What did *you* hear, Marcus?
2. *We* heard nothing because we were asleep, but the girls were awake. *They* heard the
   rumbling of wagons in the street.

3. He didn't see *me*, but I saw *him*.
4. He gave the book *to me*, not *to you*, Cornelia.
5. No, he gave it *to us*.
6. It is really *his* book.
7. But he gave it *to them*.
8. The girls are in the house. I saw *them* there.
9. Did you see *her*?
10. No, Marcus and Sextus, but I saw *you*.
11. The dog is yours, Marcus and Cornelia. Father gave it *to you*.

Exercise VId: Personal Pronouns, Reflexive Pronouns, and Possessive Adjectives

 pp. 120–122

Select the correct form to translate the English word or phrase in italics:

1. I have *my* book. (mihi/meum/meī)
2. Did he give you *your* book, Marcus? (vestrum/tuum/tibi)
3. She hurt *herself* when she fell. (eī/sibi/eae)
4. She saw *herself* in the mirror. (sē/eam/eum)
5. Did you leave *your* books at school, girls? (vōs/vestrum/vestrōs)
6. Yes, we left *our* books there. (nostrōs/nōs/vestrōs)
7. He has *his own* book. (eius/suum/sē)
8. No, he doesn't. He has *her* book. (eius/suum/suam)
9. Do the boys all have *their own* books? (eōrum/suōs/sibi)
10. No, the boys took the girls' books by mistake. So now they have *their* books. (eārum/suōs/eōrum)

Exercise VIe: Verb Forms

 pp. 16–17, 26, 31–33, 67, 69, 79, 84

Give the requested forms of the following verbs in the present, imperfect, future, perfect, pluperfect, and future perfect tenses:

	Present	Imperfect	Future	Perfect	Pluperfect	Future Perfect
1. vetāre (*1st pl.*)						
2. aperīre (*3rd pl.*)						
3. stertere (*2nd pl.*)						
4. esse (*3rd sing.*)						
5. emere (*3rd sing.*)						
6. ferre (*2nd sing.*)						
7. arripere (*1st sing.*)						
8. docēre (*1st sing.*)						
9. posse (*2nd sing.*)						
10. velle (*1st pl.*)						

Exercise VIf: Reading Comprehension

Read the following passage and answer the questions below with full sentences in Latin:

ROMAN INFLUENCE IN THE EAST: 168 B.C.

Ōlim, ubi Lūcius Aemilius Paulus et Pūblius Licinius cōnsulēs Rōmānī erant, cīvēs Alexandrīnī auxilium ā Rōmānīs petīvērunt. Obsidēbat enim urbem Alexandrīam magnō exercitū Antiochus, rēx Syriae. Hic rēx superbus erat et, quod rēgnum suum augēre in animō habēbat, Aegyptiōs vincere volēbat. Rōmānī Aegyptiīs favēbant, sed exercitum ad Aegyptum mittere nōn poterant. Erat tamen 5
senātor quīdam cōnsulāris, Gāius Popilius Laenās nōmine, quī eō ipsō tempore iter in illīs partibus faciēbat. Hunc senātōrem ad Aegyptum mīsit senātus Rōmānus quod auxilium Aegyptiīs offerre voluit.

Antiochus, ubi Popilius advēnit, ad eum nūntiōs mīsit, nam hunc senātōrem cōnsulere volēbat. Vēnit rēx Syriae ad congressum vestibus magnificīs indūtus 10
cum magnā multitūdine mīlitum. Vēnit Popilius sōlus, togā praetextā indūtus, cum duodecim modo līctōribus. Rēgī appropinquāvit et statim, "Necesse est mihi," inquit, "ad senātum respōnsum tuum, Antioche, referre. Quid ā Rōmānīs petis, bellum aut pācem?"

Stupuit Antiochus et sēcum cogitābat: "Cūr ille Rōmānus mē nōn timet? 15
Nūllum exercitum habet, sed neque commōtus neque sollicitus est." Antiochus ipse vērō commōtus sollicitusque erat et Popiliō igitur respondit, "Necesse est dē hāc rē cum amīcīs meīs cōnsulere."

Habēbat in manū Popilius baculum quod omnēs lēgātī Rōmānī sēcum ferre solēbant. Hōc baculō Popilius circulum in arēnā circum rēgem Syriae scrīpsit. 20
Rēgī, "Antequam ē circulō exierīs," inquit, "mihi respōnsum dabis." Attonitus erat Antiochus. Popilium et imperium Rōmānum valdē timēbat. "Faciam," inquit, "id quod cēnset senātus Rōmānus." Ad mīlitēs rediit et exercitum ad Syriam statim redūxit. Tanta erat dignitās et auctōritās huius lēgātī et senātūs Rōmānī.

1 cōnsul, cōnsulis, m., *consul (one of* *the two chief annual magistrates of* *the Roman state)*	10 congressus, -ūs, m., *meeting* vestis, vestis, gen. pl., vestium, f., *garment, clothes*
2 Alexandrīnus, -a, -um, *of Alexandria* *(a city in Egypt)*	indūtus, -a, -um + abl., *dressed (in)*
3 exercitus, -ūs, m., *army* rēx, rēgis, m., *king* superbus, -a, -um, *arrogant, haughty*	12 duodecim, *twelve* līctor, līctōris, m., *lictor (official* *attendant)*
4 rēgnum, -ī, n., *kingdom* Aegyptiī, -ōrum, m. pl., *the Egyptians*	13 respōnsum, -ī, n., *answer*
5 Aegyptus, -ī, f., *Egypt*	14 bellum, -ī, n., *war* pāx, pācis, f., *peace*
6 cōnsulāris, -is, -e, *having the status* *of an ex-consul*	17 vērō, adv., *truly* -que, enclitic conj., *and*

20 circulus, -ī, m., *small circle*
   arēna, -ae, f., *sand*
21 antequam, conj., *before*
22 imperium, -ī, n., *empire, power*

24 dignitās, dignitātis, f., *honor, status, dignity*
   auctōritās, auctōritātis, f., *influence, prestige, authority*

2 obsideō, obsidēre, obsēdī, obsessus, *to besiege*
4 augeō, augēre, auxī, auctus, *to increase*
8 offerō, offerre, obtulī, oblātus, irreg., *to provide*
13 referō, referre, rettulī, relātus, irreg., *to bring back*
23 cēnseō, cēnsēre, cēnsuī, cēnsus, *to decree*

1. When did the citizens of Alexandria seek help from the Romans?
2. Who was besieging Alexandria?
3. Why was he wanting to conquer the Egyptians?
4. Whom did the Senate send to Egypt?
5. How did Antiochus come to his meeting with Popilius?
6. How did Popilius come?
7. Was Popilius afraid of Antiochus?
8. Was Antiochus afraid of Popilius?
9. What did Popilius do? What did he say?
10. How did Antiochus respond?
11. What did Popilius do and say in reply?
12. What did Antiochus do?

Exercise VIg: 4th and 5th Declension Nouns

1. In the first, second, and fourth paragraphs of the story above, locate four different 4th declension nouns.
2. In the third paragraph of the story, locate one 5th declension noun.

FORMS

The following charts show the forms of typical Latin nouns, adjectives, pronouns, and verbs in the cases and tenses presented in this book. As an aid in pronunciation, markings of long vowels and of accents are included.

I. Nouns

Number Case	1st Declension	2nd Declension			
	Fem.	Masc.	Masc.	Masc.	Neut.
Singular					
Nominative	puélla	sérvus	púer	áger	báculum
Genitive	puéllae	sérvī	púerī	ágrī	báculī
Dative	puéllae	sérvō	púerō	ágrō	báculō
Accusative	puéllam	sérvum	púerum	ágrum	báculum
Ablative	puéllā	sérvō	púerō	ágrō	báculō
Vocative	puélla	sérve	púer	áger	báculum
Plural					
Nominative	puéllae	sérvī	púerī	ágrī	bácula
Genitive	puellárum	servórum	puerórum	agrórum	baculórum
Dative	puéllīs	sérvīs	púerīs	ágrīs	báculīs
Accusative	puéllās	sérvōs	púerōs	ágrōs	bácula
Ablative	puéllīs	sérvīs	púerīs	ágrīs	báculīs
Vocative	puéllae	sérvī	púerī	ágrī	bácula

Number Case	3rd Declension			4th Declension		5th Declension	
	Masc.	Fem.	Neut.	Masc.	Neut.	Masc.	Fem.
Singular							
Nominative	páter	vōx	nómen	árcus	génū	díēs	rēs
Genitive	pátris	vócis	nóminis	árcūs	génūs	diéī	réī
Dative	pátrī	vócī	nóminī	árcuī	génū	diéī	réī
Accusative	pátrem	vócem	nómen	árcum	génū	díem	rem
Ablative	pátre	vóce	nómine	árcū	génū	díē	rē
Vocative	páter	vōx	nómen	árcus	génū	díēs	rēs
Plural							
Nominative	pátrēs	vócēs	nómina	árcūs	génua	díēs	rēs
Genitive	pátrum	vócum	nóminum	árcuum	génuum	diérum	rérum
Dative	pátribus	vócibus	nōmínibus	árcibus	génibus	diébus	rébus
Accusative	pátrēs	vócēs	nómina	árcūs	génua	díēs	rēs
Ablative	pátribus	vócibus	nōmínibus	árcibus	génibus	diébus	rébus
Vocative	pátrēs	vócēs	nómina	árcūs	génua	díēs	rēs

II. Adjectives

Number Case	1st and 2nd Declensions			3rd Declension		
	Masc.	Fem.	Neut.	Masc.	Fem.	Neut.
Singular						
Nominative	mágn**us**	mágn**a**	mágn**um**	ómn**is**	ómn**is**	ómn**e**
Genitive	mágn**ī**	mágn**ae**	mágn**ī**	ómn**is**	ómn**is**	ómn**is**
Dative	mágn**ō**	mágn**ae**	mágn**ō**	ómn**ī**	ómn**ī**	ómn**ī**
Accusative	mágn**um**	mágn**am**	mágn**um**	ómn**em**	ómn**em**	ómn**e**
Ablative	mágn**ō**	mágn**ā**	mágn**ō**	ómn**ī**	ómn**ī**	ómn**ī**
Vocative	mágn**e**	mágn**a**	mágn**um**	ómn**is**	ómn**is**	ómn**e**
Plural						
Nominative	mágn**ī**	mágn**ae**	mágn**a**	ómn**ēs**	ómn**ēs**	ómn**ia**
Genitive	magn** órum**	magn**árum**	magn**órum**	ómn**ium**	ómn**ium**	ómn**ium**
Dative	mágn**īs**	mágn**īs**	mágn**īs**	ómn**ibus**	ómn**ibus**	ómn**ibus**
Accusative	mágn**ōs**	mágn**ās**	mágn**a**	ómn**ēs**	ómn**ēs**	ómn**ia**
Ablative	mágn**īs**	mágn**īs**	mágn**īs**	ómn**ibus**	ómn**ibus**	ómn**ibus**
Vocative	mágn**ī**	mágn**ae**	mágn**a**	ómn**ēs**	ómn**ēs**	ómn**ia**

III. Numbers

Case	Masc.	Fem.	Neut.
Nominative	ū́n**us**	ū́n**a**	ū́n**um**
Genitive	ūn**íus**	ūn**íus**	ūn**íus**
Dative	ū́n**ī**	ū́n**ī**	ū́n**ī**
Accusative	ū́n**um**	ū́n**am**	ū́n**um**
Ablative	ū́n**ō**	ū́n**ā**	ū́n**ō**

Case	Masc.	Fem.	Neut.	Masc.	Fem.	Neut.
Nominative	dúo	dúae	dúo	trēs	trēs	tría
Genitive	du**órum**	du**árum**	du**órum**	trí**um**	trí**um**	trí**um**
Dative	du**óbus**	du**ábus**	du**óbus**	trí**bus**	trí**bus**	trí**bus**
Accusative	dú**ōs**	dú**ās**	dúo	trēs	trēs	tría
Ablative	du**óbus**	du**ábus**	du**óbus**	trí**bus**	trí**bus**	trí**bus**

In addition to **ūnus, -a, -um**, the following other adjectives have **-īus** in the genitive singular and **-ī** in the dative singular: **alius, -a, -ud**, *another, other*; **alter, altera, alterum**, *second, one (of two), the other (of two), another*; **nūllus, -a, -um**, *no, not any*; **sōlus, -a, -um**, *alone*; and **tōtus, -a, -um**, *all, the whole*.

IV. Personal Pronouns

Number Case	1st	2nd	3rd		
			Masc.	Fem.	Neut.
Singular					
Nominative	égo	tū	is	éa	id
Genitive	méī	túī	éius	éius	éius
Dative	míhi	tíbi	éī	éī	éī
Accusative	mē	tē	éum	éam	id
Ablative	mē	tē	éō	éā	éō
Plural					
Nominative	nōs	vōs	éī	éae	éa
Genitive	nóstrī	véstrī	eórum	eárum	eórum
	nóstrum	véstrum			
Dative	nṓbīs	vṓbīs	éīs	éīs	éīs
Accusative	nōs	vōs	éōs	éās	éa
Ablative	nṓbīs	vṓbīs	éīs	éīs	éīs

V. Reflexive Pronouns

	Singular	Plural
Nominative	—	—
Genitive	súī	súī
Dative	síbi	síbi
Accusative	sē	sē
Ablative	sē	sē

VI. Relative Pronoun

Number Case	Masc.	Fem.	Neut.
Singular			
Nominative	quī	quae	quod
Genitive	cúius	cúius	cúius
Dative	cui	cui	cui
Accusative	quem	quam	quod
Ablative	quō	quā	quō
Plural			
Nominative	quī	quae	quae
Genitive	quórum	quárum	quórum
Dative	quíbus	quíbus	quíbus
Accusative	quōs	quās	quae
Ablative	quíbus	quíbus	quíbus

VII. Interrogative Pronoun

Number Case	Singular			Plural		
	Masc.	Fem.	Neut.	Masc.	Fem.	Neut.
Nominative	quis	quis	quid	quī	quae	quae
Genitive	cúius	cúius	cúius	quōrum	quārum	quōrum
Dative	cui	cui	cui	quíbus	quíbus	quíbus
Accusative	quem	quem	quid	quōs	quās	quae
Ablative	quō	quō	quō	quíbus	quíbus	quíbus

VIII. Indefinite Adjective

Number Case	Masc.	Fem.	Neut.
Singular			
Nominative	quídam	quaédam	quóddam
Genitive	cuiúsdam	cuiúsdam	cuiúsdam
Dative	cúidam	cúidam	cúidam
Accusative	quéndam	quándam	quóddam
Ablative	quódam	quádam	quódam
Plural			
Nominative	quídam	quaédam	quaédam
Genitive	quōrúndam	quārúndam	quōrúndam
Dative	quibúsdam	quibúsdam	quibúsdam
Accusative	quósdam	quásdam	quaédam
Ablative	quibúsdam	quibúsdam	quibúsdam

IX. Demonstrative Adjectives and Pronouns

Number Case	Masc.	Fem.	Neut.	Masc.	Fem.	Neut.
Singular						
Nominative	hic	haec	hoc	ílle	ílla	íllud
Genitive	húius	húius	húius	illíus	illíus	illíus
Dative	húic	húic	húic	íllī	íllī	íllī
Accusative	hunc	hanc	hoc	íllum	íllam	íllud
Ablative	hōc	hāc	hōc	íllō	íllā	íllō
Plural						
Nominative	hī	hae	haec	íllī	íllae	ílla
Genitive	hórum	hárum	hórum	illórum	illárum	illórum
Dative	hīs	hīs	hīs	íllīs	íllīs	íllīs
Accusative	hōs	hās	haec	íllōs	íllās	ílla
Ablative	hīs	hīs	hīs	íllīs	íllīs	íllīs

X. Regular Verbs

		1st Conjugation	2nd Conjugation	3rd Conjugation		4th Conjugation
	Infinitive	par*á*re	hab*é*re	mítt*ere*	iác*ere* (-iō)	aud*í*re
	Imperative	pár*ā* par*á*te	háb*ē* hab*é*te	mítt*e* mítt*ite*	iác*e* iác*ite*	aúd*ī* aud*í*te
Present	Sing. 1 2 3	pár*ō* pár*ā*s pár*at*	hábe*ō* háb*ē*s hábe*t*	mítt*ō* mítt*is* mítt*it*	iáci*ō* iáci*s* iáci*t*	aúd*iō* aúd*ī*s aúd*it*
	Pl. 1 2 3	par*á*mus par*á*tis pár*ant*	hab*é*mus hab*é*tis háb*ent*	mítt*imus* mítt*itis* mítt*unt*	iáci*mus* iáci*tis* iáci*unt*	aud*í*mus aud*í*tis aúd*iunt*
Imperfect	Sing. 1 2 3	par*á*bam par*á*bās par*á*bat	hab*é*bam hab*é*bās hab*é*bat	mitt*é*bam mitt*é*bās mitt*é*bat	iaci*é*bam iaci*é*bās iaci*é*bat	audi*é*bam audi*é*bās audi*é*bat
	Pl. 1 2 3	par*ā*bámus par*ā*bátis par*á*bant	hab*ē*bámus hab*ē*bátis hab*é*bant	mitt*ē*bámus mitt*ē*bátis mitt*é*bant	iaci*ē*bámus iaci*ē*bátis iaci*é*bant	audi*ē*bámus audi*ē*bátis audi*é*bant
Future	Sing. 1 2 3	par*á*bō par*á*bis par*á*bit	hab*é*bō hab*é*bis hab*é*bit	mítt*am* mítt*ēs* mítt*et*	iáci*am* iáci*ēs* iáci*et*	aúd*iam* aúd*iēs* aúd*iet*
	Pl. 1 2 3	par*á*bimus par*á*bitis par*á*bunt	hab*é*bimus hab*é*bitis hab*é*bunt	mitt*é*mus mitt*é*tis mítt*ent*	iaci*é*mus iaci*é*tis iáci*ent*	audi*é*mus audi*é*tis aúd*ient*
Perfect	Sing. 1 2 3	par*á*vī parāv*í*stī par*á*vit	hábu*ī* habu*í*stī hábu*it*	m*í*sī mīs*í*stī m*í*sit	i*é*cī iēc*í*stī i*é*cit	aud*í*vī audīv*í*stī aud*í*vit
	Pl. 1 2 3	par*á*vimus parāv*í*stis parāv*é*runt	habú*imus* habu*í*stis habu*é*runt	m*í*simus mīs*í*stis mīs*é*runt	i*é*cimus iēc*í*stis iēc*é*runt	aud*í*vimus audīv*í*stis audīv*é*runt
Pluperfect	Sing. 1 2 3	par*á*veram par*á*verās par*á*verat	habú*eram* habú*erās* habú*erat*	m*í*seram m*í*serās m*í*serat	i*é*ceram i*é*cerās i*é*cerat	aud*í*veram aud*í*verās aud*í*verat
	Pl. 1 2 3	parāver*á*mus parāver*á*tis par*á*verant	habuer*á*mus habuer*á*tis habú*erant*	mīser*á*mus mīser*á*tis m*í*serant	iēcer*á*mus iēcer*á*tis i*é*cerant	audīver*á*mus audīver*á*tis aud*í*verant
Future Perfect	Sing. 1 2 3	par*á*verō par*á*veris par*á*verit	habú*erō* habú*eris* habú*erit*	m*í*serō m*í*seris m*í*serit	i*é*cerō i*é*ceris i*é*cerit	aud*í*verō aud*í*veris aud*í*verit
	Pl. 1 2 3	parāv*é*rimus parāv*é*ritis par*á*verint	habu*é*rimus habu*é*ritis habú*erint*	mīs*é*rimus mīs*é*ritis m*í*serint	iēc*é*rimus iēc*é*ritis i*é*cerint	audīv*é*rimus audīv*é*ritis aud*í*verint

XI. Irregular Verbs

		Infinitive	pósse	vélle	nõlle
	Infinitive	ésse	pósse	vélle	nõlle
	Imperative	es éste	— —	— —	nõlī nõlíte
Present	Sing. 1 2 3	sum es est	póssum pótes pótest	vólō vīs vult	nõlō nõn vīs nõn vult
	Pl. 1 2 3	súmus éstis sunt	póssumus potéstis póssunt	vólumus vúltis vólunt	nõlumus nõn vúltis nõlunt
Imperfect	Sing. 1 2 3	éram érās érat	póteram póterās póterat	volébam volébās volébat	nõlébam nõlébās nõlébat
	Pl. 1 2 3	erámus erátis érant	poterámus poterátis póterant	volēbámus volēbátis volébant	nõlēbámus nõlēbátis nõlébant
Future	Sing. 1 2 3	érō éris érit	pótero póteris póterit	vólam vólēs vólet	nõlam nõlēs nõlet
	Pl. 1 2 3	érimus éritis érunt	potérimus potéritis póterunt	volémus volétis vólent	nõlémus nõlétis nõlent
Perfect	Sing. 1 2 3	fúī fuístī fúit	pótuī potuístī pótuit	vóluī voluístī vóluit	nõluī nõluístī nõluit
	Pl. 1 2 3	fúimus fuístis fuérunt	potúimus potuístis potuérunt	volúimus voluístis voluérunt	nõlúimus nõluístis nõluérunt
Pluperfect	Sing. 1 2 3	fúeram fúerās fúerat	potúeram potúerās potúerat	volúeram volúerās volúerat	nõlúeram nõlúerās nõlúerat
	Pl. 1 2 3	fuerámus fuerátis fúerant	potuerámus potuerátis potúerant	voluerámus voluerátis volúerant	nõluerámus nõluerátis nõlúerant
Future Perfect	Sing. 1 2 3	fúerō fúeris fúerit	potúerō potúeris potúerit	volúerō volúeris volúerit	nõlúerō nõlúeris nõlúerit
	Pl. 1 2 3	fuérimus fuéritis fúerint	potuérimus potuéritis potúerint	voluérimus voluéritis volúerint	nõluérimus nõluéritis nõlúerint

		ferre	īre	
	Infinitive	férre	íre	
	Imperative	fer férte	ī íte	
Present	**Sing. 1** 2 3	férō fers fert	éō īs it	
	Pl. 1 2 3	férimus fértis férunt	ímus ítis éunt	
Imperfect	**Sing. 1** 2 3	ferḗbam ferḗbās ferḗbat	íbam íbās íbat	
	Pl. 1 2 3	ferēbā́mus ferēbā́tis ferḗbant	ībā́mus ībā́tis íbant	
Future	**Sing. 1** 2 3	féram téres féret	íbō íbis íbit	
	Pl. 1 2 3	ferḗmus ferḗtis férent	íbimus íbitis íbunt	
Perfect	**Sing. 1** 2 3	túlī tulístī túlit	ī́vī īvístī ī́vit	or, more usually íī iístī > ī́stī íit
	Pl. 1 2 3	túlimus tulístis tulḗrunt	ī́vimus īvístis īvḗrunt	íimus iístis > ī́stis iḗrunt
Pluperfect	**Sing. 1** 2 3	túleram túlerās túlerat	ī́veram ī́verās ī́verat	íeram íerās íerat
	Pl. 1 2 3	tulerā́mus tulerā́tis túlerant	īverā́mus īverā́tis ī́verant	ierā́mus ierā́tis íerant
Future Perfect	**Sing. 1** 2 3	túlerō túleris túlerit	ī́verō ī́veris ī́verit	íerō íeris íerit
	Pl. 1 2 3	tulḗrimus tulḗritis túlerint	īvḗrimus īvḗritis ī́verint	iḗrimus iḗritis íerint

BUILDING THE MEANING

I. Parts of Speech

The following are eight basic parts of speech:

Nouns: names of persons, places, things, qualities, or acts (see Book IA, page 4)

Pronouns: words that stand in place of nouns, e.g., *she* in place of *Cornelia* (see Book IB, pages 118–119)

Adjectives: words that describe persons, places, things, qualities, or acts (see Book IA, page 4)

Verbs: words that denote actions (e.g., *sits*) or existence (e.g., *is*) (see Book IA, page 4)

Adverbs: words that modify verbs, adjectives, or other adverbs (see Book IA, pages 100–101)

Prepositions: words such as *from*, *in*, and *at*, which introduce prepositional phrases (see Book IA, page 64)

Conjunctions: words that link other words, phrases, or clauses (see Book IB, pages 150–152)

Interjections: words that can stand alone and that call attention to a statement or express an emotion, e.g., *Look! Alas!*

II. Core Elements of Latin Sentences

You have met Latin sentences with the following combinations of core elements:

A. Subject and Intransitive Verb (see Book IA, page 20)

    Cornēlia **sedet.** (1:3)   **Sedet** Cornēlia.   *Cornelia **sits.***

This sentence has only a subject (S) and an intransitive verb (IV). **Cornēlia** is in the nominative case and is therefore the subject of the sentence.

    The verb in the above sentence expresses an action that simply tells what the subject is doing. The action of the verb does not affect anyone or anything else. Verbs when so used are called intransitive verbs (IV).

B. Subject, Linking Verb, and Complement (see Book IA, page 8)

    Cornēlia **est** puella.   *Cornelia **is** a girl.*
    Cornēlia puella **est.**

This sentence has a subject, **Cornēlia**, and a verb, **est**, as well as another word in the nominative case, **puella**. This word is linked to the subject by the verb **est**. The word **puella** is called a complement (C), because it completes the meaning of the sentence. **Est** is called a linking verb (LV) because it links the subject with the complement. The complement may appear before the linking verb, as in the second example above.

The linking verb in the following sentence links the subject with an adjective, which serves as a complement:

Cornēlia **est** <u>laeta</u>. (1:2–3)   *Cornelia is happy*.
Cornēlia <u>laeta</u> **est**.
<u>Laeta</u> **est** <u>Cornēlia</u>.
<u>Laeta</u> <u>Cornēlia</u> **est**.

C. Est/Sunt, Subject, No Complement (see Book IA, page 8)

In pictūrā **est** <u>puella</u>. (1:1)   In pictūrā **sunt** <u>puellae</u>.
There is <u>*a girl*</u> *in the picture*.   ***There are*** <u>*girls*</u> *in the picture*.

Note that **est** and **sunt** come before their subjects here.

D. Subject, Direct Object, and Transitive Verb (see Book IA, page 20)

<u>Sextus</u> <u>Cornēliam</u> **vexat**. (4:1)   <u>*Sextus*</u> ***annoys*** <u>*Cornelia*</u>.

In this sentence there is a subject, a direct object (DO: see Book IA, pages 20 and 40), and a verb. The direct object is in the accusative case, and it names the person or thing that receives the action of the verb. The verbs in such sentences are said to be transitive verbs (TV). The words in the Latin sentence could be arranged in any order and would express essentially the same meaning.

E. Subject, Dative, and Intransitive Verb (see Book IB, pages 78–79, 118, and 148)

1. Dative with Intransitive Compound Verbs (see Book IB, pages 78 and 148)

    Ibi fortasse <u>patrī tuō</u> **occurēmus**. (24:17)
    Perhaps ***we will meet*** <u>*your father*</u> *there*.

2. Dative with Special Intransitive Verbs (see Book IB, pages 118 and 148)

    Sī <u>mihi</u> **nocueritis**, pater meus certē vōs pūniet. (26:26–27)
    If ***you do harm*** <u>*to me*</u>, *my father will certainly punish you*.
    If ***you harm*** <u>*me*</u>, *my father will certainly punish you*.

III. Sentence Types

Every Latin sentence expresses a statement, a command, an exclamation, or a question.

A. The following are statements:

In pictūrā est puella. (1:1)
There is a girl in the picture.

Flāvia scrībit. (1:5)
Flavia writes.

Sextus Cornēliam vexat. (4:1)
Sextus annoys Cornelia.

B. Sentences may express commands and have their verbs in the imperative (see Book IA, page 74):

Dēscende, Sexte! (4:6)
Come down, Sextus!

Abīte, molestī! (3:8)
Go away, pests!

Negative commands are expressed with **nōlī** (singular) or **nōlīte** (plural) plus an infinitive (see page 74):

Nōlī servōs **excitāre!** (9:9)
Don't wake up the slaves!

C. A sentence may express an exclamation:

Quam celeriter appropinquat! (15:12)
How quickly it is approaching!

D. Statements can be turned into questions by placing an important word (often the verb) first and attaching the letters **-ne** to it (see Book IA, page 13):

Puer ignāvus est.
The boy is cowardly.
(statement)

Est**ne** puer ignāvus? (5:4)
Is the boy cowardly?
(question)

Questions are introduced by the word **Nōnne...?** when the speaker clearly expects the answer "yes":

Nōnne cēnāre vultis? (19:2)
*Surely you want to eat, **don't you?***

Questions are often introduced by interrogative words such as the following:

Cui...? *To whom...? (sing.)*
Cuius...? *Whose...? (sing.)*
Cūr...? *Why...?*
Quālis...? *What sort of ...?*
Quandō...? *When...?*
Quem...? *Whom...? (sing.)*
Quī...? *Who...? (pl.)*
Quibus...? *To whom...? (pl.)*
Quid...? *What...?*
Quis...? *Who...? (sing.)*

Quō...? *Where... to?*
Quō īnstrūmentō...? *With what instrument...? By what means...? How...?*
Quōcum...? *With whom...? (sing.)*
Quōmodo...? *In what manner...? How...?*
Quōs...? *Whom...? (pl.)*
Quot...? *How many...?*
Ubi...? *Where...?*
Unde...? *From where...?*

IV. More About Verbs

A. Tenses of Verbs

1. Verbs can be in the present tense, describing actions or situations in present time (see Book IA, page 73):

    a. in a simple statement of fact:

      Cornēliī Rōmam redīre **parant.**
      *The Cornelii **prepare** to return to Rome.*

    b. in a description of an ongoing action:

      Hodiē Cornēliī Rōmam redīre **parant.**
      *Today the Cornelii **are preparing** to return to Rome.*

    c. in a question:

      Audītne Dāvus clāmōrem?
      ***Does** Davus **hear** the shouting?*

    d. in an emphatic statement:

      Clāmōrem *audit.*
      *He **does hear** the shouting.*

    e. in a denial:

      Clāmōrem nōn **audit.**
      *He **does** not **hear** the shouting.*

2. The imperfect tense (see Book IA, pages 98 and 106–107) shows action in the past that was:

    a. going on for a time:

      Ego et Mārcus **spectābāmus** cisium. (14:10)
      *Marcus and I **were watching** the carriage.*

      Cornēlia dormīre **volēbat.** (13:8)
      *Cornelia **wanted** to sleep.*

    b. repeated:

      Mārcus **vexābat** Cornēliam. (13:7–8)
      *Marcus **kept annoying** Cornelia.*

    c. habitual or customary:

      Dāvus in Britanniā **habitābat.**
      *Davus **used to live** in Britain.*

d. beginning to happen:

>   Equōs ad raedam nostrum **dēvertēbat.** (14:11)
>   *He **began to turn** the horses **aside** in the direction of our carriage.*

3. The future tense indicates an action that will take place at some time subsequent to the present (see Book IB, page 67):

>   Brevī tempore ad Portam Capēnam **adveniēmus.** (22:26)
>   *In a short time **we will arrive** at the Porta Capena.*

4. The perfect, pluperfect, and future perfect tenses are formed from the perfect stem, which is found by dropping the *-ī* from the third principal part of the verb, e.g., **parāvī**, perfect stem **parāv-.** These tenses describe completed actions.

5. The perfect tense refers to an action that happened or to something that someone did in past time (see Book IB, page 16):

>   Eō ipsō tempore ad iānuam caupōnae **appāruit** homō obēsus. (18:12)
>   *At that very moment a fat man **appeared** at the door of the inn.*

>   The perfect tense may also refer to an action that someone has completed as of present time (see Book IB, page 17):

>   Servī meī alium lectum tibi **parāvērunt.** (19:17–18)
>   *My slaves **have prepared** another bed for you.*

6. The pluperfect tense describes an action that was completed before some other action in the past took place (see Book IB, page 79):

>   Titus in itinere mōnstrāvit puerīs mīra aedificia quae prīncipēs in Palātīnō **aedificāverant.** (24:19–20)
>   *Along the way Titus showed the boys the wonderful buildings that the emperors **had built** on the Palatine.*
>   (The emperors had built the buildings *before* Titus showed them to the boys.)

7. The future perfect tense describes an action that will have been completed before some other action in future time begins (see Book IB, page 84):

>   Cum **intrāverimus**, tandem aurīgās ipsōs spectābimus. (26:17–18)
>   *When we **enter/will have entered**, we will finally watch the charioteers themselves.*
>   (The speakers will have entered the Circus Maximus *before* they will watch the charioteers.)

B. Infinitives

The infinitive is the form of the verb marked by "to..." in English (e.g., "to walk") and by the letters *-re* in Latin (e.g., **errāre, rīdēre,**

ascende*re*, and **dormī*re*)** (see Book IA, page 26 and Book IB, page 28). You have seen four uses of the infinitive in Latin sentences:

1. The complementary infinitive (see Book IA, page 26 and Book IB, page 28):

    Sextus arborēs **ascendere** <u>*vult*</u>.   *Sextus <u>wants</u> **to climb** trees.*

    Here the infinitive completes the meaning of the main verb. Other verbs and verbal phrases that are often completed with infinitives are: **nōlle, posse, parāre, solēre, timēre,** and **in animō habēre.**

2. The infinitive with impersonal verbal phrase and impersonal verbs:

    Nōbīs <u>necesse est</u> statim **discēdere.** (9.13)   <u>Licet</u>ne nōbīs hīc **cēnāre?** (20:7)
    To leave *immediately <u>is necessary</u> for us.*   *Is **to dine** here <u>allowed</u> for us?*
    *<u>It is necessary</u> for us **to leave** immediately.*   *Is <u>it allowed</u> for us **to dine** here?*
                                                           May we dine here?

    The verbal phrase **necesse est** and the verb **licet** are said to be impersonal, because we may translate them with the impersonal phrases *it is necessary* and *it is allowed.* In the Latin sentences, however, the infinitives are the grammatical subjects of the verbs.

3. The infinitive as subject of the verb **est** (see Book IB, page 28):

    Etiam in caupōnā **pernoctāre** saepe <u>est</u> perīculōsum. (20:19)
    To spend the night *in an inn <u>is</u> also often dangerous.*
    *<u>It is</u> also often dangerous **to spend the night** in an inn.*

    Here **pernoctāre,** *to spend the night,* is the subject of the sentence, and **perīculōsum** is a complement after the linking verb. It is neuter in gender because the infinitive used as subject functions as a neuter verbal noun.

4. Accusative and infinitive with **docet** and **iubet** (see Book IA, page 72 and Book IB, page 28):

    Aurēlia **Cornēliam** <u>docet</u> vīllam **cūrāre.** (6:11)
    *Aurelia <u>teaches</u> **Cornelia** (how) **to take care of** the country house.*

    Ancillam <u>iubet</u> aliās tunicās et stolās et pallās in cistam **pōnere.** (10:2)
    *<u>She orders</u> **the slave-woman to put** other tunics and stolas and pallas into a chest.*

    Cūr pater meus **nōs exīre** <u>vetat</u>? (26:12)
    *Why <u>does</u> my father <u>forbid</u> **us to go out?***

V. Modifiers

There are many ways in which the thought expressed by a sentence can be elaborated and made fuller and clearer. For example, various kinds of modifiers can be used. Any noun or verb in a sentence can have modifiers.

A. Modifiers of Nouns

1. Adjectives may be used to modify nouns. They must agree with the nouns they modify in gender, case, and number (see Book IA, pages 34–35 and 120–122, and Book IB, pages 5–6):

   Flāvia in vīllā **vīcīnā** habitat. (1:4)
   *Flavia lives in a **neighboring** country house.*

   Cum senātōre **Rōmānō** iter facit. (see Book IA, page 121)
   *He travels with a **Roman** senator.*

   Omnēs vīllās, **omnēs** agrōs, **omnēs** arborēs vident. (see Book IB, page 5)
   *They see **all** the country houses, **all** the fields, **all** the trees.*

2. Adjectives that modify the subject of the verb may sometimes best be translated as adverbs:

   Brevī tempore, ubi Mārcus advenit, eum **laetae** excipiunt. (5:12–13)
   *In a short time, when Marcus arrives, they welcome him **happily.***

3. The Genitive Case

   a. You have also seen a word or phrase in the genitive case used as a modifier (see Book IA, page 80), usually with another noun. The genitive case relates or attaches one noun or phrase to another:

   Dāvus ad portam **vīllae** stat. (11.17)
   *Davus stands near the door **of the country house.***

   The genitive case sometimes indicates possession:

   Vīlicus ipse vīllam **dominī** cūrat. (11:3)
   *The overseer himself looks after **the master's** country house.*

   b. Genitive with Adjectives

   You have also seen words or phrases in the genitive case used with adjectives, such as **plēnus** (see Book IA, page 80):

   Brevī tempore ārea est plēna **servōrum** et **ancillārum.** (11:4)
   *In a short time the space is full **of slaves** and **slave-women.***

   A word or phrase in the genitive is usually used with adjectives of remembering and forgetting:

<u>immemor</u> **terrōris nocturnī** (22:3)
forgetful of his fear during the night

   c. Partitive Genitive or Genitive of the Whole

The genitive case may be used to indicate the whole of which something is a part (partitive genitive or genitive of the whole) (see Book IB, page 95):

"<u>Nihil</u> **malī**," inquit. (21:7)
"*<u>Nothing</u> of a bad thing*," *he said.*
"*Nothing bad*" or "*There is nothing wrong.*"

Crās <u>satis</u> **temporis** habēbimus. (23f:14)
Tomorrow we will have <u>enough</u> (of) time.

<u>Nihil</u> **pecūniae** habeō. (26:26)
I have <u>nothing</u> of money.
I have no money.

With numbers and the words **paucī,** *a few,* **quīdam,** *a certain,* and **nūllus,** *no, no one,* the preposition **ex** or **dē** + ablative is used instead of the partitive genitive:

<u>ūnus</u> **ē praedōnibus** (26:24), <u>*one*</u> *of the pirates*

   4. For subordinate clauses that modify nouns, see section VIII: Main and Subordinate Clauses.

B. Modifiers of Verbs

   1. Adverbs may be used to modify verbs (see Book IA, page 100):

Laeta est Flāvia quod Cornēlia **iam** in vīllā <u>habitat</u>. (1:5)
*Flavia is happy because Cornelia <u>is</u> **now** <u>living</u> in the country house.*

Adverbs may express time (e.g., **adhūc,** *still*), place (e.g., **hīc,** *here*), or manner (e.g., **celeriter,** *quickly*) (see Book IA, pages 100–101).

   2. Dative Case
     a. Indirect Object
       You have met sentences like the following:

Sextus Cornēliam <u>vexat</u>. (4:1)   *Sextus <u>annoys</u> Cornelia.*

These sentences consist of a subject (S) in the nominative case, a direct object (DO) in the accusative case, and a transitive verb (TV).
This pattern may be expanded with a word or phrase in the dative case (as indirect object, IO; see Book IB, page 55):

Servī cistās Cornēliōrum **raedāriō** <u>trādidērunt</u>. (22:2)
*The slaves <u>handed</u> the chests of the Cornelii <u>over</u> **to the coachman.***

(The indirect object, **raedāriō,** tells to whom the slaves handed over the chests.)

b. Dative with Intransitive Verbs

Intransitive verbs (IV) and verbs that may be transitive but are used without a direct object may be accompanied by words or phrases in the dative case (see Book IB, page 55):

(Aulus) **Septimō** clāmāvit. (21:8–9)   *(Aulus) shouted **to Septimus.***

Aulus in somnō **eī** appāruit. (21:4)   *Aulus appeared **to him** in (his) sleep.*

c. Dative with Intransitive Compound Verbs

Many intransitive compound verbs are accompanied by words or phrases in the dative case (see Book IB, page 78):

Iam **urbī** appropinquābant. (22:12)
*Already they were coming near **to the city**/approaching **the city.***

Ibi fortasse **patrī tuō** occurrēmus. (24:17)
*Perhaps we will meet **your father** there.*

d. Dative with Special Intransitive Verbs (see Book IB, page 118)

The dative case is also used with special intransitive verbs, such as **nocēre,** *to do harm (to), harm,* **cōnfīdere,** *to give trust (to), trust,* and **favēre,** *to (give) favor (to), favor, support:*

"Sī **mihi** nocueritis, pater meus certē vōs pūniet." (26:26–27)
*"If you do harm **to me,** my father will certainly punish you."*
*"If you harm **me,** my father will certainly punish you."*

Frātrī Titō nōn cōnfīdō. (26e:14)
*I do not give trust **to (my) brother Titus.***
*I do not trust **(my) brother Titus.***

Ego **russātīs** favēbō. (27:25)
*I will give favor **to the reds.**   I will favor/support **the reds.***

e. You have seen the following use of the dative case with the impersonal verbal phrase **necesse est:**

Cūr **mihi** quoque necesse est ad urbem redīre? (8:13–14)
*Why is it necessary **for me** too to return to the city?*

You have met a similar use of the dative with impersonal verbs such as **licet** (see Book IB, page 56):

"Licetne **nōbīs**," inquit Mārcus, "hīc cēnāre?" (20:7)
*"Is it allowed **for us,**" said Marcus, "to eat here?"*
"May we eat here?"

3. Nouns or phrases in the ablative case without a preposition may be used to modify verbs (see Book IA, pages 90–91). Such nouns or phrases may indicate any of the following:

Cause (see Book IB, page 79):

Tuā culpā raeda <u>est</u> in fossā. (14:7)
Because of your fault the carriage is in the ditch.
It's your fault that the carriage is in the ditch.

Instrument or Means:

Dāvus Getam **baculō** <u>verberat</u>. (12:17–18)
*Davus <u>beats</u> Geta **with his stick**.*

Dāvus Getam **tunicā** <u>arripit</u>. (12:17)
*Davus <u>grabs hold of</u> Geta **by the tunic**.*

Manner: a phrase consisting of a noun and adjective in the ablative case may be used to indicate *how* something happens. This is called the ablative of manner:

Tum venit Dāvus ipse et, "Tacēte, omnēs!" **magnā vōce** <u>clāmat</u>. (11:6)
*Then Davus himself comes, and <u>he shouts</u> **in a loud voice**, "Be quiet, everyone!"*

The preposition **cum** may be found in this construction when the noun is modified by an adjective, e.g., **magnā cum vōce.**

Respect:

In pictūrā est puella, **nōmine** Cornēlia. (1:1)
*There is a girl in the picture, Cornelia **with respect to her name/by name**.*
*There is a girl in the picture, **named** Cornelia.*

Time When:

Etiam in pictūrā est vīlla rūstica ubi Cornēlia **aestāte** <u>habitat</u>. (1:2)
*Also in the picture there is a country house and farm where Cornelia <u>lives</u> **in the summer**.*

Time within Which:

Brevī tempore Flāvia quoque <u>est</u> dēfessa. (2:4–5)
In a short time Flavia <u>is</u> also tired.

4. Prepositional phrases usually modify verbs. Some prepositions are used with the accusative case (see Book IA, page 64):

<u>ad</u> **vīllam** (2:7)	*to/toward **the country house***
Iānitor <u>ad</u> **iānuam** vīllae dormit. (9:3)	*The doorkeeper sleeps <u>near/at</u> **the door** of the country house.*
<u>in</u> **piscīnam** (3:8)	*<u>into</u> **the fishpond***
<u>per</u> **agrōs** (9:1)	*<u>through</u> **the fields***
<u>prope</u> **rīvum** (5:3)	*<u>near</u> **the stream***

With names of cities and the word **domus**, *home*, the accusative case is used without the preposition **ad** to express the idea "to":

"Eugepae!" clāmat Sextus, quī **Rōmam** īre vult. (7:14)
*"Hurray!" shouts Sextus, who wants to go **to Rome**.*

Prīmum Aurēliam et Cornēliam **domum** dūcam. (23:10)
*First I will take Aurelia and Cornelia **home**.*

Some prepositions are used with the ablative case (see Book IA, pages 64 and 90):

<u>ab</u> **urbe** (13:12)	<u>*from*</u> **the city**
<u>cum</u> **canibus** (12:9)	<u>*with*</u> **dogs**
<u>ē</u> **silvā**	<u>*out of*</u> **the woods**
<u>ex</u> **agrīs** (2:7)	<u>*out of*</u> **the fields**
<u>in</u> **pictūrā** (1:1)	<u>*in*</u> **the picture**
<u>sub</u> **arbore** (1:3)	<u>*under*</u> **the tree**

5. For subordinate clauses that modify verbs, see section VIII: Main and Subordinate Clauses.

VI. Other Uses of Cases

A. The accusative case is used in exclamations:

Ō mē miseram! (9:18)   ***Poor me!***

B. The vocative case is used when addressing a person or persons directly (see page 56):

Dēscende, **Sexte!** (4:7)   *Come down, **Sextus!***

VII. Conjunctions

Conjunctions (Latin **con-**, *together* + **iungere**, *to join*) are words that join things together. A conjunction may show a relationship between sentences. For example, **igitur**, *therefore*, indicates that a sentence describes the result or consequence of what was said in the previous sentence:

Sextus est puer molestus quī semper Cornēliam vexat. Cornēlia **igitur** Sextum nōn amat. (4:1–2)
*Sextus is an annoying boy who always annoys Cornelia. Cornelia, **therefore**, does not like Sextus.*

Other conjunctions may join elements within sentences that are added to one another and are of equal grammatical importance:

Cīvēs, mercātōrēs, servī per portam <u>ībant</u> **atque** hūc illūc <u>currēbant</u>. (23:2)
*Citizens, merchants, slaves <u>were going</u> through the gate **and** <u>were running</u> this way and that.*

Cornēlia <u>sedet</u> **et** <u>legit</u>. (1:3)
*Cornelia <u>sits</u> **and** <u>reads</u>.*

Etiam Sextus <u>dormit</u> **neque** Cornēliam <u>vexat</u>. (6:2)
*Even Sextus <u>is sleeping</u> **and** <u>is **not** annoying</u> Cornelia.*

Mārcus **neque** <u>ignāvus</u> **neque** <u>temerārius</u> est. (5:5–6)
*Marcus is **neither** <u>cowardly</u> **nor** <u>rash</u>.*

Hodiē puellae nōn <u>sedent</u> **sed** in agrīs <u>ambulant</u>. (2:2–3)
*Today the girls <u>are not sitting</u> **but** <u>are walking</u> in the fields.*

VIII. Main and Subordinate Clauses

A clause is a group of words containing a verb. The following sentence contains two clauses, each of which is said to be a *main clause* because each could stand by itself as a complete sentence:

Rīdent Mārcus et Cornēlia, sed nōn rīdet Sextus. (4:10–11)
Marcus and Cornelia laugh, but Sextus does not laugh.

The clauses in this sentence are said to be *coordinate* (Latin **co-**, *together, same* + **ōrdō**, *order, rank*), and the conjunction that joins them, **sed**, is said to be a *coordinating conjunction*. For other coordinating conjunctions, see the examples in section VII: Conjunctions.

Subordinate (Latin **sub-**, *below* + **ōrdō**, *order, rank*) clauses are clauses that are of less grammatical importance than the main clause in a sentence. They are sometimes called dependent (Latin **dē-**, *down from* + **pendēre**, *to hang*) clauses because they hang down from the main clause and cannot stand by themselves. They are joined to the main clause by pronouns, adverbs, or conjunctions.

Subordinate clauses are modifiers. They may be descriptive, like adjectives, and modify nouns:

Cornēlia est puella Rōmāna **quae** in Italiā habitat. (1:1–2)
*Cornelia is a Roman girl **who** <u>lives in Italy</u>.*

Etiam in pictūrā est vīlla rūstica **ubi** Cornēlia aestāte habitat. (1:2)
*Also in the picture there is a country house and farm **where** <u>Cornelia lives in the summer</u>.*

But most subordinate clauses are adverbial, that is, they modify the verb of the main clause or the action of the main clause as a whole and are introduced by subordinating conjunctions that express ideas such as the following:

Cause:

Cornēlia est laeta **quod** iam in vīllā habitat. (1:2–3)
*Cornelia is happy **because** <u>she now lives in the country house</u>.*

Concession:

Quamquam dominus abest, necesse est nōbīs strēnuē labōrāre. (11:7)
Although the master is away, it is necessary for us to work hard.

Condition:

Sī tū puer strēnuus es, ascende arborem!
If you are an energetic boy, climb a tree!

Time:

Dum Cornēlia legit, Flāvia scrībit. (1:4–5)
While Cornelia reads, Flavia writes.

Dum per viam ībant, Aurēlia et Cornēlia spectābant rūsticōs quī in agrīs labōrābant. (13:3–4)
While/As long as they were going along the road, Aurelia and Cornelia were looking at the peasants who were working in the fields.

Dum puerī cibum dēvorant, subitō intrāvit mīles quīdam. (20:13)
While the boys were devouring their food, a certain soldier suddenly entered.
(Here the present tense verb in the **dum** clause is to be translated with the English past tense that describes ongoing action.) (See Book IB, page 27.)

Puerī, **ubi** clāmōrem audiunt, statim ad puellās currunt. (5:10)
The boys, when they hear the shout, immediately run to the girls.

Crās, **ubi** surgētis, puerī, clāmōrem et strepitum audiētis.
Tomorrow, when you get up/will get up, boys, you will hear shouting and noise.

Cum intrāverimus, tandem aurīgās ipsōs spectābimus. (26:17–18)
When we enter/will have entered, we will finally watch the charioteers themselves.
(While the verbs of the subordinate clauses in the two Latin sentences just above are in the future, **surgētis**, and future perfect, **intrāverimus**, we translate them into English as presents; see Book IB, page 84. The use of the tenses is more exact in Latin.)

Words you have met that may introduce subordinate clauses are:

cum, *when* (22:12)
dum, *as long as* (15:1)
dum, *while* (20:13)
nisi, *if not, unless* (18:16)
postquam, *after* (20b:6)
quamquam, *although* (11:7)
quī, masc., **quae,** fem., **quod,**
    neut., *who, which, that* (1:1)

quod, *because* (1:3)
sī, *if* (5:1)
simulac, *as soon as* (24:1)
ubi, *when* (5:10)
ubi, *where* (1:2)
ut, *as* (16:17)

PRONUNCIATION OF LATIN

Consonants

The Latin alphabet does not have the letters *j* or *w*; the letter *i* before a vowel is a consonant and is pronounced as *y*, and *v* is pronounced as *w*. The letters *k*, *y*, and *z* occur in few Latin words, the latter two letters only in words taken over by the Romans from their neighbors the Greeks.

In pronouncing Latin you will find the following rules of use.

Most consonants are pronounced as in English, but the following should be noted:
b before **s** or **t** is pronounced as English *p*: **urbs, observat.**
c is always hard and pronounced as English *k*: **cadit.**
g is hard, as in English "get": **gemit.**
gn in the middle of a word may be pronounced as the *ngn* in English "hangnail": **magnus.**
i before a vowel is a consonant and is pronounced as English *y*: **iam.**
r should be rolled: **rāmus.**
s is pronounced as in English "sing," never as in "roses": **servus.**
v is pronounced as English *w*: **vīlla.**

Vowels

The following approximations are offered for the pronunciation of short and long vowels. In addition, long vowels should be held approximately twice as long as short vowels.

Short	Long
a = English "aha" (**ad**)	**ā** = English "father" (**clāmat**)
e = English "pet" (**ex**)	**ē** = English "date" (**dēscendit**)
i = English "sip" (**Italia**)	**ī** = English "sleep" (**īrātus**)
o = English "for" (**arborem**)	**ō** = English "holy" (**in hortō**)
u = English "foot" (**ubi**)	**ū** = English "boot" (**fūrtim**)

The diphthong **ae** is pronounced as the *y* in English "sky" (**amīcae**). The diphthong **au** is pronounced as the *ow* in English "how" (**audit**). The diphthong **ei** is pronounced as the "ay" in English "say" (**deinde**).

Syllables

In dividing Latin words into syllables, note the following rules:

1. A single consonant between two vowels usually goes with the second vowel:

    nō-mi-ne   Rō-mā-na   vī-cī-na

2. Two consonants between vowels are usually divided between the syllables:

    pu-el-la   pic-tū-ra   rūs-ti-ca

Accents

Latin words are accented according to simple rules:

1. If the next to the last syllable (the *penult*) has a long vowel or a diphthong, it will receive the accent:

    discédō

2. If the penult has a short vowel followed by two consonants, it will usually receive the accent:

    exténdō

3. Otherwise, the accent falls on the third syllable from the end (the *antepenult*):

    Británnicus

4. Almost all words of two syllables are accented on the first syllable:

    For example: **légit**   Exception: **adhúc**

Careful observation of the long marks (macrons) over vowels will thus help with both pronunciation and accenting of Latin words.

Latin to English Vocabulary

Latin words in boldface are for mastery; those not in boldface are for recognition. Numbers in parentheses at the end of entries refer to the chapters in which the words appear in vocabulary entries or in Building the Meaning or Forms sections. Roman numerals refer to Review chapters.

A

ā or **ab**, prep. + abl., *from* (13)

ábeō, abíre, ábiī or **abívī, abitúrus,** irreg., *to go away* (3, 9)

  Ábī!/Abíte! *Go away!* (3)

abhínc, adv., *ago, previously* (25)

ábsum, abésse, áfuī, āfutúrus, irreg., *to be away, be absent, be distant* (11, 25)

áccidit, accídere, áccidit, *(it) happens* (14, 26)

accúsō, -áre, -ávī, -átus, *to accuse* (21)

ad, prep. + acc., *to, toward, at, near* (2, 9)

adhúc, adv., *still* (5, 13)

ádiuvō, adiuváre, adiúvī, adiútus, *to help* (6, 21)

admóveō, admovére, admóvī, admótus, *to move toward* (22)

ádsum, adésse, ádfuī, adfutúrus, irreg., *to be present* (26)

advéniō, adveníre, advénī, adventúrus, *to reach, arrive (at)* (5, 23)

advesperáscit, advesperáscere, advesperávit, *it gets dark* (17)

aedifícium, -ī, n., *building* (17)

aedíficō, -áre, -ávī, -átus, *to build* (24)

aéstās, aestátis, f., *summer* (1)

  aestáte, *in the summer* (1, 12)

aéstus, -ūs, m., *heat* (24, 25)

áger, ágrī, m., *field* (2)

agnóscō, agnóscere, agnóvī, ágnitus, *to recognize* (18)

ágō, ágere, égī, áctus, *to do, drive* (8, 14, 23)

  Áge!/Ágite! *Come on!* (8)

  Grátiās tíbi ágō! *I thank you! Thank you!* (26)

  Quid ágis? *How are you?* (18)

albátus, -a, -um, *white* (27)

áliquid, *something* (25)

áliter, adv., *otherwise* (26)

álius, ália, áliud, *another, other* (10)

  áliī...áliī..., *some...others...* (9)

  álius...álius, *one...another*

álter, áltera, álterum, *second, one (of two), the other (of two), another* (1)

  álter...álter, *the one...the other* (16)

ámbulō, -áre, -ávī, -atúrus, *to walk* (2)

amíca, -ae, f., *friend* (2)

amícus, -ī, m., *friend* (3)

ámō, -áre, -ávī, -átus, *to like, love* (4)

amphitheátrum, -ī, n., *amphitheater* (25)

ancílla, -ae, f., *slave-woman* (6)

ánimus, -ī, m., *mind* (16)

  ánimum recuperáre, *to regain one's senses, wake up* (21)

  in ánimō habére, *to intend* (16)

ánteā, adv., *previously, before* (20)

antíquus, -a, -um, *ancient* (26)

apériō, aperíre, apéruī, apértus, *to open* (16, 26)

appáreō, -ére, -uī, -itúrus, *to appear* (15, 18)

appéllō, -áre, -ávī, -átus, *to call, name* (21)

appropínquō, -áre, -ávī, -atúrus + dat. or **ad** + acc., *to approach, come near (to)* (4, 22)

ápud, prep. + acc., *at the house of, with, in front of, before* (16, 26)

áqua, -ae, f., *water* (6)

aquaedúctus, -ūs, m., *aqueduct* (23, 25)

árbor, árboris, f., *tree* (1)

árcus, -ūs, m., *arch* (24, 25)

área, -ae, f., *open space, threshing floor* (11)

arrípiō, arrípere, arrípuī, arréptus, *to grab hold of, snatch, seize* (5, 19, 26)

ars, ártis, gen. pl., **ártium,** f., *skill* (14)

ascéndō, ascéndere, ascéndī, ascénsus, *to climb, climb into (a carriage)* (4, 22)

Ásia, -ae, f., *Asia (Roman province in western Asia Minor)* (21)

at, conj., *but* (23)

átque, conj., *and, and also* (22)

átrium, -ī, n., *atrium, main room* (26)

atténtē, adv., *attentively, closely* (20)

attónitus, -a, -um, *astonished, astounded* (24)

aúdiō, -íre, -ívī, -ítus, *to hear, listen to* (4, 20)

aúreus, -a, -um, *golden* (25)

auríga, -ae, m., *charioteer* (13)

aúrum, -ī, n., *gold* (21)

aut... aut..., conj., *either...or...* (26)

auxílium, -ī, n., *help* (5, 15)

    Fer/Férte auxílium! *Bring help! Help!* (5)

B

báculum, -ī, n., *stick, staff* (10, 15)

Báiae, -árum, f. pl., *Baiae*

béne, adv., *well* (22)

bónus, -a, -um, *good* (12)

    bóna, -órum, n. pl., *goods, possessions* (26)

bōs, bóvis, m./f., *ox, cow* (15)

brévis, -is, -e, *short* (2)

    brévī témpore, *in a short time, soon* (2, 12)

Británnia, -ae, f., *Britain* (8)

Británnicus, -a, -um, *British* (3)

C

cádō, cádere, cécidī, cāsúrus, *to fall* (3, 22)

caélum, -ī, n., *sky* (17)

Caésar, Caésaris, m., *Caesar, emperor* (27)

cálidus, -a, -um, *warm* (5)

Calígula, -ae, m., *Caligula (emperor, A.D. 37–41)* (27)

cánis, cánis, m./f., *dog* (12)

cántō, -áre, -ávī, -átus, *to sing* (21)

cápiō, cápere, cépī, cáptus, *to take, catch capture* (21)

captívus, -ī, m., *prisoner* (26)

cáput, cápitis, n., *head* (25)

cāríssimus, -a, -um, *dearest* (16)

caúda, -ae, f., *tail* (18)

caúpō, caupónis, m., *innkeeper* (17)

caupóna, -ae, f., *inn* (17, 20)

caúsa, -ae, f., *reason* (25)

cáveō, cavére, cávī, caútus, *to be careful, watch out (for), beware (of)* (4, 13, 23)

    Cávē!/Cavéte! *Be careful! Watch out (for)! Beware (of)!* (4, 13, 23)

celériter, adv., *quickly* (8, 13)

    celérrimē, adv., *very fast, very quickly* (14)

célō, -áre, -ávī, -átus, *to hide* (11)

céna, -ae, f., *dinner* (19)

cénō, -áre, -ávī, -átus, *to dine, eat dinner* (19)

céntum, *a hundred* (15)

cértē, adv., *certainly* (19)

céssō, -áre, -ávī, -ātúrus, *to be idle, do nothing, delay* (14)

cíbus, -ī, m., *food* (6)

circénsis, -is, -e, *in/of the circus* (27)

    lúdī circénsēs, *games in the circus, chariot races* (27)

circúmeō, circumíre, circúmiī or **circumívī, circúmitus,** irreg., *to go around* (24)

Círcus Máximus, -ī, m., *Circus Maximus (a stadium in Rome)* (23)

císium, -ī, n., *light two-wheeled carriage* (14, 15)

císta, -ae, f., *trunk, chest* (10)

cívis, cívis, gen. pl., **cívium,** m./f., *citizen* (13)

clámō, -áre, -ávī, -ātúrus, *to shout* (3)

clámor, clāmóris, m., *shout, shouting* (5)

claúdō, claúdere, claúsī, claúsus, *to shut* (26)

    claúsus, -a, -um, *shut, closed* (24)

clíēns, cliéntis, gen. pl., **cliéntium,** m., *client, dependent* (25)

cógitō, -áre, -ávī, -átus, *to think* (21)

collóquium, -ī, n., *conversation* (26)

cólō, cólere, cóluī, cúltus, *to cultivate* (23)

commótus, -a, -um, *moved* (14)

compléxus, -ūs, m., *embrace* (9, 25)

    compléxū, *in an embrace* (9)

cóncidō, concídere, cóncidī, *to fall down* (14)

condúcō, condúcere, condúxī, condúctus, *to hire* (23)

cōnfíciō, cōnfícere, cōnfḗcī, cōnféctus, *to finish* (25)

cōnfídō, cōnfídere + dat., *to give trust (to), trust* (26)

coníciō, conícere, coniḗcī, coniéctus, *to throw* (21)

cóniūnx, cóniugis, m./f., *husband, wife* (26)

cōnsídō, cōnsídere, cōnsḗdī, *to sit down* (23)

cōnspíciō, cōnspícere, cōnspéxī, cōnspéctus, *to catch sight of* (4, 21)

cōnstítuō, cōnstitúere, cōnstítuī, cōnstitútus, *to decide* (23)

cōnsulō, cōnsúlere, cōnsúluī, cōnsúltus, *to consult* (7)

cónvocō, -áre, -ávī, -átus, *to call together* (12)

cóquō, cóquere, cóxī, cóctus, *to cook* (6)

Cornēliánus, -a, -um, *belonging to Cornelius, Cornelian* (10)

Cornéliī, -órum, m. pl., *the Cornelii* (10)

córpus, córporis, n., *body* (21)

crās, adv., *tomorrow* (10, 13)

crótalum, -ī, n., *castanet* (21)

cubículum, -ī, n., *room, bedroom* (8, 15)

cúbitum íre, *to go to bed* (19)

cui, *to whom, to him, to her* (19)

Cúius…? *Whose…?* (22)

culína, -ae, f., *kitchen* (21)

cúlpa, -ae, f., *fault, blame* (14)

cum, conj., *when* (22)

cum, prep. + abl., *with* (12)

cúnctī, -ae, -a, *all* (14)

Cūr…? adv., *Why…?* (1)

Cúria, -ae, f., *Senate House* (23)

cúrō, -áre, -ávī, -átus, *to look after, take care of* (6)

currículum, -ī, n., *racetrack* (27)

cúrrō, cúrrere, cucúrrī, cursúrus, *to run* (2, 23)

custódiō, -íre, -ívī, -ítus, *to guard* (17)

cústōs, custódis, m., *guard* (26)

D

dē, prep. + abl., *down from, concerning, about* (16)

débeō, -ére, -uī, -itúrus + infin., *ought* (26)

décem, *ten* (15)

dēféndō, dēféndere, dēféndī, dēfḗnsus, *to defend* (1)

dēféssus, -a, -um, *tired* (2)

deínde, adv., *then, next* (8, 13)

dēmónstrō, -áre, -ávī, -átus, *to show* (24)

dēscéndō, dēscéndere, dēscéndī, dēscēnsúrus, *to come/go down, climb down* (4, 23)

dēsíderō, -áre, -ávī, -átus, *to long for, miss* (26)

dēvértō, dēvértere, dēvértī, dēvérsus, *to turn aside* (14, 27)

dévorō, -áre, -ávī, -átus, *to devour* (20)

dícō, dícere, díxī, díctus, *to say, tell* (20, 21)

díēs, diḗī, m., *day* (5, 13, 25)

éō díē, *on that day* (25)

dīligénter, adv., *carefully* (19)

discédō, discédere, discéssī, discessúrus, *to go away, depart* (9, 22)

díū, adv., *for a long time* (15)

dō, dáre, dédī, dátus, *to give* (21)

sē quiétī dáre, *to rest* (23)

dóceō, docére, dócuī, dóctus, *to teach* (6, 21)

dóleō, -ére, -uī, -itúrus, *to be sad* (18)

dómina, -ae, f., *mistress, lady of the house* (17)

dóminus, -ī, m., *master, owner* (11)

dómus, -ūs, f., *house, home* (23, 25)

dómī, *at home* (26)

dómum, *homeward, hence* (23)

dórmiō, -íre, -ívī, -itúrus, *to sleep* (4)

dúcō, dúcere, dúxī, dúctus, *to lead, take, bring* (7, 19, 20)

dum, conj., *while, as long as* (1)

dúo, dúae, dúo, *two* (15)

E

ē or ex, prep. + abl., *from, out of* (2, 5, 9)

éam, *her, it* (9, 16)

eárum, *their* (27)

Écce! interj., *Look! Look at!* (1)

effúgiō, effúgere, effúgī, *to flee, run away, escape* (11, 21)

égo, *I* (5, 27)

Éheu! interj., *Alas! oh no!* (7)

Ého! interj., *Hey!* (25)

éī, *to him/her/it* (21)

éī, éae, éa, *they* (22, 27)

éīs, *to them* (22)

éius, *his, her(s), its* (2, 27)

émō, émere, émī, émptus, *to buy* (21)

énim, conj., *for* (20)

éō, íre, íī or **ívī, itúrus,** irreg., *to go* (7, 17, 19, 20, 21)

    cúbitum íre, *to go to bed* (19)

éō, adv., *there, to that place* (23)

éō díē, *on that day* (25)

éō ípsō témpore, *at that very moment* (10)

eórum, *their* (25, 27)

éōs, *them* (5)

epístula, -ae, f., *letter* (7)

équus, -ī, m., *horse* (10)

érat, *(he/she/it) was* (13)

érrō, -áre, -ávī, -ātúrus, *to wander, be mistaken* (5, 18)

ērúptiō, ēruptiónis, f., *eruption* (26)

ésse (see **sum**)

est, *(he/she/it) is* (1)

Éstō! *All right!* (20)

ēsúriō, -íre, _____, -ītúrus, *to be hungry* (19)

et, conj., *and* (1)

étiam, adv., *also, even* (1, 6, 13)

Eúgepae! interj., *Hurray!* (7)

éum, *him, it* (5)

ex or **ē,** prep. + abl., *from, out of* (2, 5, 9)

excípiō, excípere, excépī, excéptus, *to welcome, receive, catch* (5, 16, 22)

éxcitō, -áre, -ávī, -átus, *to rouse, wake (someone) up* (8)

    excitátus, -a, -um, *wakened, aroused* (25)

exclámō, -áre, -ávī, -átus, *to exclaim, shout out* (10)

éxeō, exíre, éxiī or **exívī, exitúrus,** irreg., *to go out* (5, 23)

éxplicō, -áre, -ávī, -átus, *to explain* (19)

    rem explicáre, *to explain the situation* (19)

exspéctō, -áre, -ávī, -átus, *to look out for, wait for* (15)

éxstāns, exstántis, *standing out, towering* (23)

exténdō, exténdere, exténdī, exténtus, *to hold out* (18)

éxtrā, prep. + acc., *outside* (23)

éxtrahō, extráhere, extráxī, extráctus, *to drag out, take out* (14, 21)

F

fábula, -ae, f., *story* (20)

fáciō, fácere, fécī, fáctus, *to make, do* (1, 23)

    íter fácere, *to travel* (13)

    Quid fácit...? *What does...do? What is... doing?* (1)

    Quid fécit...? *What did...do?* (19)

fáctiō, factiónis, f., *company (of charioteers)* (27)

fátuus, -a, -um, *stupid* (13)

fáveō, favére, fávī, fautúrus + dat., *to give favor (to), favor, support* (27)

félēs, félis, gen. pl., félium, f., *cat* (21)

fémina, -ae, f., *woman* (3)

fériae, -árum, f. pl., *holiday, festival day* (27)

fēriátus, -a, -um, *celebrating a holiday* (27)

fériō, -íre, *to hit, strike* (16)

férō, férre, túlī, látus, irreg., *to bring, carry, bear* (5, 12, 17, 21)

    Fer/Férte auxílium! *Bring help! Help!* (5)

feróciter, adv., *fiercely* (13)

festínō, -áre, -ávī, -átúrus, *to hurry* (9)

fília, -ae, f., *daughter* (11)

fílius, -ī, m., *son* (11)

fíniō, -íre, -ívī, -ítus, *to finish* (21)

fortásse, adv., *perhaps* (15)

fórtis, -is, -e, *brave, strong* (18)

Fórum, -ī, n., *the Forum (city center of Rome)* (25)

fóssa, -ae, f., *ditch* (12)

frágor, fragóris, m., *crash, noise, din* (4)

fráter, frátris, m., *brother* (11)

frígidus, -a, -um, *cool, cold* (5)

frōns, fróntis, gen. pl., fróntium, f., *forehead* (12)

frústrā, adv., *in vain* (14)

fúgiō, fúgere, fúgī, fugitúrus, *to flee* (18, 25)

fúī (see **sum**)

fúrtim, adv., *stealthily* (4, 13)

G

Gádēs, Gádium, f. pl., *Gades (Cadiz, a town in Spain)* (21)

gaúdeō, gaudére, *to be glad, rejoice* (14)

gaúdium, -ī, n., *joy* (23)

gémō, gémere, gémuī, gémitus, *to groan* (3)

gérō, gérere, géssī, géstus, *to wear* (10)

gládius, -ī, m., *sword* (26)

  gládium stríngere, *to draw a sword* (26)

Graécia, -ae, f., *Greece* (21)

Graécus, -a, -um, *Greek* (17)

  Graécī, -órum, m. pl., *the Greeks* (I)

grátia, -ae, f., *gratitude, thanks* (26)

  Grátiās tíbi ágō! *I thank you! Thank you!* (26)

H

habénae, -árum, f. pl., *reins* (22)

hábeō, -ére, -uī, -itus, *to have, hold* (10, 20, 26)

  in ánimō habére, *to intend* (16)

  ōrātiónem habére, *to deliver a speech* (26)

hábitō, -áre, -ávī, -átus, *to live, dwell* (1)

hāc, *this* (25)

haéreō, haerére, haésī, haesúrus, *to stick* (14)

héri, adv., *yesterday* (20)

hī, *these* (18)

hīc, adv., *here* (9, 13)

hic, haec, hoc, *this, the latter* (18, 19, 20, 25, 26)

hódiē, adv., *today* (2, 13)

hómō, hóminis, m., *man* (18)

  hóminēs, hóminum, m. pl., *people* (15)

hóra, -ae, f., *hour* (9)

hórtus, -ī, m., *garden* (3)

hóspes, hóspitis, m./f., *host, guest, friend* (16)

hūc illúc, adv., *here and there, this way and that* (23)

húius (genitive of **hic**) (25)

húmī, *on the ground* (27)

I

iáceō, -ére, -uī, -itúrus, *to lie, be lying down* (26)

iáciō, iácere, iécī, iáctus, *to throw* (10, 20)

iam, adv., *now, already* (1, 8, 13)

  nōn iam, adv., *no longer* (2, 13)

iánitor, iānitóris, m., *doorkeeper* (9)

iánua, -ae, f., *door* (9)

íbi, adv., *there* (5, 13)

id (see **is**)

  id quod, *that which, what* (11)

ídem, éadem, ídem, *the same* (3)

idéntidem, adv., *again and again, repeatedly* (13)

ígitur, conj., *therefore* (4)

ignávus, -a, -um, *cowardly, lazy* (5)

ílle, ílla, íllud, *that, he, she, it, the former* (11, 15, 16, 20, 22, 25, 26)

illúc, adv., *there, to that place* (23)

  hūc illúc, adv., *here and there, this way and that* (23)

ímber, ímbris, gen. pl., **ímbrium** m., *rain* (23)

ímmemor, immémoris + gen., *forgetful* (22)

immóbilis, -is, -e, *motionless* (12)

impédiō, -íre, -ívī, -ítus, *to hinder, prevent* (11)

in, prep. + abl., *in, on* (1, 9)

  in ánimō habére, *to intend* (16)

  in itínere, *on a journey* (10)

in, prep. + acc., *into, against* (3, 9)

íncitō, -áre, -ávī, -átus, *to spur on, urge on, drive* (10)

incólumis, -is, -e, *unhurt, safe and sound* (14)

índuō, indúere, índuī, indútus, *to put on* (8, 23)

īnfírmus, -a, -um, *weak, shaky* (4)

íngēns, ingéntis, *huge* (22)

innocéntia, -ae, f., *innocence* (21)

ínquit, *(he/she) says, said* (7)

īnspíciō, īnspícere, īnspéxī, īnspéctus, *to examine* (21)

intérdiū, adv., *during the day, by day* (23)

intéreā, adv., *meanwhile* (10, 13)

interpéllō, -áre, -ávī, -átus, *to interrupt* (14)

íntrā, prep. + acc., *inside* (22)

íntrō, -áre, -ávī, -átus, *to enter, go into* (8, 19)

inū́rō, inū́rere, inū́ssī, inū́stus, *to brand* (12)

invéniō, invenī́re, invḗnī, invéntus, *to come upon, find* (12, 21)

invī́tus, -a, -um, *unwilling* (21)

iócus, -ī, m., *joke, prank* (16)

per iócum, *as a prank* (16)

ípse, ípsa, ípsum, *himself, herself, itself, themselves, very* (6, 10)

íra, -ae, f., *anger* (11)

īrátus, -a, -um, *angry* (3)

íre (see **éō**) (7, 17)

is, ea, id, *he, she, it; this, that* (27)

íta, adv., *thus, so, in this way* (3, 13, 21)

Íta vḗrō! adv., *Yes! Indeed!* (3, 13)

Itália, -ae, f., *Italy* (1)

ítaque, adv., *and so, therefore* (16)

íter, itíneris, n., *journey* (10, 13, 15)

íter fácere, *to travel* (13)

íterum, adv., *again, a second time* (8, 13)

iúbeō, iubḗre, iússī, iússus, *to order, bid* (10, 19, 21)

L

lábor, labóris, m., *work, toil* (24)

labórō, -áre, -ávī, -átus, *to work* (3)

labōrántēs, *working* (7)

lácrimō, -áre, -ávī, -átus, *to weep, cry* (9)

lácrimāns, *weeping* (9)

laétus, -a, -um, *happy, glad* (1)

lā́na, -ae, f., *wool* (6)

lā́nam tráhere, *to spin wool* (6)

lápis, lápidis, m., *stone* (25)

lā́trō, -áre, -ávī, -ātū́rus, *to bark* (12)

lātrántēs, *barking* (18)

laúdō, -áre, -ávī, -átus, *to praise* (18)

lávō, laváre, lā́vī, laútus, *to wash* (20)

lectī́ca, -ae, f., *litter* (23)

lectīcárius, -ī, m., *litter-bearer* (23)

léctus, -ī, m., *bed, couch* (19)

lēgátus, -ī, m., *envoy* (18)

légō, légere, lḗgī, léctus, *to read* (1, 24)

léntē, adv., *slowly* (2, 13)

líber, líbrī, m., *book* (24)

líberī, -órum, m. pl., *children* (10, 11)

lībértās, lībertátis, f., *freedom* (21)

lícet, licére, lícuit + dat., *it is allowed* (20, 24)

lícet nóbīs, *we are allowed, we may* (20)

líttera, -ae, f., *letter (of the alphabet)* (12)

lóngus, -a, -um, *long* (15)

lū́cet, lūcére, lū́xit, *it is light, it is day* (6)

lū́dī, -órum, m. pl., *games* (24)

lū́dī circénsēs, *games in the circus, chariot races* (27)

lū́dō, lū́dere, lū́sī, lūsū́rus, *to play* (16)

pílā lū́dere, *to play ball* (16)

lū́dus, -ī, m., *school* (26)

lúpa, -ae, f., *she-wolf* (II)

lúpus, -ī, m., *wolf* (5)

lútum, -ī, n., *mud* (26)

lūx, lū́cis, f., *light* (21)

prī́mā lū́ce, *at dawn* (21)

M

magníficus, -a, -um, *magnificent* (24)

mágnus, -a, -um, *big, great, large, loud (voice, laugh)* (4)

mágnā vóce, *in a loud voice* (4)

mágnō rī́sū, *with a loud laugh* (13)

málus, -a, -um, *bad* (21)

níhil málī, *nothing of a bad thing, there is nothing wrong* (21)

mandátum, -ī, n., *order, instruction* (22)

mā́nc, adv., *early in the day, in the morning* (21)

máneō, manére, mā́nsī, mā́nsus, *to remain, stay, wait (for)* (9, 20, 23)

mánus, -ūs, f., *hand* (18, 25)

máppa, -ae, f., *napkin, white cloth* (27)

máter, mátris, f., *mother* (6, 11)

máximus, -a, -um, *greatest, very great, very large* (23)

mē, *me* (4)

mécum, *with me* (9)

médius, -a, -um, *mid-, middle of* (20)

média nox, médiae nóctis, f., *midnight* (20)

Mégara, -ae, f., *Megara (a city in Greece)* (21)

Mehércule! interj., *By Hercules! Goodness me!* (18)

mélior, mélius, gen., **melióris,** *better* (19)

mercátor, mercātóris, m., *merchant* (22)

méta, -ae, f., *mark, goal, turning post* (27)

métus, -ūs, m., *fear* (26)
méus, -a, -um, *my, mine* (7)
míhi, *for me, to me* (8)
míles, mílitis, m., *soldier* (20)
mílle, *a thousand* (15)
Mínimē! *No! Not at all!* (3, 13)
mírus, -a, -um, *wonderful, marvelous,*
   strange (23)
míser, mísera, míserum, *unhappy,*
   miserable, wretched (9)
míttō, míttere, mísī, míssus, *to send* (9, 20)
módo, adv., *only* (18)
mólēs, mólis, gen. pl., **mólium,** f., *mass,*
   huge bulk (24)
moléstus, -a, -um, *troublesome, annoying* (4)
  moléstus, -ī, m., *pest* (3)
mōns, móntis, gen. pl., **móntium,** m.,
   mountain, hill (24)
   Mōns Vesúvius, Montis Vesúviī, m., *Mount*
    Vesuvius (a volcano in southern Italy) (26)
mónstrō, -áre, -ávī, -átus, *to show* (22)
mors, mórtis, gen. pl., **mórtium,** f., *death*
   (21)
mórtuus, -a, -um, *dead* (16)
móveō, movére, móvī, mótus, *to move*
   (14, 24)
mox, adv., *soon, presently* (6, 13)
múlier, mulíeris, f., *woman* (27)
múltī, -ae, -a, *many* (3)
multitúdō, multitúdinis, f., *crowd* (23)
múrmur, múrmuris, n., *murmur,*
   rumble (15)
múrus, -ī, m., *wall* (23)
mūs, múris, m., *mouse* (21)
mússō, -áre, -ávī, -atúrus, *to mutter* (11)

N

nam, conj., *for* (8)
nārrátor, nārrātóris, m., *narrator* (8)
nárrō, -áre, -ávī, -átus, *to tell (a story)* (20)
  nārrátus, -a, -um, *told* (20)
-ne (indicates a yes or no question) (3)
Neápolis, Neápolis, f., *Naples* (15)
necésse, adv. or indeclinable adj.,
   necessary (6)
nécō, -áre, -ávī, -átus, *to kill* (20)

némō, néminis, m./f., *no one* (9)
néque, conj., *and...not* (6)
  néque...néque, conj., *neither...nor* (5)
nésciō, -íre, -ívī, -ítus, *to be ignorant, not to*
   know (9)
níhil, *nothing* (4)
  níhil málī, *nothing of a bad thing, there is*
   nothing wrong (21)
nísi, conj., *unless, if...not, except* (18, 26)
nóbīs, *for us, to us* (9)
  nōbíscum, *with us* (16)
nóceō, -ére, -uī, -itúrus + dat., *to do harm*
   (to), harm (26)
nócte, *at night* (12)
noctúrnus, -a, -um, *happening during the night* (22)
nólō, nólle, nóluī, irreg., *not to wish, not to*
   want, to be unwilling (5, 17, 21)
  Nólī/Nólíte + infin., *Don't...!* (9)
nómen, nóminis, n., *name* (1, 15)
  nómine, *by name, named* (1)
nōn, adv., *not* (2, 13)
  nōn iam, adv., *no longer* (2, 13)
nóndum, adv., *not yet* (6, 13)
Nónne...? *Surely...?* (introduces a question that
   expects the answer "yes") (19)
nōnnúmquam, adv., *sometimes* (26)
nónus, -a, -um, *ninth* (16)
nōs, *we, us* (8, 27)
nóster, nóstra, nóstrum, *our* (14, 27)
nóvem, *nine* (15)
nóvus, -a, -um, *new* (16)
nox, nóctis, gen. pl., **nóctium,** f., *night* (11)
  íllā nócte, *that night* (11)
  média nox, *midnight* (20)
  nócte, *at night* (12)
núbēs, núbis, gen. pl., **núbium,** f., *cloud* (15)
núllus, -a, -um, *no, not any* (9)
númerus, -ī, m., *number* (11)
númquam, adv., *never* (20)
nunc, adv., *now* (6, 13)
núntius, -ī, m., *messenger* (7)

O

ō, interj., used with vocative and in
   exclamations (9)
  Ō mē míseram! *Poor me! Oh dear me!* (9)

obdórmiō, -íre, -ívī, -ītū́rus, *to go to sleep* (21)

obḗsus, -a, -um, *fat* (18)

obsérvō, -áre, -ávī, -átus, *to watch* (6)

occupátus, -a, -um, *busy* (7)

occúrrō, occúrrere, occúrrī, occursū́rus + dat., *to meet, encounter* (24)

óctō, *eight* (15)

óculus, -ī, m., *eye* (26)

olfáciō, olfácere, olfḗcī, olfáctus, *to catch the scent of, smell, sniff* (12)

ólim, adv., *once (upon a time)* (18)

olīvḗtum, -ī, n., *olive grove* (14, 15)

ómnis, -is, -e, *all, the whole, every, each* (6, 18)

  ómnēs, *all, everyone* (6)

  ómnia quae, *everything that* (6)

ónus, óneris, n., *load, burden* (15)

oppréssus, -a, -um, *crushed* (25)

óptimus, -a, -um, *best, very good* (20)

  vir óptime, *sir* (20)

ōrátiō, ōrātiṓnis, f., *oration, speech* (26)

  ōrātiṓnem habḗre, *to deliver a speech* (26)

ōrátor, ōrātṓris, m., *orator, speaker* (22)

os, óssis, n., *bone* (18)

P

Palātínus, -a, -um, *Palatine, belonging to the Palatine Hill* (24)

pálla, -ae, f., *palla* (10)

parátus, -a, -um, *ready, prepared* (10)

párēns, paréntis, m./f., *parent* (11)

párō, -áre, -ávī, -átus, *to prepare, get ready* (5, 20)

  sē paráre, *to prepare oneself, get ready* (22)

pars, pártis, gen. pl., **pártium,** f., *part, direction, region* (13)

párvulus, -a, -um, *small, little* (26)

páter, pátris, m., *father* (6, 11)

patrṓnus, -ī, m., *patron* (25)

pátruus, -ī, m., *uncle* (22)

paulísper, adv., *for a short time* (20)

pecū́nia, -ae, f., *money* (21)

per, prep. + acc., *through, along* (6, 9)

  per iócum, *as a prank* (16)

perīculṓsus, -a, -um, *dangerous* (17)

perículum, -ī, n., *danger* (14, 15)

pernóctō, -áre, -ávī, -átū́rus, *to spend the night* (17, 18)

pertérritus, -a, -um, *frightened, terrified* (5)

pervéniō, pervenī́re, pervḗnī, perventū́rus, *to arrive (at), reach* (25)

pēs, pédis, m., *foot* (13)

pétō, pétere, petī́vī, petítus, *to look for, seek, head for, aim at, attack* (5, 21)

pictū́ra, -ae, f., *picture* (1)

píla, -ae, f., *ball* (16)

  pílā lū́dere, *to play ball* (16)

pīráta, -ae, m., *pirate* (21)

piscína, -ae, f., *fishpond* (3)

plácidē, adv., *gently, peacefully* (14)

plaústrum, -ī, n., *wagon, cart* (15)

plḗnus, -a, -um, *full* (11)

plúit, plúere, plúit, *it rains, is raining* (23)

poḗta, -ae, m., *poet* (25)

Pompḗiī, -ṓrum, m. pl., *Pompeii*

pṓnō, pṓnere, pósuī, pósitus, *to put, place* (10, 21)

pōns, póntis, gen. pl., **póntium,** m., *bridge* (23)

pórta, -ae, f., *gate* (11)

pórtō, -áre, -ávī, -átus, *to carry* (6)

póssum, pósse, pótuī, irreg., *to be able; I can* (5, 14, 21)

  póterat, *(he/she/it) was able, could* (13)

  pótest, *(he/she/it) is able, can* (5)

post, prep. + acc., *after* (20)

póstis, póstis, gen. pl., póstium, m., *doorpost* (25)

póstquam, conj., *after* (20)

postrídiē, adv., *on the following day* (26)

praecípitō, -áre, -ávī, -átus, *to hurl* (18)

  sē praecipitáre, *to hurl oneself, rush* (18)

praeclárus, -a, -um, *distinguished, famous* (13)

praecúrrō, praecúrrere, praecúrrī, praecursū́rus, *to run ahead* (18)

praḗdō, praedṓnis, m., *robber* (26)

praéter, prep. + acc., *except* (21)

praetéreā, adv., *besides, too, moreover* (15)

praetéreō, praeterī́re, praetériī or **praeterī́vī, praetéritus,** irreg., *to go past* (15)

praetéxta, tóga, -ae, f., *toga with purple border* (10)

prásinus, -a, -um, *green* (27)

prímus, -a, -um, *first* (21)
  prímā lúce, *at dawn* (21)
  prímum, adv., *first* (23)
prínceps, príncipis, m., *emperor* (7)
prócul, adv., *in the distance, far off, far* (15)
prōmíttō, prōmíttere, prōmísī, prōmíssus, *to promise* (9)
própe, prep. + acc., *near* (5, 9)
própter, prep. + acc., *on account of, because of* (26)
puélla, -ae, f., *girl* (1)
púer, púerī, m., *boy* (3)
púlvis, púlveris, m., *dust* (15)
púniō, -íre, -ívī, -ítus, *to punish* (21)
púrgō, -áre, -ávī, -átus, *to clean* (6)

Q

quadrátus, -a, -um, *squared* (25)
quadrígae, -árum, f. pl., *team of four horses, chariot* (27)
quae, *who* (1, 11)
Quális...? Quális...? Quále...? *What sort of...?* (4, 18)
Quam...! adv., *How....!* (13)
Quam...? adv., *How...?*
quámquam, conj., *although* (11)
Quándō...? adv., *When...?* (12, 21)
quáttuor, *four* (15)
Quem...? *Whom...?* (5)
quem, *whom, which, that* (24)
quī, quae, quod, *who, which, that* (1, 3, 14)
Quī...? *Who...?* (pl.) (6)
Quibúscum...? *With whom...?* (12)
Quid...? *What...?* (1, 4)
  Quid ágis? *How are you?* (18)
  Quid fácit...? *What does...do? What is...doing?* (1)
  Quid fécit...? *What did...do?* (19)
quídam, quaédam, quóddam, *(a) certain* (10)
quiḗs, quiḗtis, f., *rest* (23)
  sē quiḗtī dáre, *to rest* (23)
quiéscō, quiéscere, quiévī, quiētúrus, *to rest, keep quiet* (13, 23)
quīngéntī, -ae, -a, *five hundred* (15)
quīnquāgíntā, *fifty* (15)

quínque, *five* (15)
quíntus, -a, -um, *fifth* (26)
Quis...? Quid...? *Who...? What...?* (1, 4)
  Quid ágis? *How are you?* (18)
  Quid fácit...? *What does...do? What is...doing?* (1)
  Quid fécit...? *What did...do?* (19)
Quō...? adv., *Where...to?* (4)
Quócum...? *With whom...?* (12)
quod (see **quī, quae, quod**)
quod, conj., *because* (1)
Quō īnstrūméntō...? *With what instrument...? By what means...? How?* (12)
Quómodo...? adv., *In what manner...? In what way...? How...?* (12)
quóque, adv., *also* (2, 13)
Quōs...? *Whom...?* (7)
Quot...? *How many...?* (15)

R

raéda, -ae, f., *carriage* (10)
raedárius, -ī, m., *coachman, driver* (10)
rámus, -ī, m., *branch* (4)
recúperō, -áre, -ávī, -átus, *to recover* (21)
  ánimum recuperáre, *to regain one's senses, wake up* (21)
rédeō, redíre, rédiī or **redívī, réditúrus,** irreg., *to return, go back* (7, 23)
réditus, -ūs, m., *return* (25)
relínquō, relínquere, relíquī, relíctus, *to leave behind* (16, 21)
remóveō, removḗre, remóvī, remótus, *to remove, move aside* (21)
repéllō, repéllere, réppulī, repúlsus, *to drive off, drive back* (5)
reprehéndō, reprehéndere, reprehéndī, reprehénsus, *to blame, scold, reprove* (6)
rēs, réī, f., *thing, matter, situation* (19, 25)
  rem explicáre, *to explain the situation* (19)
respóndeō, respondḗre, respóndī, respōnsúrus, *to reply* (5, 21)
révocō, -áre, -ávī, -átus, *to recall, call back* (7)
rídeō, rīdḗre, rísī, rísus, *to laugh (at), smile* (3, 21)

rīmṓsus, -a, -um, *full of cracks, leaky* (23)
rī́sus, -ūs, m., *smile, laugh* (13, 25)
  mágnō rī́sū, *with a loud laugh* (13)
rī́vus, -ī, m., *stream* (5)
rógō, -áre, -ā́vī, -ā́tus, *to ask* (12)
Rṓma, -ae, f., *Rome* (7)
  Rṓmam, *to Rome* (7)
Rōmā́nus, -a, -um, *Roman* (1)
  Rōmā́nī, -ṓrum, m. pl., *the Romans* (III)
róta, -ae, f., *wheel* (15)
russā́tus, -a, -um, *red* (27)
rū́stica, vī́lla, -ae, f., *country house and farm* (1)
rū́sticus, -ī, m., *peasant* (13)

S

saépe, adv., *often* (2, 13)
saltā́trīx, saltātrī́cis, f., *dancer* (21)
sáltō, -áre, -ā́vī, -ātū́rus, *to dance* (21)
salū́tō, -áre, -ā́vī, -ā́tus, *to greet, welcome* (7)
Sálvē!/Salvḗte! *Greetings! Hello!* (7)
sálvus, -a, -um, *safe* (5)
sátis, adv., indeclinable substantive, *enough* (23)
  sátis témporis, *enough time* (23)
scelḗstus, -a, -um, *wicked* (10)
scíō, -íre, -ī́vī, -ī́tus, *to know* (16)
scrī́bō, scrī́bere, scrī́psī, scrī́ptus, *to write* (1, 24)
sē, *himself, herself, oneself, itself, themselves* (11, 27)
secúndus, -a, -um, *second* (9)
sed, conj., *but* (2)
sédeō, sedḗre, sḗdī, sessū́rus, *to sit* (1, 21)
sēmisómnus, -a, -um, *half-asleep* (9)
sémper, adv., *always* (4, 13)
senā́tor, senātṓris, m., *senator* (7)
sēnā́tus, -ūs, m., *Senate* (25)
sénex, sénis, m., *old man* (I)
séptem, *seven* (15)
séptimus, -a, -um, *seventh* (13)
sepúlcrum, -ī, n., *tomb* (22)
séquēns, sequéntis, *following* (25)
sḗrō, adv., *late* (21)
sérvō, -áre, -ā́vī, -ā́tus, *to save* (26)
sérvus, -ī, m., *slave* (3)

sex, *six* (15)
sī, conj., *if* (5)
  sī vīs, *if you wish, please* (26)
sígnum, -ī, n., *signal* (27)
siléntium, -ī, n., *silence* (15)
sílva, -ae, f., *woods, forest* (5)
símul, adv., *together, at the same time* (9, 13)
símulac, conj., *as soon as* (24)
símulō, -áre, -ā́vī, -ā́tus, *to pretend* (21)
síne, prep. + abl., *without* (26)
sóleō, solḗre + infin., *to be accustomed (to), be in the habit (of)* (10)
sollícitus, -a, -um, *anxious, worried* (4)
sṓlus, -a, -um, *alone* (3)
sómnium, -ī, n., *dream* (21)
sómnus, -ī, m., *sleep* (21)
sónitus, -ūs, m., *sound* (21, 25)
sórdidus, -a, -um, *dirty* (19)
sóror, sorṓris, f., *sister* (11)
spectā́tor, spectātṓris, m., *spectator* (27)
spéctō, -áre, -ā́vī, -ā́tus, *to watch, look at* (7)
spī́na, -ae, f., *barrier (of a racetrack)* (27)
státim, adv., *immediately* (5, 13)
státua, -ae, f., *statue* (3)
stércus, stércoris, n., *dung, manure* (21)
stértō, stértere, stértuī, *to snore* (25)
stílus, -ī, m., *pen* (25)
stō, stáre, stétī, statū́rus, *to stand* (10, 22)
stóla, -ae, f., *stola (a woman's outer garment)* (10)
strḗnuus, -a, -um, *active, energetic* (2)
  strḗnuē, adv., *strenuously, hard* (6, 13)
strépitus, -ūs, m., *noise, clattering* (23, 25)
strī́ngō, strī́ngere, strī́nxī, strī́ctus, *to draw* (26)
  gládium strī́ngere, *to draw a sword* (26)
stúltus, -a, -um, *stupid, foolish* (23)
stúpeō, -ére, -uī, *to be amazed, gape* (23)
sub, prep. + abl., *under, beneath* (1, 9)
súbitō, adv., *suddenly* (3, 13)
súī, síbi, sē, sē, *himself, herself, oneself, itself, themselves* (27)
sum, ésse, fúī, futū́rus, irreg., *to be* (1, 14, 20, 21)
sū́mō, sū́mere, sū́mpsī, sū́mptus, *to take, take up, pick out* (22)

sunt, *(they) are* (2)

súprā, adv., *above, on top* (21)

súprā, prep. + acc., *above* (23)

súrgō, súrgere, surréxī, surrēctúrus,
  to get up, rise (6, 21)

súus, -a, -um, *his, her, one's, its, their (own)*
  (9, 27)

T

tabellárius, -ī, m., *courier* (13)

tabérna, -ae, f., *shop* (25)

tablínum, -ī, n., *study* (26)

táceō, -ére, -uī, -itus, *to be quiet* (9)
  Tácē!/Tacéte! *Be quiet!* (9)

tácitē, adv., *silently* (9, 13)

taédet, taedére, *it bores* (16)

tális, -is, -e, *such, like this, of this kind* (23)

támen, adv., *however, nevertheless* (6, 13)

tándem, adv., *at last, at length* (2, 13)

tántus, -a, -um, *so great, such a big* (24)
  tántum, adv., *only* (15)

tárdus, -a, -um, *slow* (15)

tē (see **tū**), *you* (4)

temerárius, -a, -um, *rash, reckless, bold* (5)

témptō, -áre, -ávī, -átus, *to try* (9)

témpus, témporis, n., *time* (2, 8, 12, 15)
  brévī témpore, *in a short time, soon*
    (2, 12)
  éō ípsō témpore, *at that very moment* (10)
  sátis témporis, *enough time* (23)

téneō, tenére, ténuī, téntus, *to hold* (9, 25)

térra, -ae, f., *earth, ground* (26)

térreō, -ére, -uī, -itus, *to frighten, terrify* (4)

térror, terróris, m., *terror, fear* (22)

tértius, -a, -um, *third* (25)

tíbi, *to you, for you* (19)

tímeō, -ére, -uī, *to fear, be afraid (to/of)* (5)

tímidus, -a, -um, *afraid, fearful, timid* (21)

tóga, -ae, f., *toga* (8)
  tóga praetéxta, -ae, f., *toga with purple border*
    (10)

tótus, -a, -um, *all, the whole* (21)

trádō, trádere, trádidī, tráditus,
  to hand over (7, 22)

tráhō, tráhere, tráxī, tráctus, *to drag,*
  pull (6, 12, 25)

lánam tráhere, *to spin wool* (6)

trémō, trémere, trémuī, *to tremble* (21)

trēs, trēs, tría, *three* (13, 15)
  tríbus diébus, *in three days* (12, 13)

Tróia, -ae, f., *Troy* (I)

Troiánus, -a, -um, *Trojan* (I)
  Troiánī, -órum, m. pl., *the Trojans* (I)

tū (acc. **tē**), *you* (sing.) (4, 27)

túlī (see **férō**)

tum, adv., *at that moment, then* (4, 13)

tumúltus, -ūs, m., *uproar, commotion* (25)

túnica, -ae, f., *tunic* (8)

túrba, -ae, f., *crowd, mob* (23)

túus, -a, -um, *your* (sing.) (9, 27)

U

úbi, conj., *where* (1), *when* (5)

Úbi...? adv., *Where...?* (10, 12)

Únde...? adv., *From where...?* (12)

ūndécimus, -a, -um, *eleventh* (17)

úndique, adv., *on all sides, from all sides* (23)

únus, -a, -um, *one* (15)

urbs, úrbis, gen. pl., **úrbium,** f., *city* (7)

ut, conj., *as* (16)

úxor, uxóris, f., *wife* (11)

V

váldē, adv., *very, very much, exceedingly* (19)

Válē!/Valéte! *Goodbye!* (9)

veheménter, adv., *very much, violently, hard*
  (19)

vehículum, -ī, n., *vehicle* (13, 15)

vélle (see **vólō**)

vénetus, -a, -um, *blue* (27)

véniō, veníre, vénī, ventúrus, *to come*
  (7, 20)

vérberō, -áre, -ávī, -átus, *to beat, whip*
  (11)

verbósus, -a, -um, *talkative* (26)

vértō, vértere, vértī, vérsus, *to turn* (16)

vésperī, *in the evening* (18)

véster, véstra, véstrum, *your* (pl.)
  (22, 27)

vēstígium, -ī, n., *track, footprint, trace*
  (12, 15)

vétō, vetā́re, vétuī, vétitus, *to forbid* (26)
véxō, -ā́re, -ā́vī, -ā́tus, *to annoy* (4)
vía, -ae, f., *road, street* (10)
    Vía Áppia, -ae, f., *the Appian Way* (11)
viátor, viātṓris, m., *traveler* (18)
vīcī́nus, -a, -um, *neighboring, adjacent* (1)
víctor, victṓris, m., *conqueror, victor* (27)
vídeō, vidḗre, vī́dī, vī́sus, *to see* (4, 21)
    vidḗtur, *he/she/it seems* (21)
vígilō, -ā́re, -ā́vī, -ātū́rus, *to stay awake* (19)
vī́licus, -ī, m., *overseer, farm manager*
    (11)
vī́lla, -ae, f., *country house* (1)
    vī́lla rústica, -ae, f., *country house and farm*
    (1)
víncō, víncere, vī́cī, víctus, *to conquer, win*
    (27)
vī́nea, -ae, f., *vineyard* (12)

vī́num, -ī, n., *wine* (25)
vir, vírī, m., *man, husband* (3, 11)
    vir óptime, *sir* (20)
vírga, -ae, f., *stick, rod, switch* (13)
vīs (from vólō), *you want* (16)
vī́sitō, -ā́re, -ā́vī, -ā́tus, *to visit* (23)
vī́tō, -ā́re, -ā́vī, -ā́tus, *to avoid* (13)
vix, adv., *scarcely, with difficulty* (24)
vṓbīs, *to you, for you* (pl.) (19)
vócō, -ā́re, -ā́vī, -ā́tus, *to call* (16)
vólō, vélle, vóluī, irreg., *to wish, want,*
    be willing (5, 17, 20, 21)
    sī vīs, *if you wish, please* (26)
vōs, *you* (pl.) (8)
vōx, vṓcis, f., *voice* (4)
    mágnā vṓce, *in a loud voice* (4)
vult (from vólō), *(he/she) wishes, wants,*
    is willing (5, 17)

English to Latin Vocabulary

All Latin words in this list are in boldface, regardless of whether they are for mastery or for recognition. Numbers in parentheses at the end of entries refer to the chapters in which the words appear in vocabulary entries or in Building the Meaning or Forms sections. Roman numerals refer to Review sections.

A

able, (he/she/it) was, **póterat** (13)

able, to be, **póssum, pósse, pótuī** (5, 14, 21)

about, **dē,** prep. + abl. (16)

above, **súprā,** adv. (21), **súprā,** prep. + acc. (23)

absent, to be, **ábsum, abésse, áfuī, āfutúrus** (11, 25)

accuse, to, **accúsō, -áre, -ávī, -átus** (21)

accustomed (to), to be, **sóleō, solére** + inf. (10)

active, **strénuus, -a, -um** (2)

adjacent, **vīcínus, -a, -um** (1)

afraid (to/of), to be, **tímeō, -ére, -uī** (5)

after, **post,** prep. + acc. (20), **póstquam,** adv. (20)

again, **íterum,** adv. (8, 13)

again and again, **idéntidem,** adv. (13)

against, **in,** prep. + acc. (3, 9)

ago, **abhínc,** adv. (25)

aim at, to, **pétō, pétere, petívī, petítus** (5, 21)

Alas! **Éheu!** interj. (7)

all, **cúnctī, -ae, -a** (14), **ómnis, -is, -e** (6, 18), **tótus, -a, -um** (21)

All right! **Éstō!** (20)

allowed, it is, **lícet, licére, lícuit** + dat. (20, 24)

allowed, we are, **lícet nóbīs** (20)

alone, **sólus, -a, -um** (3)

along, **per,** prep. + acc. (6, 9)

already, **iam,** adv. (1, 8, 13)

also, **átque,** conj. (22), **étiam,** adv. (1, 6, 13), **quóque,** adv. (2, 13)

although, **quámquam,** conj. (11)

always, **sémper,** adv. (4, 13)

amazed, to be, **stúpeō, -ére, -uī** (23)

amphitheater, **amphitheátrum, -ī,** n. (25)

ancient, **antíquus, -a, -um** (26)

and, **átque,** conj. (22), **et,** conj. (1)

and also, **átque,** conj. (22)

and...not, **néque,** conj. (6)

and so, **ítaque,** adv. (16)

anger, **íra, -ae,** f. (11)

angry, **īrátus, -a, -um** (3)

annoy, to, **véxō, -áre, -ávī, -átus** (4)

annoying, **moléstus, -a, -um** (4)

another, **álius, ália, áliud** (10)

anxious, **sollícitus, -a, -um** (4)

appear, to, **appáreō, -ére, -uī, -itúrus** (15, 18)

Appian Way, the, **Vía Áppia, -ae,** f. (11)

approach, to, **appropínquō, -áre, -ávī, -atúrus** + dat. or **ad** + acc. (4, 22)

aqueduct, **aquaedúctus, -ūs,** m. (23, 25)

arch, **árcus, -ūs,** m. (24, 25)

are, they, **sunt** (2)

aroused, **excitátus, -a, -um** (25)

arrive (at), to, **advéniō, advenīre, advénī, adventúrus** (5, 23)

as, **ut,** conj. (16)

as a prank, **per iócum** (16)

as long as, **dum,** conj. (1)

Asia, **Ásia, -ae,** f. (21)

ask, to, **rógō, -áre, -ávī, -átus** (12)

astonished, **attónitus, -a, -um** (24)

astounded, **attónitus, -a, -um** (24)

at, **ad,** prep. + acc. (2, 9)

at last, **tándem,** adv. (2, 13)

at length, **tándem,** adv. (2, 13)

at night, **nócte** (12)

at the house of, **ápud**, prep. + acc. (16)

atrium, **átrium, -ī,** n. (26)

attack, to, **pétō, pétere, petīvī, petītus** (5, 21)

attend to, to, **cúrō, -áre, -ávī, -átus** (6)

attentively, **atténtē,** adv. (20)

avoid, to, **vítō, -áre, -ávī, -átus** (13)

awake, to stay, **vígilō, -áre, -ávī, -ātū́rus** (19)

away, to be, **ábsum, abésse, áfuī, āfutū́rus** (11, 25)

B

bad, **málus, -a, -um** (21)

Baiae, **Báiae, -árum,** f. pl.

ball, **píla, -ae,** f. (16)

ball, to play, **pílā lúdere** (16)

bark, to, **látrō, -áre, -ávī, -ātū́rus** (12)

barking, **látrāns** (18)

barrier (of a racetrack), **spína, -ae,** f. (27)

be, to, **sum, ésse, fúī, futū́rus** (1, 14, 20, 21)

be away, to, **ábsum, abésse, áfuī, āfutū́rus** (11, 25)

Be careful! **Cávē!/Cavéte!** (4, 13, 23)

be careful, to, **cáveō, cavére, cā́vī, caútus** (4, 13, 23)

Be quiet! **Tácē!/Tacéte!** (9)

bear, to, **férō, férre, túlī, látus** (16)

beat, to, **vérberō, -áre, -ávī, -átus** (11)

because, **quod,** conj. (1, 13)

because of, **própter,** prep. + acc. (26)

bed, **léctus, -ī,** m. (19)

bed, to go to, **cúbitum íre** (19)

bedroom, **cubículum, -ī,** n. (8, 15)

before, **ánteā,** adv. (20), **ápud,** prep. + acc. (26)

beneath, **sub,** prep. + abl. (1, 9)

besides, **praetéreā,** adv. (15)

best, **óptimus, -a, -um** (20)

better, **mélior, mélius,** gen., melióris (19)

Beware (of)! **Cávē!/Cavéte!** (4, 13, 23)

beware (of), to, **cáveō, cavére, cā́vī, caútus** (4, 13, 23)

bid, to, **iúbeō, iubére, iússī, iússus** (10, 19, 21)

big, **mágnus, -a, -um** (4)

big, such a, **tántus, -a, -um** (24)

blame, **cúlpa, -ae,** f. (14)

blame, to, **reprehéndō, reprehéndere, reprehéndī, reprehénsus** (6)

blue, **vénetus, -a, -um** (27)

body, **córpus, córporis,** n. (21)

bold, **temerárius, -a, -um** (5)

bone, **os, ossis,** n. (18)

book, **líber, líbrī,** m. (24)

bores, it, **taédet, taedére** (16)

boy, **púer, púerī,** m. (3)

branch, **rámus, -ī,** m. (4)

brand, to, **inū́rō, inū́rere, inū́ssī, inū́stus** (12)

brave, **fórtis, -is, -e** (18)

bridge, **pōns, póntis,** gen. pl., **póntium,** m. (23)

bring, to, **dū́cō, dū́cere, dū́xī, dúctus** (7, 19, 20)

Bring help! **Fer/Férte auxílium!** (5)

Britain, **Británnia, -ae,** f. (8)

British, **Británnicus, -a, -um** (3)

brother, **fráter, frátris,** m. (11)

build, to, **aedíficō, -áre, -ávī, -átus** (24)

building, **aedifícium, -ī,** n. (17)

bulk, huge, **mólēs, mólis,** gen. pl., **mólium,** f. (24)

burden, **ónus, óneris,** n. (15)

busy, **occupátus, -a, -um** (7)

but, **at,** conj. (23), **sed,** conj. (2)

buy, to, **émō, émere, ḗmī, ḗmptus** (21)

By Hercules! **Mehércule!** interj. (18)

By what means...? **Quō īnstrūméntō...?** (12)

C

Caesar, **Cáesar, Caésaris,** m. (27)

Caligula, **Calígula, -ae,** m. (27)

call, to, **appéllō, -áre, -ávī, -átus** (21), **vócō, -áre, -ávī, -átus** (16)

call back, to, **révocō, -áre, -ávī, -átus** (7)

call together, to, **cónvocō, -áre, -ávī, -átus** (12)

can, I, **póssum, pósse, pótuī** (5, 14, 21)

can, he/she/it, **pótest** (5)

capture, to, **cápiō, cápere, cḗpī, cáptus** (21)

careful! Be, **Cávē!/Cavéte!** (4, 13, 23)

careful, to be, **cáveō, cavére, cávī, caútus** (4, 13, 23)

carefully, **dīligénter**, adv. (19)

carriage, **raéda, -ae**, f. (10)

carriage, light two-wheeled, **císium, -ī**, n. (14, 15)

carry, to, **férō, férre, túlī, látus** (5, 12, 17, 21), **pórtō, -áre, -ávī, -átus** (6)

cart, **plaústrum, -ī**, n. (15)

castanet, **crótalum, -ī**, n. (21)

cat, **félēs, félis**, gen. pl., **félium**, f. (21)

catch, to, **cápiō, capere, cépī, captus** (21), **excípiō, excípere, excépī, excéptus** (5, 16, 22)

catch sight of, to, **cōnspíciō, cōnspícere, cōnspéxī, cōnspéctus** (4, 21)

catch the scent of, to, **olfáciō, olfácere, olfécī, olfáctus** (12)

certain, (a), **quídam, quaédam, quóddam** (10)

certainly, **cértē**, adv. (19)

chariot, **quadrígae, -árum**, f. pl. (27)

chariot races, **lúdī circénsēs** (27)

charioteer, **auríga, -ae**, m. (13)

chest, **císta, -ae**, f. (10)

children, **líberī, -órum**, m. pl. (10, 11)

circus, in the, **circénsis, -is, -e** (27)

Circus Maximus, **Círcus Máximus, -ī**, m. (23)

citizen, **cívis, cívis**, gen. pl., **cívium**, m./f. (13)

city, **urbs, úrbis**, gen. pl., **úrbium**, f. (7)

clattering, **strépitus, -ūs**, m. (23, 25)

clean, to, **púrgō, -áre, -ávī, -átus** (6)

client, **clíēns, cliéntis**, gen. pl., **cliéntium**, m. (25)

climb, to, **ascéndō, ascéndere, ascéndī, ascénsus** (4, 21)

climb down, to, **dēscéndō, dēscéndere, dēscéndī, dēscēnsúrus** (4, 23)

climb into (a carriage), to, **ascéndō, ascéndere, ascéndī, ascénsus** (4, 21)

closed, **claúsus, -a, -um** (24)

closely, **atténtē**, adv. (20)

cloud, **núbēs, núbis**, gen. pl., **núbium**, f. (15)

coachman, **raedárius, -ī**, m. (10)

cold, **frígidus, -a, -um** (5)

come, to, **véniō, veníre, vénī, ventúrus** (7, 25)

come down, to, **dēscéndō, dēscéndere, dēscéndī, dēscēnsúrus** (4, 23)

come near (to), to, **appropínquō, -áre, -ávī, -átus** + dat. or **ad** + acc. (4, 22)

Come on! **Áge!/Ágite!** (8)

come upon, to, **invéniō, inveníre, invénī, invéntus** (12, 21)

commotion, **tumúltus, -ūs**, m. (25)

company (of charioteers), **fáctiō, factiónis**, f. (27)

concerning, **dē**, prep. + abl. (16)

conquer, to, **víncō, víncere, vícī, víctus** (27)

conqueror, **víctor, victóris**, m. (27)

consult, to, **cónsulō, cōnsúlere, cōnsúluī, cōnsúltus** (7)

conversation, **collóquium, -ī**, n. (26)

cook, to, **cóquō, cóquere, cóxī, cóctus** (6)

cool, **frígidus, -a, -um** (5)

Cornelian, **Cornēliánus, -a, -um** (10)

Cornelii, the, **Cornéliī, -órum**, m. pl. (10)

Cornelius, belonging to, **Cornēliánus, -a, -um** (10)

couch, **léctus, -ī**, m. (19)

could, (he/she/it), **póterat** (13)

country house, **vílla, -ae**, f. (1)

country house and farm, **vílla rústica, -ae**, f. (1)

courier, **tabellárius, -ī**, m. (13)

cow, **bōs, bóvis**, m./f. (15)

cowardly, **ignávus, -a, -um** (5)

cracks, full of, **rīmósus, -a, -um** (23)

crash, **frágor, fragóris**, m. (4)

crowd, **multitúdō, multitúdinis**, f. (23), **túrba, -ae**, f. (23)

crushed, **oppréssus, -a, -um** (25)

cry, to, **lácrimō, -áre, -ávī, -átus** (9)

cultivate, to, **cólō, cólere, cóluī, cúltus** (23)

D

dance, to, **sáltō, -áre, -ávī, -ātúrus** (21)

dancer, **saltátrīx, saltātrícis**, f. (21)

danger, **perículum, -ī**, n. (14, 15)

dangerous, **perīculósus, -a, -um** (17)

dark, it gets, **advesperáscit, advesperáscere, advesperávit** (17) daughter, **fília, -ae,** f. (11)

dawn, at, **prímā lúce** (21)

day, **díēs, diḗī,** m. (5, 13, 25)

day, by/during the, **intérdiū,** adv. (23)

day, it is, **lúcet, lūcḗre, lúxit** (6)

day, on that, **éō díē** (25)

day, on the following, **postrídiē,** adv. (26)

dead, **mórtuus, -a, -um** (16)

dearest, **cāríssimus, -a, -um** (16)

death, **mors, mórtis,** gen. pl., **mórtium,**
    f. (21)

decide, to, **cōnstítuō, cōnstitúere, cōnstítuī,**
    cōnstitū́tus (23)

defend, to, **dēféndō, dēféndere, dēféndī,**
    dēfénsus (I)

delay, to, **céssō, -áre, -ávī, -ātū́rus** (14)

deliver a speech, to, **ōrātiṓnem habḗre** (26)

depart, to, **discḗdō, discḗdere, discéssī,**
    discessū́rus (9, 22)

dependent, **clíēns, cliéntis,** gen. pl.,
    cliéntium, m. (25)

devour, to, **dḗvorō, -áre, -ávī, -átus** (20)

difficulty, with, **vix,** adv. (24)

din, **frágor, fragóris,** m. (4)

dine, to, **cḗnō, -áre, -ávī, -átus** (19)

dinner, **cḗna, -ae,** f. (19)

direction, **pars, pártis,** gen. pl., **pártium,**
    f. (13)

dirty, **sórdidus, -a, -um** (19)

distance, in the, **prócul,** adv. (15)

distant, to be, **ábsum, abésse, áfuī, āfutū́rus**
    (11, 25)

distinguished, **praeclárus, -a, -um** (13)

ditch, **fóssa, -ae,** f. (12)

do, to, **ágō, ágere, ḗgī, áctus** (8, 14, 23),
    fáciō, fácere, fḗcī, fáctus (1, 23)

do?, What did… **Quid fḗcit…?** (19)

do?, What does… **Quid fácit…?** (1)

do nothing, to, **céssō, -áre, -ávī, -ātū́rus** (14)

dog, **cánis, cánis,** m./f. (12)

doing?, What is… **Quid fácit…?** (1)

Don't…! **Nṓlī!/Nōlíte!** + infinitive (9)

door, **iánua, -ae,** f. (9)

doorkeeper, **iánitor, iānitóris,** m. (9)

doorpost, **póstis, póstis,** gen. pl., **póstium,**
    m. (25)

down from, **dē,** prep. + abl. (16)

drag, to, **tráhō, tráhere, tráxī, tráctus**
    (6, 12, 25)

drag out, to, **éxtrahō, extráhere, extráxī,**
    extráctus (14, 21)

draw, to, **stríngō, stríngere, strínxī, stríctus**
    (26)

draw a sword, to, **gládium stríngere** (26)

dream, **sómnium, -ī,** n. (21)

drive, to, **ágō, ágere, ḗgī, áctus** (8, 14, 23),
    íncitō, -áre, -ávī, -átus (10)

drive off/back, to, **repéllō, repéllere,**
    réppulī, repúlsus (5)

driver, **raedárius, -ī,** m. (10)

dung, **stércus, stércoris,** n. (21)

dust, **púlvis, púlveris,** m. (15)

dwell, to, **hábitō, -áre, -ávī, -átus** (1)

E

each, **ómnis, -is, -e** (6, 18)

early in the day, **máne,** adv. (21)

earth, **térra, -ae,** f. (26)

eat dinner, to, **cḗnō, -áre, -ávī, -átus** (19)

eight, **óctō** (15)

either…or, **aut…aut,** conj. (26)

eleventh, **ūndécimus, -a, -um** (17)

embrace, **compléxus, -ūs,** m. (9, 25)

embrace, in an, **compléxū** (9)

emperor, **Caésar, Caésaris,** m. (27),
    prínceps, príncipis, m. (7)

encounter, to, **occúrrō, occúrrere, occúrrī,**
    occursū́rus + dat. (24)

energetic, **strḗnuus, -a, -um** (2)

enough, **sátis,** adv., indeclinable substantive
    (23)

enter, to, **íntrō, -áre, -ávī, -átus** (8, 19)

envoy, **lēgátus, -ī,** m. (18)

eruption, **ērúptiō, ēruptiónis,** f. (26)

escape, to, **effúgiō, effúgere, effū́gī** (11, 21)

even, **étiam,** adv. (1, 6, 13)

evening, in the, **vésperī** (18)

every, **ómnis, -is, -e** (6, 18)

everyone, **ómnēs** (6)

everything, **ómnia** (6)

everything that, **ómnia quae** (6)

examine, to, **īnspíciō, īnspícere, īnspḗxī,**
    īnspéctus (21)

exceedingly, **váldē,** adv. (19)

except, **nísi,** conj. (18, 26), **praéter,**
   prep. + acc. (21)

exclaim, to, **exclámō, -áre, -ávī, -átus** (10)

explain, to, **éxplicō, -áre, -ávī, -átus** (19)

eye, **óculus, -ī,** m. (26)

F

fall, to, **cádō, cádere, cécidī, cāsúrus**
   (3, 22)

fall down, to, **cóncidō, concídere, cóncidī**
   (14)

famous, **praeclárus, -a, -um** (13)

far (off), **prócul,** adv. (15)

farm manager, **vílicus, -ī,** m. (11)

fast, very, **celérrimē,** adv. (14)

fat, **obésus, -a, -um** (18)

father, **páter, pátris,** m. (6, 11)

fault, **cúlpa, -ae,** f. (14)

favor, to, **fáveō, favére, fávī, fautúrus** + dat.
   (27)

fear, **métus, -ūs,** m. (26), **térror, terróris,** m.
   (22)

fear, to, **tímeō, timére, tímuī** (5)

festival day, **fériae, -árum,** f. pl. (27)

field, **áger, ágrī,** m. (2)

fiercely, **feróciter,** adv. (13)

fifth, **quíntus, -a, -um** (26)

fifty, **quīnquāgíntā** (15)

find, to, **invéniō, inveníre, invénī, invéntus**
   (12, 21)

finish, to, **cōnfíciō, cōnfícere, cōnfécī,**
   cōnféctus (25), **fíniō, -íre, -ívī,**
   -ítus (21)

first, **prímus, -a, -um** (21)
   first, **prímum,** adv. (23)

fishpond, **piscína, -ae,** f. (3)

five, **quínque** (15)

flee, to, **fúgiō, fúgere, fúgī, fugitúrus** (18,
   25)

following, **séquēns, sequéntis** (25)

following day, on the, **postrídiē,** adv.
   (26)

food, **cíbus, -ī,** m. (6)

foolish, **stúltus, -a, -um** (23)

foot, **pēs, pédis,** m. (13)

footprint, **vēstígium, -ī,** n. (12, 15)

for, **énim,** conj. (20), **nam,** conj. (8)

forbid, to, **vétō, vetáre, vétuī,**
   vétitus (26)

forehead, **frōns, fróntis,** f. (12)

forest, **sílva, -ae,** f. (5)

forgetful, **ímmemor, immémoris +**
   gen. (22)

former, the, **ílle, ílla, íllud** (11, 15, 16, 20, 22,
   25, 26)

Forum, **Fórum, -ī,** n. (25)

four, **quáttuor** (15)

freedom, **lībértās, lībertátis,** f. (21)

friend, **amíca, -ae,** f. (2), **amícus, -ī,**
   m. (3), **hóspes, hóspitis,** m./f. (16)

frighten, to, **térreō, -ére, -uī, -itus** (4)

frightened, **pertérritus, -a, -um** (5)

from, **ā** or **ab,** prep. + abl. (13), **ē** or **ex,** prep.
   + abl. (2, 5, 9)

From where...? **Únde...?** adv. (12)

full, **plénus, -a, -um** (11)

G

games, **lúdī, -órum,** m. pl. (24)

gape, to, **stúpeo, -ére, -uī** (23)

garden, **hórtus, -ī,** m. (3)

gate, **pórta, -ae,** f. (11)

gently, **plácidē,** adv. (14)

get ready, to, **(sē) paráre** (22)

get up, to, **súrgō, súrgere, surréxī,**
   surrēctúrus (6, 21)

gets dark, it, **advesperáscit, advesperáscere,**
   advesperávit (17)

girl, **puélla, -ae,** f. (1)

give, to, **dō, dáre, dédī, dátus** (21)

give favor (to), to, **fáveō, favére, fávī,**
   fautúrus + dat. (27)

glad, **laétus, -a, -um** (1)

glad, to be, **gaúdeō, gaudére** (14)

go, to, **éō, íre, íī** or **ívī, itúrus** (7, 17, 19, 20,
   21)

go around, to, **circúmeō, circumíre,**
   circúmiī or **circumívī, circúmitus**
   (24)

Go away! **Ábī!/Abíte!** (3)

go away, to, **ábeō, abíre, ábiī** or **abívī, abitúrus** (3, 9) **discédō, discédere, discéssī, discessurus** (9, 22)

go back, to, **rédeō, redíre, rédiī** or **redívī, reditúrus** (7, 23)

go down, to, **dēscéndō, dēscéndere, dēscéndī, dēscēnsúrus** (4, 23)

go into, to, **íntrō, -áre, -ávī, -átus** (8, 19)

go out, to, **éxeō, exíre, éxiī** or **exívī, exitúrus** (5, 23)

go past, to, **praetéreō, praeteríre, praetériī** or **praeterívī, praeteritúrus** (15)

goal, **méta, -ae**, f. (27)

gold, **aúrum, -ī**, n. (21)

golden, **aúreus, -a, -um** (25)

good, **bónus, -a, -um** (12)

good, very, **óptimus, -a, -um** (20)

Goodbye! **Válē!/Valéte!** (9)

Goodness me! **Mehércule!** interj. (18)

goods, **bóna, -órum**, n. pl. (26)

grab hold of, to, **arrípiō, arrípere, arrípuī, arréptus** (5, 9, 26)

great, **mágnus, -a, -um** (4)

great, very, **máximus, -a, -um** (23)

greatest, **máximus, -a, -um** (23)

Greece, **Graécia, -ae**, f. (21)

Greek, **Graécus, -a, -um** (17)

Greeks, the, **Graécī, -órum**, m. pl. (I)

green, **prásinus, -a, -um** (27)

greet, to, **salútō, -áre, -ávī, -átus** (7)

Greetings! **Sálvē!/Salvéte!** (7)

groan, to, **gémō, gémere, gémuī, gémitus** (3)

ground, **térra, -ae**, f. (26)

ground, on the, **húmī** (27)

guard, **cústōs, custódis**, m. (26)

guard, to, **custódiō, -íre, -ívī, -ítus** (17)

guest, **hóspes, hóspitis**, m./f. (16)

H

habit (of), to be in the, **sóleō, solére** + infin. (10)

half-asleep, **sēmisómnus, -a, -um** (9)

hand, **mánus, -ūs**, f. (18, 25)

hand over, to, **trádō, trádere, trádidī, tráditus** (7, 22)

happens, (it), **áccidit, accídere, áccidit** (14, 26)

happy, **laétus, -a, -um** (1)

hard, **strénuē**, adv. (6, 13)

harm, to, **nóceō, -ére, -uī, -itúrus** + dat. (26)

have, to, **hábeō, -ére, -uī, -itus** (10, 20, 26)

he, **ílle** (11, 15, 16, 20, 22, 26), **is** (2, 7)

head, **cáput, cápitis**, n. (25)

head for, to, **pétō, pétere, petívī, petítus** (5, 21)

hear, to, **aúdiō, -íre, -ívī, -ítus** (4, 20)

heat, **aéstus, -ūs**, m. (24, 25)

Hello! **Sálvē!/Salvéte!** (7)

help, **auxílium, -ī**, n. (5,15)

Help! **Fer/Férte auxílium!** (5)

help, to, **ádiuvō, adiuváre, adiúvī, adiútus** (6, 21)

her, **éam** (9, 16), **éius** (2, 27)

her (own), **súus, -a, -um** (9, 27)

her, to, **cui, éī** (19, 21)

here, **hīc**, adv. (9, 13)

here and there, **hūc illúc**, adv. (23)

herself, **ípsa** (6, 10), **sē** (27)

Hey! **Ého!** interj. (25)

hide, to, **célō, -áre, -ávī, -átus** (11)

hill, **mōns, móntis**, gen. pl., **móntium**, m. (24)

him, **éum** (5)

him, to, **cui, éī** (19, 21)

himself, **ípse** (6, 10), **sē** (11, 27)

hinder, to, **impédiō, -íre, -ívī, -ítus** (11)

hire, to, **condúcō, condúcere, condúxī, condúctus** (23)

his, **éius** (27)

his (own), **súus, -a, -um** (9, 27)

hit, to, **fériō, -íre**, (16)

hold, to, **hábeō, -ére, -uī, -itus** (10, 20, 26), **téneō, tenére, ténuī, téntus** (9, 25)

hold out, to, **exténdō, exténdere, exténdī, exténtus** (18)

holiday, **fériae, -árum**, f. pl. (27)

holiday, celebrating a, **fēriátus, -a, -um** (27)

home, **domus, -ūs**, f. (25)

home, at, **dómī** (26)

home(ward), **dómum** (23)

horse, **équus, -ī**, m. (10)

host, **hóspes, hóspitis**, m./f. (16)

hour, **hóra, -ae**, f. (9)

house, **dómus, -ūs**, f. (23, 25)

house, country, **vílla, -ae**, f. (1)

house of, at the, **ápud**, prep. + acc. (16)

How...! **Quam...!** adv. (13)

How...? **Quam...?** adv., **Quō instrūméntō...? Quómodo...?** adv. (12)

How are you? **Quid ágis?** (18)

How many...? **Quot...?** (15)

however, **támen,** adv. (6, 13)

huge, **íngēns, ingéntis** (22)

hundred, five, **quīngéntī, -ae, -a** (15)

hundred, one, **céntum** (15)

hungry, to be, **ēsúriō, -íre,   , -ītúrus** (19)

hurl, to, **praecípitō, -áre, -ávī, -átus** (18)

hurl oneself, to, **sē praecipitáre** (18)

Hurray! **Eúgepae!** interj. (7)

hurry, to, **festínō, -áre, -ávī, -ātúrus** (9)

husband, **cóniūnx, cóniugis,** m. (26), **vir, vírī,** m. (3, 11)

I

I, **égo** (5, 27)

I thank you! **Grátiās tíbi ágō!** (26)

idle, to be, **céssō, -áre, -ávī, -ātúrus** (14)

if, **sī,** conj. (5)

if... not, **nísi,** conj. (18, 26)

ignorant, to be, **néscio, -íre, -ívī, -ítus** (9)

immediately, **státim,** adv. (5, 13)

in, **in,** prep. + abl. (1, 9)

in a loud voice, **mágnā vóce** (4)

in front of, **ápud,** prep. + acc. (26)

in this way, **íta,** adv. (3, 13, 21)

in three days, **tríbus diébus** (12, 13)

in vain, **frústrā,** adv. (14)

In what manner/way...? **Quómodo...?** adv. (12)

Indeed! **Íta vérō!** adv. (3, 13)

inn, **caupóna, -ae,** f. (17, 20)

innkeeper, **caúpō, caupónis,** m. (17)

innocence, **innocéntia, -ae,** f. (21)

inside, **íntrā,** prep. + acc. (22)

instruction, **mandátum, -ī,** n. (22)

instrument...? With what, **Quō instrūméntō...?** (12)

intend, to, **in ánimō habére** (16)

interrupt, to, **interpéllō, -áre, -ávī, -átus** (8, 19)

into, **in,** prep. + acc. (3, 9)

is, (he/she/it), **est** (1)

is able, (he/she/it), **pótest** (5)

Italy, **Itália, -ae,** f. (1)

its, **éius** (2, 27)

its (own), **súus, -a, -um** (27)

J

joke, **iócus, -ī,** m. (16)

journey, **íter, itíneris,** n. (10, 13, 15)

joy, **gaúdium, -ī,** n. (23)

K

keep quiet, to, **quiéscō, quiéscere, quiévī, quiētúrus** (13, 23)

kill, to, **nécō, -áre, -ávī, -átus** (20)

kind, of this, **tális, -is, -e** (23)

kitchen, **culína, -ae,** f. (21)

know, not to, **néscio, -íre, -ívī, -ítus** (9)

know, to, **scíō, -íre, -ívī, -ítus** (16)

L

lady of the house, **dómina, -ae,** f. (17)

large, **mágnus, -a, -um** (4)

large, very, **máximus, -a, -um** (23)

late, **sérō,** adv. (21)

latter, the, **hic, haec, hoc** (18, 19, 20, 25, 26)

laugh, **rísus -ūs,** m. (13, 25)

laugh, with a loud, **mágnō rísū** (13)

laugh (at), to, **rídeō, rīdére, rísī, rísus** (3, 21)

lazy, **ignávus, -a, -um** (5)

lead, to, **dúcō, dúcere, dúxī, dúctus** (7, 19, 20)

leaky, **rīmósus, -a, -um** (23)

leave behind, to, **relínquō, relínquere, relíquī, relíctus** (16, 21)

letter, **epístula, -ae,** f. (7)

letter (of the alphabet), **líttera, -ae,** f. (12)

lie, to, **iáceō, -ére, -uī, -itúrus** (26)

light, **lūx, lúcis,** f. (21)

light, it is, **lúcet, lūcére, lúxit** (6)

light two-wheeled carriage, **císium, -ī,** n. (14, 15)

like, to, **ámō, -áre, -ávī, -átus** (4)

like this, **tális, -is, -e** (23)

listen to, to, **aúdiō, -íre, -ívī, -ítus** (4, 20)

litter, **lectíca, -ae,** f. (23)

litter-bearer, **lectīcárius, -ī**, m. (23)

little, **párvulus, -a, -um** (26)

live, to, **hábitō, -áre, -ávī, -átus** (1)

load, **ónus, óneris**, n. (15)

long, **lóngus, -a, -um** (15)

long for, to, **dēsíderō, -áre, -ávī, -átus** (26)

long time, for a, **díū**, adv. (15)

look after, to, **cúrō, -áre, -ávī, -átus** (6)

Look (at...)! **Écce!** interj. (1)

look at, to, **spéctō, -áre, -ávī, -átus** (7)

look for, to, **pétō, pétere, petívī, petítus** (5, 21)

look out for, to, **exspéctō, -áre, -ávī, -átus** (15)

Look (at...)! **Écce!** interj. (1)

loud laugh, with a, **mágnō rísū** (13)

loud voice, with a, **mágnā vóce** (4)

love, to, **ámō, -áre, -ávī, -átus** (4)

M

magnificent, **magníficus, -a, -um** (24)

main room, **átrium, -ī**, n. (26)

make, to, **fáciō, fácere, fḗcī, fáctus** (1, 23)

man, **vir, vírī**, m. (3, 11), **hómō, hóminis**, m. (18)

man, old, **sénex, sénis**, m. (I)

manager, farm, **vílicus, -ī**, m. (11)

manner...?, In what, **Quómodo...?** adv. (12)

manure, **stércus, stércoris**, n. (21)

many, **múltī, -ae, -a** (3)

mark, **méta, -ae**, f. (27)

marvelous, **mírus, -a, -um** (23)

mass, **mólēs, mólis**, gen. pl., **mólium**, f. (24)

master, **dóminus, -ī**, m. (11)

matter, **rēs, réī**, f. (19, 25)

may, we, **lícet nóbīs** (20)

me, **mē** (4)

me, to/for, **míhi** (8)

me, with, **mécum** (9)

means...?, By what, **Quō īnstrūméntō...?** (12)

meanwhile, **intéreā**, adv. (10, 13)

meet, to, **occúrrō, occúrrere, occúrrī, occursúrus** + dat. (24)

Megara, **Mégara, -ae**, f. (21)

merchant, **mercátor, mercātóris**, m. (22)

messenger, **núntius, -ī**, m. (7)

mid-, **médius, -a, -um** (20)

middle of, **médius, -a, -um** (20)

midnight, **média nox, médiae nóctis**, f. (20)

mind, **ánimus, -ī**, m. (16)

mine, **méus, -a, -um** (7)

miserable, **míser, mísera, míserum** (9)

miss, to, **dēsíderō, -áre, -ávī, -átus** (26)

mistaken, to be, **érrō, -áre, -ávī, -ātúrus** (5, 18)

mistress, **dómina, -ae**, f. (17)

mob, **túrba, -ae**, f. (23)

moment, at that, **tum**, adv. (4, 13)

moment, at that very, **éō ípsō témpore** (10)

money, **pecúnia, -ae**, f. (21)

moreover, **praetéreā**, adv. (15)

morning, in the, **máne**, adv. (21)

mother, **máter, mátris**, f. (6, 11)

motionless, **immóbilis, -is, -e** (12)

Mount Vesuvius, **Mōns Vesúvius, Móntis Vesúviī**, m. (26)

mountain, **mōns, móntis**, gen. pl., **móntium**, m. (24)

mouse, **mūs, múris**, m. (21)

move, to, **móveō, movére, móvī, mótus** (14, 24)

move aside, to, **remóveō, removére, remóvī, remótus** (21)

move toward, to, **admóveō, admovére, admóvī, admótus** (22)

moved, **commótus, -a, -um** (14)

mud, **lútum, -ī**, n. (26)

murmur, **múrmur, múrmuris**, n. (15)

mutter, to, **mússō, -áre, -ávī, -ātúrus** (11)

my, **méus, -a, -um** (7)

N

name, **nómen, nóminis**, n. (1, 15)

name, by, **nómine** (1)

name, to, **appéllō, -áre, -ávī, -átus** (21)

napkin, **máppa, -ae**, f. (27)

Naples, **Neápolis, Neápolis,** f. (15)
narrator, **nārrátor, nārrātóris,** m. (8)
near, **ad,** prep. + acc. (15), **própe,** prep. + acc.
  (5, 9)
necessary, **necésse,** adv. or indeclinable adj.
  (6)
neighboring, **vīcínus, -a, -um** (1)
neither...nor, **néque...néque,** conj. (5)
never, **númquam,** adv. (20)
nevertheless, **támen,** adv. (6, 13)
new, **nóvus, -a, -um** (16)
next, **deínde,** adv. (8, 13)
night, **nox, nóctis,** gen. pl., **nóctium,**
  f. (11)
night, at, **nócte** (12)
night, happening during the, **noctúrnus,**
  -a, -um (22)
night, that, **íllā nócte** (11)
nine, **nóvem** (15)
ninth, **nónus, -a, -um** (16)
no, **núllus, -a, -um** (9)
No! **Mínimē!** adv. (3, 13)
no longer, **nōn iam,** adv. (2, 13)
no one, **némō, néminis,** m./f. (9)
noise, **frágor, frāgóris,** m. (4), **strépitus, -us,**
  m. (23, 25)
not, **nōn,** adv. (2, 13)
not any, **núllus, -a, -um** (9)
Not at all! **Mínimē!** adv. (3, 13)
not to wish/want, **nólō, nólle, nóluī**
  (5, 17, 21)
not yet, **nóndum,** adv. (6, 13)
nothing, **níhil** (4)
nothing, to do, **céssō, -áre, -ávī, -ātúrus** (14)
nothing wrong, there is, **níhil málī** (21)
now, **iam,** adv. (1, 8, 13), **nunc,** adv. (6, 13)
number, **númerus, -ī,** m. (11)

O

often, **saépe,** adv. (2, 13)
Oh dear me! **Ō mē míseram!** (9)
Oh no! **Éheu!** interj. (7)
old man, **sénex, sénis,** m. (I)
olive grove, **olīvétum, -ī,** n. (14, 15)
on, **in,** prep. + abl. (1, 9)
on account of, **própter,** prep. + acc. (26)
on top, **súprā,** adv. (21)

once (upon a time), **ólim,** adv. (18)
one, **únus, -a, -um** (15)
one (of two), **álter, áltera, álterum** (1)
one...the other, the, **álter...álter** (16)
oneself, **sē** (11)
only, **módo,** adv. (18), **tántum,** adv. (15)
open, to, **apériō, aperíre, apéruī, apértus**
  (16, 26)
open space, **área, -ae,** f. (11)
oration, **ōrátiō, ōrātiónis,** f. (26)
orator, **ōrátor, ōrātóris,** m. (22)
order, **mandátum, -ī,** n. (22)
order, to, **iúbeō, iubére, iússī, iússus** (10, 19,
  21)
other, **álius, ália, áliud** (10), **álter, áltera,**
  álterum (1)
other (of two), the, **álter, áltera, álterum** (1)
otherwise, **áliter,** adv. (26)
ought, **débeō, -ére, -uī, -itúrus** + infin. (26)
our, **nóster, nóstra, nóstrum** (14, 27)
out of, **ē** or **ex,** prep. + abl. (2, 5, 9)
outer garment, woman's, **stóla, -ae,**
  f. (10)
outside, **éxtrā,** prep. + acc. (23)
overseer, **vílicus, -ī,** m. (11)
owner, **dóminus, -ī,** m. (11)
ox, **bōs, bóvis,** m./f. (15)

P

Palatine, belonging to the Palatine Hill,
  Palātínus, -a, -um (24)
palla, **pálla, -ae,** f. (10)
parent, **párēns, paréntis,** m./f. (11)
part, **pars, pártis,** gen. pl., **pártium,** f. (13)
patron, **patrónus, -ī,** m. (25)
peacefully, **plácidē,** adv. (14)
peasant, **rústicus, -ī,** m. (13)
pen, **stílus, -ī,** m. (25)
people, **hóminēs, hóminum,** m. pl. (15)
perhaps, **fortásse,** adv. (15)
pest, **moléstus, -ī,** m. (3)
pick out, to, **súmō, súmere, súmpsī,**
  súmptus (22)
picture, **pictúra, -ae,** f. (1)
pirate, **pīráta, -ae,** m. (21)
place, to, **pónō, pónere, pósuī, pósitus**
  (10, 21)

place, to that, **éō**, adv. (23), **illúc,** adv. (23)

play, to, **lúdō, lúdere, lúsī, lūsúrus** (16)

play ball, to, **pílā lúdere** (16)

please, **sī vīs** (26)

poet, **poéta, -ae,** m. (25)

Pompeii, **Pompéiī, Pompeiórum,** m. pl.

Poor me! **Ō mē míseram!** (9)

possessions, **bóna, -órum,** n. pl. (26)

praise, to, **laúdō, -áre, -ávī, -átus** (18)

prank, **iócus, -ī,** m. (16)

prepare, to, **párō, -áre, -ávī, -átus** (5, 20)

prepare oneself, to, **sē paráre** (22)

prepared, **parátus, -a, -um** (10)

present, to be, **ádsum, adésse, ádfuī, adfutúrus** (26)

presently, **mox,** adv. (6, 13)

pretend, to, **símulō, -áre, -ávī, -átus** (21)

prevent, to, **impédiō, -íre, -ívī, -ítus** (11)

previously, **abhínc,** adv. (25), **ánteā,** adv. (20)

prisoner, **captívus, -ī,** m. (26)

promise, to, **prōmíttō, prōmíttere, prōmísī, prōmíssus** (9)

pull, to, **tráhō, tráhere, tráxī, tráctus** (6, 12, 25)

punish, to, **púniō, -íre, -ívī, -ítus** (21)

purple-bordered toga, **tóga praetéxta, tógae praetéxtae,** f. (10)

put, to, **pónō, pónere, pósuī, pósitus** (10, 21)

put on, to, **índuō, indúere, índuī, indútus** (8, 23)

Q

quickly, **celériter,** adv. (8, 13)

quickly, very, **celérrimē,** adv. (14)

quiet, to be, **táceō, -ére, -uī, -itus** (9)

quiet, to keep, **quiéscō, quiéscere, quiévī, quiētúrus** (13, 23)

R

race track, **currículum, -ī,** n. (27)

rain, **ímber, ímbris,** gen. pl., **ímbrium,** m. (23)

rains/is raining, it, **plúit, plúere, plúit** (23)

rash, **temerárius, -a, -um** (5)

reach, to, **advéniō, adveníre, advénī, adventúrus** (5, 23), **pervéniō, perveníre, pervénī, perventúrus** + ad + acc. (25)

read, to, **légō, légere, légī, léctus** (1, 24)

ready, **parátus, -a, -um** (10)

ready, to get, **párō, -áre, -ávī, -átus** (5)

ready, to get (oneself), **sē paráre** (22)

reason, **caúsa, -ae,** f. (25)

recall, to, **révocō, -áre, -ávī, -átus** (7)

receive, to, **excípiō, excípere, excépī, excéptus** (5, 16, 22)

reckless, **temerárius, -a, -um** (5)

recognize, to, **agnóscō, agnóscere, agnóvī, ágnitus** (18)

recover, to, **recúperō, -áre, -ávī, -átus** (21)

red, **russátus, -a, -um** (27)

regain one's senses, to, **ánimum recuperáre** (21)

region, **pars, pártis,** gen. pl., **pártium,** f. (13)

reins, **habénae, -árum,** f. pl. (22)

rejoice, to, **gaúdeō, gaudére** (14)

remain, to, **máneō, manére, mánsī, mánsurus** (9, 20, 23)

remove, to, **remóveō, removére, remóvī, remótus** (21)

repeatedly, **idéntidem,** adv. (13)

reply, to, **respóndeō, respondére, respóndī, respōnsúrus** (5, 21)

rest, **quíēs, quiétis,** f. (23)

rest, to, **quiéscō, quiéscere, quiévī, quiētúrus** (13, 23), **sē quiétī dáre** (23)

return, **réditus, -ūs,** m. (25)

return, to, **rédeō, redíre, rédiī** or **redívī, reditúrus** (7, 23)

rise, to, **súrgō, súrgere, surréxī, surrēctúrus** (6, 21)

road, **vía, -ae,** f. (10)

robber, **praédō, praedónis,** m. (26)

rod, **vírga, -ae,** f. (13)

Roman, **Rōmánus, -a, -um** (1)

Romans, the, **Rōmánī, -órum,** m. pl. (III)

Rome, **Róma, -ae,** f. (7)

Rome, to, **Rómam** (7)

room, **cubículum, -ī,** n. (8, 15)

room, main, **átrium, -ī,** n. (26)

rouse, to, **éxcitō, -áre, -ávī, -átus** (8)

rumble, **múmur, múrmuris,** n. (15)

run, to, **cúrrō, cúrrere, cucúrrī, cursúrus** (2, 23)

run ahead, to, **praecúrrō, praecúrrere, praecúrrī, praecursúrus** (18)

run away, to, **effúgiō, effúgere, effúgī** (11, 21)

rush, to, **sē praecipitáre** (18)

S

sad, to be, **dóleo, -ére, -uī, -itúrus** (18)

safe, **sálvus, -a, -um** (5)

safe and sound, **incólumis, -is, -e** (14)

said, (he/she), **ínquit** (7)

same, the, **ídem, éadem, ídem** (3)

same time, at the, **símul,** adv. (9, 13)

save, to, **sérvō, -áre, -ávī, -átus** (26)

say, to, **dícō, dícere, díxī, díctus** (20, 21)

says, (he/she), **ínquit** (7)

scarcely, **vix,** adv. (24)

scent of, to catch the, **olfáciō, olfácere, olféci, olfáctus** (12)

school, **lúdus, -ī,** m. (26)

scold, to, **reprehéndō, reprehéndere, reprehéndī, reprehénsus** (6)

second, **álter, áltera, álterum** (1), **secúndus, -a, -um** (9)

second time, a, **íterum,** adv. (8, 13)

see, to, **vídeō, vidére, vídī, vísus** (4, 21)

seek, to, **pétō, pétere, petívī, petítus** (5, 21)

seems, he/she/it, **vidétur** (21)

seize, to, **arrípiō, arrípere, arrípuī, arréptus** (5, 19, 26)

-self, -selves, **ípse, ípsa, ípsum** (6, 10), **sē** (11, 27)

Senate, **senátus, -ūs,** m. (25)

Senate House, **Cúria, -ae,** f. (23)

senator, **senátor, senātóris,** m. (7)

send, to, **míttō, míttere, mísī, míssus** (9, 20)

seven, **séptem** (15)

seventh, **séptimus, -a, -um** (13)

shaky, **īnfírmus, -a, -um** (4)

she, **éa** (27), **ílla** (11, 15, 16, 20, 22, 25, 26)

she-wolf, **lúpa, -ae,** f. (II)

shop, **tabérna, -ae,** f. (25)

short, **brévis, -is, -e** (2)

short time, for a, **paulísper,** adv. (20)

short time, in a, **brévī témpore** (2, 12)

shout, to, **clámō, -áre, -ávī, -ātúrus** (3)

shout out, to, **exclámō, -áre, -ávī, -ātúrus** (10)

shout(ing), **clámor, clāmóris,** m. (5)

show, to, **dēmónstrō, -áre, -ávī, -átus** (24), **mónstrō, -áre, -ávī, -átus** (22)

shut, **claúsus, -a, -um** (24)

shut, to, **claúdō, claúdere, claúsī, claúsus** (26)

sides, from on/all, **úndique,** adv. (23)

signal, **sígnum, -ī,** n. (27)

silence, **siléntium, -ī,** n. (15)

silently, **tácitē,** adv. (9, 13)

sing, to, **cántō, -áre, -ávī, -átus** (21)

sir, **vir óptime** (20)

sister, **sóror, soróris,** f. (11)

sit, to, **sédeō, sedére, sédī, sessúrus** (1, 21)

sit down, to, **cōnsídō, cōnsídere, cōnsédī** (23)

situation, **rēs, réī,** f. (19, 25)

six, **sex** (15)

skill, **ars, ártis,** gen. pl., **ártium,** f. (14)

sky, **caélum, -ī,** n. (17)

slave, **sérvus, -ī,** m. (3)

slave-woman, **ancílla, -ae,** f. (6)

sleep, **sómnus, -ī,** m. (21)

sleep, to, **dórmiō, -íre, -ívī, -ītúrus** (4)

sleep, to go to, **obdórmiō, -íre, -ívī, -ītúrus** (21)

slow, **tárdus, -a, -um** (15)

slowly, **léntē,** adv. (2, 13)

small, **párvulus, -a, -um** (26)

smell, to, **olfáciō, olfácere, olféci, olfáctus** (12, 18)

smile, **rísus, -ūs,** m. (13, 25)

smile, to, **rídeō, rīdére, rísī, rísus** (3, 21)

snatch, to, **arrípiō, arrípere, arrípuī, arréptus** (5, 19, 26)

sniff, to, **olfáciō, olfácere, olféci, olfáctus** (12, 18)

snore, to, **stértō, stértere, stértuī** (25)

so, **íta,** adv. (3, 13, 21)

so great, **tántus, -a, -um** (24)

soldier, **míles, mílitis,** m. (20)

some...others, **áliī...áliī** (9)

something, **áliquid** (25)

sometimes, **nōnnúmquam,** adv. (26)

son, **fílius, -ī,** m. (11)

soon, **brévī témpore** (2, 12), **mox,** adv. (6, 13)

sound, **sónitus, -ūs,** m. (21, 25)

space, open, **área, -ae,** f. (11)

speaker, **ōrátor, ōrātóris,** m. (22)

spectator, **spectátor, spectātóris,** m. (27)

speech, **ōrátiō, ōrātiónis,** f. (26)

speech, to deliver a, **ōrātiónem habére** (26)

spend the night, to, **pernóctō, -áre, -ávī, -ātúrus** (17, 18)

spin wool, to, **lánam tráhere** (6)

spur on, to, **íncitō, -áre, -ávī, -átus** (10)

squared, **quadrátus, -a, -um** (25)

staff, **báculum, -ī,** n. (10, 15)

stand, to, **stō, stáre, stétī, statúrus** (10, 22)

standing out, **éxstāns, exstántis** (23)

statue, **státua, -ae,** f. (3)

stay, to, **máneō, manére, mánsī, mánsus** (9, 20, 23)

stay awake, to, **vígilō, -áre, -ávī, -ātúrus** (19)

stealthily, **fúrtim,** adv. (4, 13)

stick, **báculum, -ī,** n. (10, 15), **vírga, -ae,** f. (13)

stick, to, **haéreō, haerére, haésī, haesúrus** (14)

still, **adhúc,** adv. (5, 13)

stola, **stóla, -ae,** f. (10)

stone, **lápis, lápidis,** m. (25)

story, **fábula, -ae,** f. (20)

strange, **mírus, -a, -um** (23)

stream, **rívus, -ī,** m. (5)

street, **vía, -ae,** f. (10)

strenuously, **strénuē,** adv. (6, 13)

strike, to, **fériō, -íre** (16)

strong, **fórtis, -is, -e** (18)

study, **tablínum, -ī,** n. (26)

stupid, **fátuus, -a, -um** (13), **stúltus, -a, -um** (23)

such, **tális, -is, -e** (23)

suddenly, **súbitō,** adv. (3, 13)

summer, **aéstās, aestátis,** f. (1)

summer, in the, **aestáte** (1)

support, to, **fáveō, favére, fávī, fautúrus** + dat. (27)

switch, **vírga, -ae,** f. (13)

sword, **gládius, -ī,** m. (26)

sword, to draw a, **gládium stríngere** (26)

T

tail, **caúda, -ae,** f. (18)

take, to, **cápiō, cápere, cépī, cáptus** (21), **dúcō, dúcere, dúxī, dúctus** (7, 19, 20)

take care of, to, **cúrō, -áre, -ávī, -átus** (6)

take out, to, **éxtrahō, extráhere, extráxī, extráctus** (14, 21)

take (up), to, **súmō, súmere, súmpsī, súmptus** (22)

talkative, **verbósus, -a, -um** (26)

teach, to, **dóceō, docére, dócuī, dóctus** (6, 21)

team of four horses, **quadrígae, -árum,** f. pl. (27)

tell, to, **dícō, dícere, díxī, díctus** (20, 21)

tell (a story), to, **nárrō, -áre, -ávī, -átus** (20)

ten, **décem** (15)

terrified, **pertérritus, -a, -um** (5)

terrify, to, **térreō, -ére, -uī, -itus** (4)

terror, **térror, terróris,** m. (22)

Thank you! **Grátiās tíbi ágō!** (26)

that, **ílle, ílla, íllud** (11, 15, 16, 20, 22, 25, 26), **is, éa, id** (27), **quī, quae, quod** (1, 3, 14)

that night, **íllā nócte** (11)

that place, to, **éō,** adv. (23), **illúc,** adv. (23)

their, **eórum, eárum, eórum** (25, 27)

their (own), **súus, -a, -um** (27)

them, **eós, eás, éa** (27)

them, of, **eórum, eárum, eórum** (27)

them, to/for, **éīs** (22, 27)

then, **deínde,** adv. (8, 13), **tum,** adv. (4, 13)

there, **éō,** adv. (23), **íbi,** adv. (5, 13), **illúc,** adv. (23)

therefore, **ígitur,** conj. (4), **ítaque,** adv. (16)

these, **hī, hae, haec** (18, 19, 20, 25, 26)

they, **éī, éae, éa** (27)

thing, **rēs, réī,** f. (19, 25)

think, to, **cốgitō, -áre, -ávī, -átus** (21)

third, **tértius, -a, -um** (25)

this, **hic, haec, hoc** (18, 19, 20, 25, 26), **is, éa, id** (27)

this way and that, **hūc illúc,** adv. (23)

thousand, one, **mílle** (15)

three, **trēs, trēs, tría** (13, 15)

threshing floor, **área, -ae,** f. (11)

through, **per,** prep. + acc. (6, 9)

throw, to, **conício, conícere, coniécī, coniéctus** (21), **iáciō, iácere, iécī, iáctus** (10, 20)

time, **témpus, témporis,** n. (2, 8, 12, 15)

time, enough, **sátis témporis** (23)

tired, **dēféssus, -a, -um** (2)

to Rome, **Rốmam** (7)

to that place, **éō,** adv. (23)

today, **hódiē,** adv. (2, 13)

toga, **tóga, -ae,** f. (8)

toga with purple border, **tóga praetéxta, tốgae praetéxtae,** f. (10)

together, **símul,** adv. (9, 13)

toil, **lábor, labóris,** m. (24)

told, **nārrátus, -a, -um** (20)

tomb, **sepúlcrum, -ī,** n. (22)

tomorrow, **crās,** adv. (10, 13)

too, **praetéreā,** adv. (15)

to(ward), **ad,** prep. + acc. (2, 9)

towering, **éxstāns, exstántis** (23)

trace, **vēstígium, -ī,** n. (12, 15)

track, **vēstígium, -ī,** n. (12, 15)

travel, to, **íter fácere** (13)

traveler, **viátor, viātóris,** m. (18)

tree, **árbor, árboris,** f. (1)

tremble, to, **trémō, trémere, trémuī** (21)

Trojan, **Troiánus, -a, -um** (I)

Trojans, the, **Troiánī, -órum,** m. pl. (I)

troublesome, **moléstus, -a, -um** (4)

Troy, **Trốia, -ae,** f. (I)

trunk, **císta, -ae,** f. (10)

trust, to, **cōnfídō, cōnfídere** + dat. (26)

try, to, **témptō, -áre, -ávī, -átus** (9)

tunic, **túnica, -ae,** f. (8)

turn, to, **vértō, vértere, vértī, vérsus** (16)

turn aside, to, **dēvértō, dēvértere, dēvértī, dēvérsus** (14, 27)

turning-post, **méta, -ae,** f. (27)

two, **dúo, dúae, dúo** (15)

U

uncle, **pátruus, -ī,** m. (22)

under, **sub,** prep. + abl. (1, 9)

unhappy, **míser, mísera, míserum** (9)

unhurt, **incólumis, -is, -e** (14)

unless, **nísi,** conj. (18, 26)

unwilling, **invítus, -a, -um** (21)

unwilling, to be, **nốlō, nốlle, nốluī** (5, 17, 21)

uproar, **tumúltus, -ūs,** m. (25)

urge on, to, **íncitō, -áre, -ávī, -átus** (10)

us, **nōs** (8)

us, to/for, **nốbīs** (9)

us, with, **nōbíscum** (16)

V

vehicle, **vehículum, -ī,** n. (13, 15)

very, **váldē,** adv. (19)

very much, **váldē,** adv. (19), **veheménter,** adv. (19)

victor, **víctor, victóris,** m. (27)

vineyard, **vínea, -ae,** f. (12)

violently, **veheménter,** adv. (19)

visit, to, **vísitō, -áre, -ávī, -átus** (23)

voice, **vōx, vócis,** f. (4)

voice, in a loud, **mágnā vóce** (4)

W

wagon, **plaústrum, -ī,** n. (15)

wait for, to, **exspéctō, -áre, -ávī, -átus** (15)

wait (for), to, **máneō, manére, mánsī, mānsúrus** (9, 20, 23)

wake up, to, **ánimum recuperáre** (21)

wake (someone) up, to, **éxcitō, -áre, -ávī, -átus** (8)

wakened, **excitátus, -a, -um** (25)

walk, to, **ámbulō, -áre, -ávī, -ātúrus** (2)

wall, **múrus, -ī,** m. (23)

wander, to, **érrō, -áre, -ávī, -ātúrus** (5, 18)

want, to, **vólō, vélle, vóluī** (5, 17, 20, 21)

want, (you), **vīs** (16)

wants, (he/she), **vult** (5, 17)

warm, **cálidus, -a, -um** (5)

was, (he/she/it), **érat** (13)

wash, to, **lávō, laváre, lávī, laútus** (20)

watch, to, **obsérvō, -áre, -ávī, -átus** (6), **spéctō, -áre, -ávī, -átus** (7)

Watch out (for)! **Cávē!/Cavéte!** (4, 13, 23)

watch out (for), to, **cáveō, cavére, cávī, caútus** (4, 13, 23)

water, **áqua, -ae,** f. (6)

way, in this, **íta,** adv. (3, 13, 21)

way...?, In what, **Quómodo...?** adv. (12)

we, **nōs** (8, 27)

weak, **īnfírmus, -a, -um** (4)

wear, to, **gérō, gérere, géssī, géstus** (10)

weep, to, **lácrimō, -áre, -ávī, -átus** (9)

weeping, **lácrimāns** (9)

welcome, to, **excípiō, excípere, excépī, excéptus** (5, 16, 22), **salútō, -áre, -ávī, -átus** (7)

well, **béne,** adv. (2)

What...? **Quid...?** (1, 4)

What sort of...? **Quális...?, Quális...? Quále...?** (4, 18)

wheel, **róta, -ae,** f. (15)

when, **cum,** conj. (22), **úbi,** conj. (5)

When...? **Quándō...?** adv. (12, 21)

where, **úbi,** conj. (1)

Where...? **Úbi...?** adv. (10, 12)

where...?, From, **Únde...?** adv. (12)

Where...to? **Quō...?** adv. (4)

which, **quī, quae, quod** (1, 3, 14, 24)

while, **dum,** conj. (1)

whip, to, **vérberō, -áre, -ávī, -átus** (11)

white, **albátus, -a, -um** (27)

white cloth, **máppa, -ae,** f. (27)

who, **quī, quae** (1, 3, 14)

Who...? (sing.) **Quis...?** (1), (pl.) **Quī...?** (6)

whole, the, **ómnis, -is, -e** (6, 18)

whom, to, (sing.) **cui** (19)

Whom...? **Quem...?** (5), **Quōs...?** (7), **Quās...?**

whom...?, With, (sing.) **Quócum...?** (12, 26), (pl.) **Quibúscum...?** (12)

Whose...? **Cúius...?** (22)

Why...? **Cūr...?** adv. (1)

wicked, **sceléstus, -a, -um** (10)

wife, **cóniūnx, cóniugis,** f. (26), **úxor, uxóris,** f. (11)

willing, (he/she) is, **vult** (5, 17)

willing, to be, **vólō, vélle, vóluī** (5, 17, 20, 21)

win, to, **víncō, víncere, vícī, víctus** (27)

wine, **vínum, -ī,** n. (25)

wish, if you, **sī vīs** (26)

wish, not to, **nólō, nólle, nóluī** (5, 17, 21)

wish, to, **vólō, vélle, vóluī** (5, 17, 20, 21)

wishes, (he/she), **vult** (5, 17)

with, **ápud,** prep. + acc. (16, 26), **cum,** prep. + abl. (12)

with a loud laugh, **mágnō rísū** (13)

With whom...? (sing.) **Quócum...?** (12, 26), (pl.) **Quibúscum...?** (12)

without, **síne,** prep. + abl. (26)

wolf, **lúpus, -ī,** m. (5)

woman, **fémina, -ae,** f. (3)

wonderful, **mírus, -a, -um** (23)

woods, **sílva, -ae,** f. (5)

wool, **lána, -ae,** f. (6)

wool, to spin, **lánam tráhere** (6)

work, **lábor, labóris,** m. (24)

work, to, **labórō, -áre, -ávī, -átus** (3)

worried, **sollícitus, -a, -um** (4)

wretched, **míser, mísera, míserum** (9)

write, to, **scríbō, scríbere, scrípsī, scríptus** (1, 24)

Y

Yes! **Íta vérō!** adv. (3, 13)

yesterday, **héri,** adv. (20)

you, (sing.) **tū, tē** (4, 27), (pl.) **vōs** (8, 27)

you, to/for, (sing.) **tíbi** (19), (pl.) **vóbīs** (19)

your, (sing.) **túus, -a, -um** (9, 27), (pl.) **véster, véstra, véstrum** (22, 27)

INDEX OF GRAMMAR

Index of Cultural Information

CREDITS

The publisher gratefully acknowledges the contributions of the agencies, institutions, and photographers listed below:

Cover
(*Left*) Faustina the Younger (139–175 A.D.) Spouse of Emperor Marc Aurel. © Bildarchiv Preussischer Kulturbesitz/Art Resource. (*Right*) So-called Brutus Minor. © Alinari/Art Resource

Frontmatter
(p. iv) Roman wall painting. Metropolitan Museum of Art, New York, USA/The Bridgeman Art Library

(p. v) Roman aqueduct, Segovia, Spain. © age footstock/SuperStock

Chapter 18
(p. 7) *Horatius Cocles Defending the Bridge*, Charles Le Brun. © Dulwich Picture Gallery, London, UK/The Bridgeman Art Library.

(p. 9) *Great Women of Antiquity*, Frederick Dudley Wallenn. © Mallett Gallery, London, UK, Private Collection/The Bridgeman Art Library.

Chapter 19
(p. 21) Mosaic. Museo Archeologico Prenestino, Palestrina, Italy/The Bridgeman Art Library.

Chapter 20
(p. 30) Open-air tricinlium. © Jim Zuckerman/Corbis.

(p. 36) *A Roman Triumph*, Peter Paul Rubens. National Gallery, London, UK/The Bridgeman Art Library.

Chapter 21
(p. 45) Silver mask. Louvre, Paris, France/The Bridgeman Art Library.

(p. 46) Roman wall painting. Metropolitan Museum of Art, New York, USA/The Bridgeman Art Library.

Chapter 22
(p. 58) © Rome, Italy/Index/The Bridgeman Art Library.

(p. 59) *Vercingetorix before Caesar* 52 B.C., Henri-Paul Motte. Bridgeman-Giraudon/Art Resource, NY.

(p. 60) © Norfolk Archaeological Trust, Artist Sue White.

Chapter 23
(p. 68) Detail of reconstructed general view of the Forum Romanum. From *The Ancient City* by Peter Connolly. akg-images/Peter Connolly.

(p. 73) Pont du Gard. ©Steve Vidler/eStock Photo.

(p. 74) ©age fotostock/SuperStock

Chapter 24
(p. 81) *Left*: © Michael Holford. *Right*: Louvre, Paris, France/The Bridgeman Art Library.

(p. 82) *Hannibal Swearing Eternal Enmity to Rome*, Jacopo Amigoni. ©Agnew's, London, UK, Private Collection/The Bridgeman Art Library.

(p. 87) Wheeled toy, Romano-German. M. Williams/Ancient Art & Architecture Collection, Ltd.

(p. 88) ©Altrendo Travel/Getty Images, Inc.

Chapter 25
(p. 96) Mosaic, Tunisia. C M Dixon/AAA Collection Ltd.

(p. 97) Roman funerary stele. ©Erich Lessing/Art Resource, NY.

(p. 98) Courtesy of Elizabeth Lyding Will.

(p. 99) *Roman Art Lover*, Sir Lawrence Alma-Tadema. ©Milwaukee Art Center, WI, USA/The Bridgeman Art Library.

(p. 101) ©Scala/Art Resource, NY.

(p. 103) akg-images/Peter Connolly.

Chapter 26
(p. 111) Fresco. ©The Art Archive/Museum of Carthage/Dagli Orti.

(p. 112) Roman Sarcophagus Showing Frieze with the Nine Muses. ©Lauros/Giraudon, Louvre, Paris, France/The Bridgeman Art Library.

Chapter 27
(p. 116) Roman relief sculpture. ©British Museum, London, UK/The Bridgeman Art Library.

(p. 117) Courtesy of Elizabeth Lyding Will.

TIMELINE

ca. 1184 B.C.   The Fall of Troy and the Wanderings of Aeneas

THE REGAL PERIOD

753 B.C.   The Founding of Rome by Romulus

753–509 B.C.   The Kings of Rome
> Romulus ▪ Numa Pompilius ▪ Tullus Hostilius ▪ Ancus Marcius ▪ Tarquinius Priscus ▪ Servius Tullius ▪ Tarquinius Superbus

THE REPUBLIC

509–264 B.C.   The Early Republic
> Legendary Heroes of Early Rome
> > Horatius ▪ Mucius Scaevola ▪ Cloelia ▪ Cincinnatus
>
> Invasion of the Gauls
> War with Pyrrhus

264–241 B.C.   The First Punic War

218–201 B.C.   The Second Punic War

201–146 B.C.   Rome in the Mediterranean World
> The Third Punic War

146–63 B.C.   Deadly Struggles within the Roman Republic
> The Gracchi ▪ Gaius Marius ▪ Lucius Cornelius Sulla ▪ Gnaeus Pompeius

63–44 B.C.   The Collapse of the Republic
> Marcus Tullius Cicero ▪ Gaius Julius Caesar ▪ Mark Antony ▪ Cleopatra ▪ Octavian

THE EMPIRE

31 B.C. – A.D. 14   The Augustan Age

A.D. 14–180   The Early Empire
> The Julio-Claudians: Tiberius ▪ Caligula ▪ Claudius ▪ Nero
> The Flavians: Vespasian ▪ Titus **OUR STORY: A.D. 80–81** ▪ Domitian
> The Five Good Emperors: Nerva ▪ Trajan ▪ Hadrian ▪ Antoninus Pius ▪ Marcus Aurelius

A.D. 211–476   The Late Empire
> Caracalla ▪ Diocletian ▪ Constantine

A.D. 330   Founding of Constantinople

A.D. 403   Legiō XX defeats Alaric the Visigoth

A.D. 476   Romulus Augustulus, last of the Roman emperors, overthrown by Odoacer the German